BOOKS BY BARRY LOPEZ

NONFICTION

About This Life:
Journeys on the Threshold of Memory (1998)

Apologia (1998)

The Rediscovery of North America (1991)

Crossing Open Ground (1988)

Arctic Dreams:
Imagination and Desire in a Northern Landscape (1986)

Of Wolves and Men (1978)

FICTION

Light Action in the Caribbean (2000)

Lessons from the Wolverine (1997),
with illustrations by Tom Pohrt

Field Notes:
The Grace Note of the Canyon Wren (1994)

Crow and Weasel (1990),
with illustrations by Tom Pohrt

Winter Count (1981)

River Notes:
The Dance of Herons (1979)

Giving Birth to Thunder, Sleeping with His Daughter:
Coyote Builds North America (1978)

Desert Notes: Reflections in the Eye of a Raven (1976)

ANTHOLOGY

Vintage Lopez (2004)

Barry Lopez

OF WOLVES AND MEN

With photographs by John Bauguess

*Including a new afterword by the author
and expanded bibliography*

SCRIBNER CLASSICS
New York   London   Toronto   Sydney

SCRIBNER
1230 Avenue of the Americas
New York, NY 10020

First Scribner Classics Edition 2004

SCRIBNER and design are trademarks of Macmillan Library Reference USA, Inc.,
used under license by Simon & Schuster, the publisher of this work.

For information regarding special discounts for bulk purchases,
please contact Simon & Schuster Special Sales:
1-800-456-6798 or business@simonandschuster.com.

Designed by Joel Schick
Text set in Janson

Manufactured in the United States of America

10 9 8 7 6 5 4 3 2 1

Library of Congress Cataloging-in-Publication Data is available.

ISBN 0-7432-4936-4

Grateful acknowledgment is made to the Memorial University of Newfoundland for permission
to quote from Georg Henriksen, *Hunters in the Barrens: the Naskapi on the Edge of the White
Man's World*, Memorial University of Newfoundland, 1973; and to Harper & Row, Publishers, Inc.,
for permission to quote from Frank B. Linderman, *American*, pp. 262–65, copyright 1930, 1957 by
Frank Linderman.

Front cover photograph © 1975 Rollie Ostermick

Photograph p. 151 copyright © 1975 John Bauguess; photographs pp. 8, 22–24, 34, 35, 40, 41,
44–46, 91, 103, 125, 136, 190 copyright © 1979 John Bauguess.

FOR WOLVES

Not the book, for which you would have little use,
but the effort at understanding.
I enjoyed your company.

We need another and a wiser and perhaps a more mystical concept of animals. Remote from universal nature, and living by complicated artifice, man in civilization surveys the creature through the glass of his knowledge and sees thereby a feather magnified and the whole image in distortion. We patronize them for their incompleteness, for their tragic fate of having taken form so far below ourselves. And therein we err, and greatly err. For the animal shall not be measured by man. In a world older and more complete than ours they move finished and complete, gifted with extensions of the senses we have lost or never attained, living by voices we shall never hear. They are not brethren, they are not underlings; they are other nations, caught with ourselves in the net of life and time, fellow prisoners of the splendour and travail of the earth.

—Henry Beston, *The Outermost House*

Presumption is our natural and original disease. The most wretched and frail of all creatures is man, and withal the proudest. He feels and sees himself lodged here in the dirt and filth of the world, nailed and riveted to the worst and deadest part of the universe, in the lowest story of the house, trapped worse than bird or fish, and yet in his imagination he places himself above the circle of the moon, bringing heaven under his feet.

By the vanity of the same imagination he equals himself to God, attributes to himself divine faculties, and withdraws and separates himself from all other creatures; he allots to these, his fellows and companions, the portion of faculties and power which he himself thinks fit.

How does he know, by the strength of his understanding, the secret and internal motions of animals, and from what comparison between them and us does he conclude the stupidity he attributes to them?

—Montaigne, *The Defense of Raymond Sebond*

The only real revolutionary stance is that "nature" is the greatest convention of all. Perhaps there are no natures, no essences—only categories and paradigms that human beings mentally and politically impose on the flux of experience in order to produce illusions of certainty, definiteness, distinction, hierarchy. Apparently, human beings do not like a Heraclitan world; they want fixed points of reference in order not to fall into vertigo, nausea. Perhaps the idea of nature or essence is man's ultimate grasp for eternity. The full impact of the theory of evolution (the mutability of species—including man) is thus still to come.

—John Rodman, *The Dolphin Papers*

ACKNOWLEDGMENTS

Many people were generous with their time, in interviews and correspondence, and generous with a bed and a meal when the situation arose. I would particularly like to thank Robert Stephenson of Fairbanks, Alaska, with whom I had the pleasure of weeks in the field, and Dave Mech, with whom I stayed in Minnesota and who directed me to a number of valuable people.

I am deeply indebted to the Nunamiut hunters of Anaktuvuk Pass, Alaska, for their ideas; to John Fentress, Department of Psychology, Dalhousie University, Nova Scotia, for his early encouragement in this project; and to the late Joseph Brown, Department of Religious Studies, University of Montana, for his direction and encouragement. To Pat Reynolds of the Naval Arctic Research Laboratory, Barrow, Alaska; Dick Coles of the Tyson Research Center, Saint Louis; and the staff of the wolf research facility, Shubenacadie, Nova Scotia, for their hospitality. And to Dale Bush, D.V.M., for his assistance.

The task of research was eased by various librarians and by the staffs of several state historical societies. I would particularly like to thank the interlibrary loan staff at the University of Oregon, Eugene; Minnie Paugh, special collections librarian at Montana State University; the staff of the Montana Historical Society, Helena; the staff of the South Dakota Historical Society, Pierre; and Marylyn Skaudis of Parkville, Minnesota.

Portions of the manuscript were critically reviewed by Robert Stephenson, Joseph Brown, and Roger Peters, and I am grateful for their insights.

Some of the ideas here first took shape in conversations with various people. In addition to those already named I would like to thank Dick Showalter, Jenny Ryon, Glynn Riley, Heather Parr, Tim Roper, Sandra Gray, and the late Dave Wallace.

Laurie Graham, my editor at Scribners, and Peter Schults, my agent, were deeply committed to the ideas here and I hope their insistence on clear and elegant expression is evident on these pages.

Sandy, my former wife, read this manuscript in progress. Her insights and the range of her vision are remarkable, and I am indebted.

CONTENTS

INTRODUCTION   1

I: *CANIS LUPUS* LINNAEUS

1.   Origin and Description   9
2.   Social Structure and Communication   31
3.   Hunting and Territory   53

II: AND A CLOUD PASSES OVERHEAD

4.   *Amaguk* and Sacred Meat   77
5.   A Wolf in the Heart   98
6.   Wolf Warriors   114

III: THE BEAST OF WASTE AND DESOLATION

7.   The Clamor of Justification   137
8.   Wolfing for Sport   153
9.   An American Pogrom   167

IV: AND A WOLF SHALL DEVOUR THE SUN

10.   Out of a Medieval Mind   203
11.   The Reach of Science   212
12.   Searching for the Beast   225
13.   Images from a Childhood   250
14.   A Howling at Twilight   271

EPILOGUE: On the Raising of Wolves
      and a New Ethology   279
AFTERWORD: A Reacquaintance with Wolves   287
BIBLIOGRAPHY   295
INDEX   309
ILLUSTRATION CREDITS   321

I am in a small cabin outside Fairbanks, Alaska, as I write these words. The cold sits down like iron here, and the long hours of winter darkness cause us to leave a light on most of the day. Outside, at thirty below, wood for the stove literally pops apart at the touch of the ax. I can see out across the short timber of the taiga when I am out there in the gray daylight.

Go out there.

Traveling for hours cross-country you see only a few animal tracks. Perhaps a single ptarmigan or a hare. Once in a while the tracks of a moose. In the dead of winter hardly anything moves. It's very hard to make a living. Yet the wolf eats. He hunts in the darkness. And stays warm. He gets on out there.

The cabin where I am writing sits a few miles north of the city, in

Goldstream Valley. This valley came briefly into the news a few years ago when wolves killed a lot of domestic dogs here. Goldstream Valley is lightly settled and lies on the edge of active wolf range, and that winter wolves got into the habit of visiting homes and killing pet dogs. A dog owner wouldn't hear a sound but the barking and growling of his dog. Then silence. He would pass a flashlight beam through the darkness and see nothing. In the morning he would find the dog's collar or a few of its bones stripped of meat. The wolves would have left behind little else but their enormous footprints in the snow.

After the wolves killed about twenty dogs like this, a petition turned up in local stores. Sign one sheet and it meant you wanted the Alaska Department of Fish and Game to kill the wolves. Sign another and it meant you didn't. The plan was defeated, five to one, and the Department of Fish and Game, for its part, declined to get involved. Some residents set out poisoned meat and steel traps on their own. The wolves went on killing dogs until spring, when the toll was something like forty-two.

When it was over some biologists, pressed for an explanation, told residents it had been a hard winter, that wolves had simply turned to dogs for food. Athabascan Indians living in Fairbanks said with a grin that that might be true—they didn't know—but wolves just naturally hate dogs, and that's all it had been about. The owner of a sled-dog team argued that the wolf was a born killer, like the wolverine and the weasel. Some creatures God put on earth to help man, he said, and others to hinder him, and the wolf was a hinderer.

The dog-killing incident in Goldstream Valley brings together the principal threads in this book. What wolves do excites men and precipitates strong emotions, especially if men feel their lives or the lives of their domestic animals are threatened. Explanations for the wolf's behavior are rampant. Biologists turn to data. Eskimos and Indians accept natural explanations but also take a wider view, that some things are inexplicable except through the metaphorical language of legend. The owner of a dog team is more righteously concerned with the safety of his animals than with understanding what motivates wolves. And everyone believes to some degree that wolves howl at the moon, or weigh two hundred pounds, or travel in packs of fifty, or are driven crazy by the smell of blood.

None of this is true. The truth is we know little about the wolf. What we know a good deal more about is what we imagine the wolf to be.

Alaska is the last North American stronghold of the wolf. With Eskimos and Indians here. with field biologists working on wolf studies, with a suburban population in Fairbanks wary of wolves on winter nights, with environmentalists pushing for protection, there is a great mix of opinion. The astounding thing is that, in large part, it is only opinion. Even biologists acknowledge that there are things about wolves and wolf behavior you just have to guess at.

Let's say there are 8,000 wolves in Alaska. Multiplying by 365, that's about 3 million wolf-days of activity a year. Researchers may see something like 75 different wolves over a period of 25 or 30 hours. That's about 90 wolf-days. Observed behavior amounts to about three one-thousandths of 1 percent of wolf behavior. The deductions made from such observations represent good guesses, and indicate how incomplete is our sense of worlds outside our own.

Wolves are extraordinary animals. In the winter of 1976 an aerial hunter surprised ten gray wolves traveling on a ridge in the Alaska Range. There was nowhere for the animals to escape to and the gunner shot nine quickly. The tenth had broken for the tip of a spur running off the ridge. The hunter knew the spur ended at an abrupt vertical drop of about three hundred feet and he followed, curious to see what the wolf would do. Without hesitation the wolf sailed off the spur, fell the three hundred feet into a snowbank, and came up running in an explosion of powder.

The Nunamiut Eskimo of the central Brooks Range speak of wolves as hunters something like themselves. They believe that wolves know where they are going when they set out to find caribou, and that perhaps wolves learn from the behavior of ravens where caribou might be. They believe certain wolves in a pack never kill, while others in the pack specialize in killing small game. Always, to requests for generalizations, they say that each wolf is a little different, that new things are always seen. If someone says big males always lead the pack and do the killing, the Eskimo shrug and say, "Maybe. Sometimes."

Wolves vary their hunting techniques, share food with the old who do not hunt, and give gifts to each other. They can live for a week without food and travel twenty miles without breaking stride. They have three systems of communication—vocal, postural, and olfactory. Their pelages range from slate blue to almost pure white, through chocolate brown, ocher, cinnamon, gray, and blond. And like primates they spend a good part of their time with their young and playing with each other. I once saw a wolf on the tundra winging a piece of caribou hide around like a Frisbee for an hour by himself.

You can look at a gray wolf standing in the snow in winter twilight and not see him at all. You may think I'm pulling your leg—I'm not. Sometimes even the Eskimos can't see them, which causes the Eskimos to smile.

Perhaps you already know some of these things, or have heard that wolves, especially in the time before the responsibility of hunting is upon them, chase through caribou herds for the fun of it. In the past twenty years biologists have given us a new wolf, one separated from folklore. But they have not found the whole truth. For example, wolves do not kill just the old, the weak, and the injured. They also kill animals in the prime of health. And they don't always kill just what they need; they sometimes kill in excess. And wolves kill each other. The reasons for these acts are not clear. No one—not biologists, not Eskimos, not backwoods hunters, not naturalist writers—knows why wolves do what they do.

The wolf exerts a powerful influence on the human imagination. It takes your stare and turns it back on you. (The Bella Coola Indians believed that someone once tried to change all the animals into men but succeeded in making human only the eyes of the wolf.) People suddenly want to explain the feelings that come over them when confronted with that stare—their fear, their hatred, their respect, their curiosity. Wolf-haters want to say they are born killers, which isn't true. Wolf-lovers want to say no healthy wolf ever killed anyone in North America, which isn't true either. They have killed Indians and Eskimos.

Everything we have been told about wolves in the past should have been said, I think, with more care, with the preface that it is only a perception in a particular set of circumstances, that in the end it is only an opinion.

To be rigorous about wolves—you might as well expect rigor of clouds.

I have looked for a wolf different from that ordinarily given us in the course of learning about animals. I have watched captive wolves in Barrow, Alaska; in Saint Louis, and in Nova Scotia. I drove across the Dakotas and Montana and Wyoming, speaking with old men who killed wolves for a living when they were young. In New York I read in libraries like the Pierpont Morgan what men thought of wolves hundreds of years ago. I read in the archives of historical societies of outlaw wolves and Indians. I went out with field biologists in Minnesota and Alaska and spoke with Eskimos. I spoke with people who loved wolves and with people who hated them.

I remember sitting in this cabin in Alaska one evening reading over the notes of all these encounters, and recalling Joseph Campbell, who wrote in the conclusion to *Primitive Mythology* that men do not discover their gods, they create them. So do they also, I thought, looking at the notes before me, create their animals.

One

CANIS LUPUS
LINNAEUS

ORIGIN AND DESCRIPTION

I MAGINE a wolf moving through the northern woods. The movement, over a trail he has traversed many times before, is distinctive, unlike that of a cougar or a bear, yet he appears, if you are watching, sometimes catlike or bearlike. It is purposeful, deliberate movement. Occasionally the rhythm is broken by the wolf's pause to inspect a scent mark, or a move off the trail to paw among stones where a year before he had cached meat.

The movement down the trail would seem relentless if it did not appear so effortless. The wolf's body, from neck to hips, appears to float over the long, almost spindly legs and the flicker of wrists, a bicycling drift through the trees, reminiscent of the movement of water or of shadows.

The wolf is three years old. A male. He is of the subspecies *occidentalis*, and the trees he is moving among are spruce and subalpine fir on the eastern slope of the Rockies in northern Canada. He is light gray; that is, there are more blond and white hairs mixed with gray in the saddle of fur that covers his shoulders and extends down his spine than there are black and brown. But there are silver and even red hairs mixed in, too.

It is early September, an easy time of year, and he has not seen the other wolves in his pack for three or four days. He has heard no howls, but he knows the others are about, in ones and twos like himself. It is not a time of year for much howling. It is an easy time. The weather is pleasant. Moose are fat. Suddenly the wolf stops in mid-stride. A moment, then his feet slowly come alongside each other. He is staring into the grass. His ears are rammed forward, stiff. His back arches and he rears up and pounces like a cat. A deer mouse is pinned between his forepaws. Eaten. The wolf drifts on. He approaches a trail crossing, an undistinguished crossroads. His movement is now slower and he sniffs the air as though aware of a possibility for scents. He sniffs a scent post, a scrawny blueberry bush in use for years, and goes on.

The wolf weighs ninety-four pounds and stands thirty inches at the shoulder. His feet are enormous, leaving prints in the mud along a creek (where he pauses to hunt crayfish but not with much interest) more than five inches long by just over four wide. He has two fractured ribs, broken by a moose a year before. They are healed now, but a sharp eye would notice the irregularity. The skin on his right hip is scarred, from a fight with another wolf in a neighboring pack when he was a yearling. He has not had anything but a few mice and a piece of arctic char in three days, but he is not hungry. He is traveling. The char was a day old, left on rocks along the river by bears.

The wolf is tied by subtle threads to the woods he moves through. His fur carries seeds that will fall off, effectively dispersed, along the trail some miles from where they first caught in his fur. And miles distant is a raven perched on the ribs of a caribou the wolf helped kill ten days ago, pecking like a chicken at the decaying scraps of meat. A smart snowshoe hare that eluded the wolf and left him exhausted when he was a pup has been dead a year now, food for an owl. The den in which he was born one April evening was home to porcupines last winter.

It is now late in the afternoon. The wolf has stopped traveling, has lain down to sleep on cool earth beneath a rock outcropping. Mosquitoes rest on his ears. His ears flicker. He begins to waken. He rolls on his back and lies motionless with his front legs pointed toward the sky but folded like wilted flowers, his back legs splayed, and his nose and tail curved toward each other on one side of his body. After a few moments he flops on his side, rises, stretches, and moves a few feet to inspect—minutely, delicately—a crevice in the rock outcropping and finds or doesn't find what draws him there. And then he ascends the rock face, bounding and balancing momentarily before bounding again, appearing slightly unsure of the process—but committed. A few minutes later he bolts suddenly into the woods, achieving full speed, almost forty miles per hour, for forty or fifty yards before he begins to skid, to lunge at a lodgepole pine cone. He trots away with it, his head erect, tail erect, his hips slightly to one side and out of line with his shoulders, as though hindquarters were impatient with forequarters, the cone inert in his mouth. He carries it for a hundred feet before dropping it by the trail. He sniffs it. He goes on.

The underfur next to his skin has begun to thicken with the coming of fall. In the months to follow it will become so dense between his shoulders it will be almost impossible to work a finger down to his skin. In seven months he will weigh less: eighty-nine pounds. He will have tried unsuccessfully to mate with another wolf in the pack. He will have helped kill four moose and thirteen caribou. He will have fallen through ice into a creek at twenty-two below zero but not frozen. He will have fought with other wolves.

He moves along now at the edge of a clearing. The wind coming down-valley surrounds him with a river of odors, as if he were a migrating salmon. He can smell ptarmigan and deer droppings. He can smell willow and spruce and the fading sweetness of fireweed. Above, he sees a hawk circling, and farther south, lower on the horizon, a flock of sharp-tailed sparrows going east. He senses through his pads with each step the dryness of the moss beneath his feet, and the ridges of old tracks, some his own. He hears the sound his feet make. He hears the occasional movement of deer mice and voles. Summer food.

Toward dusk he is standing by a creek, lapping the cool water, when a wolf howls—a long wail that quickly reaches pitch and then tapers, with several harmonics, long moments to a tremolo. He recognizes his sister. He waits a few moments, then, throwing his head back and closing his eyes, he howls. The howl is shorter and it changes pitch twice in the beginning, very quickly. There is no answer.

The female is a mile away and she trots off obliquely through the trees. The other wolf stands listening, laps water again, then he too departs, moving quickly, quietly through the trees, away from the trail he had been on. In a few minutes the two wolves meet. They approach each other briskly, almost formally, tails erect and moving somewhat as deer move. When they come together they make high squeaking noises and encircle each other, rubbing and pushing, poking their noses into each other's neck fur, backing away to stretch, chasing each other for a few steps, then standing quietly together, one putting a head over the other's back. And then they are gone, down a vague trail, the female first. After a few hundred yards they begin, simultaneously, to wag their tails.

In the days to follow, they will meet another wolf from the pack, a second female, younger by a year, and the three of them will kill a caribou. They will travel together ten or twenty miles a day, through the country where they live, eating and sleeping, birthing, playing with sticks, chasing ravens, growing old, barking at bears, scent-marking trails, killing moose, and staring at the way water in a creek breaks around their legs and flows on.

This is the animal Linnaeus called *Canis lupus* in 1758. In recent years the wolf has been studied enough by biologists to produce this picture, but his numbers have dwindled and his range has shrunk, and as is the case with so many things, deep appreciation and a sense of loss have arrived simultaneously.

Wolves, twenty or thirty subspecies of them, are Holarctic—that is, they once roamed most of the Northern Hemisphere above thirty degrees north latitude. They were found throughout Europe, from the Zezere River Valley of Portugal north to Finland and south to the Mediterranean. They roamed eastern Europe, the Balkans, and the Near and Middle East south into Arabia. They were found in Afghanistan and northern India, throughout Russia north into Siberia, south again as far as China, and east into the islands of Japan. In North America the wolf reached a southern limit north of Mexico City and ranged north as far as Cape Morris Jesup, Greenland, less than four hundred miles from the North Pole. Outside of Iceland and North Africa, and such places as the Gobi Desert, wolves—if you imagine the differences in geography it seems astounding—had adapted to virtually every habitat available to them.

Today they have been exterminated in the British Isles and Scandinavia and throughout most of Europe. There are a few wolves left in northern Spain, some in the Apennines in Italy, and a few in Germany and eastern Europe. Populations in the Near and Middle East and in northern India are greatly reduced. The present, or even past, populations of Russia and China are undetermined.

Mexico still has a small population of wolves, and large populations—perhaps twenty to twenty-five thousand—remain in Alaska and Canada. The largest concentrations of wolves in the lower forty-eight states are in northeastern Minnesota (about one thousand) and on Isle Royale in Lake Superior (about thirty). There is a very small wolf population in Glacier National Park in Montana and a few in Michigan's Upper Peninsula. Occasionally lone wolves show up in the western states along the Canadian border; most are young animals dispersing from packs in British Columbia, Alberta, and Saskatchewan.

The red wolf, *Canis rufus*, a little known but distinct species of wolf found only in America, has been exterminated across virtually all its former range in the southeastern United States. A small population of perhaps one hundred survives in the swamp thickets of extreme southeastern Texas and adjacent Cameron Parish, Louisiana.

Of the twenty-three subspecies of wolf (too many to be meaningful) that taxonomist Edward Goldman identified in North America in 1945, seven are no longer around. These include the Great Plains wolf (also called the lobo wolf, the loafer wolf, or simply the buffalo runner), the Cascade Mountain wolf, the Texas gray wolf, the Mogollon Mountain wolf of central Arizona and New Mexico, the Newfoundland wolf, and the northern Rocky Mountain wolf. The southern Rocky Mountain wolf, last reported alive in 1970, is now also believed to be extinct.

Japan's two wolves, *Canis lupus hattai* and *Canis lupus hodophilax*, are probably extinct. And another wolf, one that lived in the Danube River

Latin nomenclature for various subspecies of wolf was not applied rigorously, but some of it is intriguing. Many of the subspecific designations, such as nubilus *(cloudy gray) for the Great Plains wolf and* fuscus *(tawny or cinnamon colored) for the Cascade Mountains wolf, refer to the color of the pelage.* Monstrabalis *(Texas gray wolf) means "unusual" or "remarkable."* Occidentalis *(Mackenzie Valley wolf) refers, of course, to the wolf of the west, while* orion *(Greenland wolf) refers to the mythic hunter and giant.* Irremotus *(Northern Rocky Mountain wolf) means something like "the wolf who is always showing up there."*

Lycaon *(Eastern timber wolf) was the Greek king of Arcadia whom Zeus turned into a wolf.* Youngi *(Southern Rocky Mountain wolf) was named for Stanley Young, a government hunter and popularizer of wolf lore in the forties and fifties.* Baileyi *(Mexican wolf) was named for a government trapper.*

Laniger *(Chinese wolf) means woolly, and* campestris *(central Asian wolf) simply "the wolf of the open plains."*

Valley and was apparently distinct enough to be classed as a subspecies, was eliminated before any specimens were examined. Other subspecies in Asia have probably disappeared, but this is hard to prove and even harder to give meaning to. They represent subtle losses. In North America, and elsewhere, as human civilization affected the distribution and food habits of wolves—by killing buffalo, for example, and putting domestic cattle in their place on the ranges—various subspecies of wolf interbred and the purity of gene pools, such as they were, was altered. The wolves that remain in North America today are often distinguished simply as tundra or timber (or gray) wolves, according to where they live.

One value of distinguishing among wolves is to set off other wolflike canids. There is, for example, a wild canid in Maine that is intermediate in size between wolf and coyote; and in Texas, red wolves and coyotes have bred to produce what biologists call a hybrid swarm. Feral dogs— pets gone wild—sometimes breed with wolves. All these creatures are wolflike but they are not wolves and it is right to keep them out of things.

Originally, distinctions were made among subspecies on the basis of cranial features, pelage (fur), relative size, and geographic distribution. But taxonomic distinction among wolves is probably most valuable for the way it distinguishes among factors other than size and color. The small Asian, or Iranian, wolf, *Canis lupus pallipes,* for example, differs from most other wolves in that it is not known to howl and apparently travels alone, or in very small packs. The Chinese wolf, *Canis lupus laniger,* also hunts alone or in small packs. And the European wolf, *Canis lupus lupus,* has adapted to living in fairly close proximity with human beings. Wolves in thinly populated areas of Canada may move out if the human density is more than three persons per square mile.

Recently the trend has been to distinguish less among subspecies of wolf and to make more of other differences—hunting techniques, pack size, range, diet—than color and size.

By whatever standard, a significant part of the genetic reservoir that once represented one of the more adaptive mammals on the face of the earth is now gone. The argument in rebuttal; that wolves in captivity represent pure strains of extinct races and therefore constitute a genetic

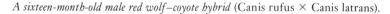

A sixteen-month-old male red wolf–coyote hybrid (Canis rufus × Canis latrans).

reservoir, is probably meaningless. Zoo populations are sometimes derived from animals of questionable genetic background and/or geographic origin, and in many cases subspecific labels are casually applied. And pups raised in captivity are virtually certain not to survive in the wild.

It would be nice to write with precision and neatness about the exact location of the last subspecific populations of wolves in the world, because we are a culture that fancies that sort of order, but the task is complicated and ultimately made impossible by two factors: wolves wander, and subspecific populations, as stated, breed with each other. Even prior to widespread human persecution, wolves disappeared from certain portions of their ranges for years at a time. No one knows why. Game thinned out, perhaps, or people moved in. Douglas Pimlott, a Canadian wildlife biologist, believes the "extinct" Newfoundland wolf, for example, simply vanished from that island as part of a natural process, that it was not hunted out. Ian MacTaggart Cowan, another Canadian, thinks that the last specimens of northern Rocky Mountain wolf bred with the Mackenzie Valley wolf to finally eliminate all vestiges of that race. These cases are important I think insofar as we blame ourselves, with a lack of humility, for every animal's demise.

A third factor to consider in trying to pinpoint world populations is the simple lack of records and research. It was not, astonishingly, until the early 1940s that anyone took a serious, scientific look at wolves, and in some parts of Eurasia (where they are still regarded as beasts of blood and darkness) specific information on their numbers, locations, and habits is lacking even now.

A fourth factor is that lone wolves disperse for considerable distances, hundreds of miles away from known wolf ranges, in search of new territories each year. In North America some generalizations can be made about the pattern—about where dispersing wolves will likely show up. But in China, for example, we still lack a general picture of primary wolf ranges.

Although the lines of descent are not entirely clear, the wolf began to develop as a specialized genus of cursorial, or hunt-by-chasing, carnivore in the Paleocene, some 60 million years ago. Its ancestors included small, rodentlike insectivores and, later, much larger creodonts, animals that walked on five toes, had partially retractile claws, partially opposable thumbs on the forefeet, and long, thick tails. They perhaps looked like long-legged otters, dwelt in forests, and may have slept in trees. Some of them, evolutionarily speaking, moved out on the plains and prairies and became wolves, bears, badgers, skunks, and weasels. The ones that stayed behind in the forests retained their retractile claws, perfected an ambush/stabbing kind of hunting, and became saber-toothed tigers, leopards, and cheetahs.

By Miocene times, 20 million years ago, these two superfamilies of carnivores, the dogs and cats, were distinct, and the more recognizable ancestors of the wolf had emerged. They had specialized shearing teeth and the bones of their lower legs had begun to fuse as flexibility in the limbs (as in the cats) gave way to rigidity for strength in the chase. In one relative, Tomarctus, the fifth toe on the hind leg became vestigial and the dewclaw was born. The legs grew longer, the feet more compact. By the Pleistocene, 1 million years ago, the wolf's immediate ancestor, *Canis*, had emerged with a larger brain and longer nose than his predecessors. Among the species of *Canis* was *dirus*, the dire wolf. *Canis* was better adapted to running and had perhaps evolved a primitive social structure and some cooperative hunting techniques. We can imagine him pulling down camels hundreds of thousands of years ago in what is now Oklahoma.

Canis sp. was parent to *Canis lupus*, the wolf (a somewhat smaller animal, with a higher forehead and more social tendencies); and the wolf was probably parent to the domestic dog, *Canis familiaris*, the first large creature who would live with men.

Today the wolf's closest relatives are the domestic dog, the dingo, the coyote, and the jackal. Then come the other members of the family Canidae: the foxes and wild dogs. The Canidae in turn are related to the Ursidae, the bears, and more distantly to animals like the raccoon, the marten, and the wolverine. There are some irregularities in popular names that should be cleared up here. The aardwolf, *Proteles cristatus*, is not a wolf but an insect-eating member of the hyena family—and hyenas are related to the cats. The maned wolf, *Chrysocyon brachyurus*, and the Andean wolf, *Dasycyon hagenbecki*, are not wolves but South American wild dogs. The extinct Falkland wolf, *Dusicyon australis,* was also a South American canid that shared but few behavioral traits with the wolf of the Northern Hemisphere. The same can be said of a rare Ethiopian canid, the Abyssinian wolf, *Canis simensis.* The Tasmanian wolf, or thylacine, *Thylacinus cynocephalus,* is a marsupial, in the same order with kangaroos and possums.

The Cape hunting dog, or African wild dog, *Lycaon pictus,* on the other hand, has much in common with the wolf in its hunting habits and social behavior, and some zoologists have suggested that it belongs in the same genus with the wolf. Another irregularity of taxonomy.

Of them all, the wolf is perhaps the most socially evolved and intelligent. Wolves have a high degree of social organization and have evolved a system of communication and communal interaction which stabilizes these social relationships. They may be unique in having markedly different individual personalities. In human terms, some are more aggressive or shyer or moodier, and pack society allows these individual temperaments to mature. In one pack, for example, one wolf may be the best hunter, another have a better sense of strategy and (again, to stretch for the human equivalent) be called upon for it by the others.

Whenever I've spoken with people who've never seen a wolf, I've found that the belief that wolves are enormous is pervasive. Even people who have considerable experience with the animal seem to want it to be, somehow, bigger than it is. A trapper in Minnesota, a man who had caught hundreds of wolves in his life, looked at one in a trap one day and judged its weight at "eighty-five or ninety pounds." When it was weighed and found to be sixty-seven pounds, he became slightly indignant with the creature and said, "He's got the frame to carry ninety pounds. Must be sick."

Wolves range in size from about 45 pounds for an adult Arabian wolf to well over 100 pounds for a large timber wolf. In Alaska, where perhaps the biggest wolves are found, a wolf that weighs more than 120 pounds is uncommon. The largest wolf on record is a 175-pound animal killed on 70 Mile River in extreme east central Alaska by a government hunter on July 12, 1939. A Canadian park ranger killed a 172-pound animal in Jasper National Park in 1945. Males are generally 5 or 10 pounds heavier than females. An average weight for a North American wolf would be 80 pounds, less in southern Canada, more in the north. A mature European wolf might weigh 85 pounds. Wolves in the Punjab in India and on the Arabian Peninsula might average 55 pounds.

I spent a couple of days south of the Alaska Range on the Susitna River one spring weighing and measuring wild wolves and when I returned home, a friend asked how wolves compared in size to his Alaskan malamute, which many people think of as a sort of carbon copy of the wolf. I took a tape measure, and using the figures from my notebook for a typical male of the same age and weight came up with the following differences: The wolf's head was wider, longer, and generally larger. Malamute and wolf were about the same in the neck, twenty inches around, but the malamute was bigger in the chest by a few inches. The wolf stood two inches taller, was three inches longer in the leg, and eight inches longer in the body. The wolf's tail was longer and had no tendency to curl over its back as the malamute's did. The wolf's track was nearly twice the size of the dog's. Both animals weighed about 100 pounds.

The wolf's coat is remarkable, a luxurious fur consisting of two layers: a soft, light-colored, dense underfur that lies beneath a covering of long guard hairs which shed moisture and keep the underfur dry. Much of the underfur and some of the guard hairs are shed in the spring and grow back in the fall. The coat is thick across the shoulders, where guard hairs may be four or five inches long, and thins out on the muzzle and legs. By placing muzzle and unprotected nose between the rear legs and overlapping the face with the thickly furred tail, wolves can turn their backs to the wind and sleep comfortably in the open at forty degrees below zero. Pound for pound a wolf's fur provides better insulation than a dog's fur, and, like the wolverine's fur, it won't collect ice when warm breath condenses against it.

Wolves in warmer climes have shorter guard hairs and less dense underfur. The red wolf, which inhabits hot, humid areas on the Gulf Coast, has a short, coarse coat and large, pointed ears in contrast to the short, rounded ears of tundra wolves. Short ears are less sensitive to the cold; long ears are efficient dissipaters of body heat.

In extreme cold the wolf can reduce the flow of blood near its skin and conserve even more heat. A team of biologists in Barrow, Alaska, found

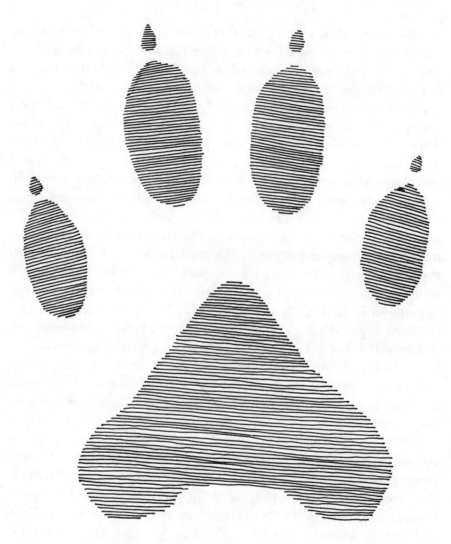

Footprint of a three-year-old Alaskan timber wolf (Canis lupus pambasileus), *actual size.*

that the temperature of the wolf's footpads was maintained at just above the tissue-freezing point where the pads came in contact with ice and snow. Warmth there was regulated independently of the rest of the body. This is a good example of the marvelous but nevertheless commonplace efficiency of design found in all wild creatures.

On warm days wolves dissipate heat by panting, a weary-looking but efficient method of cooling by evaporation. And by flopping in creeks and rivers. In the 1920s a Montana cattleman wrote that the wolves on his ranch "would lay up in the damp cool dirt among the reeds and cat-tails below some spring or in the cedar clumps and thickets on the north side of a high butte" on a hot day.

During hot spells wolves travel much less and restrict their hunting to the coolest hours of the night.

The wolf's ability to regulate its body temperature no doubt helped it survive in a wide variety of climates, each with a wide range of temperature. In the Northwest Territories it may reach seventy degrees below zero or climb to ninety degrees on a summer day. In the northern plains it gets nearly as cold and twenty degrees hotter. The Cascade wolf had to contend with deep snows, the British Columbia wolf with forty to fifty inches of rain in the winter. No one knows how wolves managed in all that moisture. Maybe they simply stayed out of the rain.

The wolf's coat ranges in color from almost pure white through various shades of blond, cream, and ocher to grays, browns, and blacks. Among the more striking are the slate blue coats of some arctic wolves. Most white wolves are found in the north, though Lewis and Clark and many mountain men, explorers, and immigrants reported large numbers of very light wolves on the Great Plains in the early 1800s. The color of the coat apparently has no camouflage function, as black wolves are commonly found on the tundra and white wolves stand out against the black soils of central Russia. In southern Canada and Minnesota the black phase is more common than the white, but grays predominate. Variety in color in the same litter is the rule, though litter mates usually have the same quality of fur. The most luxuriant pelages show up among adults on the tundra, the difference between a tundra wolf pelt and a timber wolf pelt being so pronounced that the former often sells for twice as much.

There are no records I know of for albino wolves, but an aerial hunter told me of one he killed twenty-five miles east of Umiat on the arctic slope in April 1957. It was a female, with pink eyes, nose, and footpads, and weighed about eighty pounds. There are no statistics to bear this

out, but when it came up in conversation, many people in Alaska—hunters, biologists, native people—volunteered the information that the biggest wolves they'd seen were blacks.

The great variety in pelage—and I know of no other mammal so variously colored—among wolves in a single area is attested to by the number of words people use to describe local wolf coloration. "Peach," "yellow," "orange," "tan," and "rusty" were all words I heard used in the Arctic. One Eskimo remembered trapping a spotted wolf, a black with white patches in its coat, in 1968 in the Brooks Range.

Eskimos are keen observers of detail and the Nunamiut people of the Brooks Range in Alaska distinguish between male and female wolves and between lactating females and other wolves partly on the basis of differences in pelage. Females tend to have more reddish tones in their fur, and the hair on their legs tends to be smooth, where the hair on a male's leg has a slightly tufted appearance. Pelage changes texture as the animal grows older, with females generally developing the smoothest coats. Older animals tend to have more white hairs in the tip of the tail and elsewhere, along the nose and on the forehead, for example. Lactating females retain their long winter fur longer than other wolves and show hair loss around their nipples. What hair remains on the belly around the mammae develops a red–brown stain.

The Nunamiut also point out that there are subtle anatomical differences between males and females. Females have a narrower muzzle and forehead, thinner neck, slightly shorter legs, and less massive shoulders, which makes the males seem slimmer in the waist by comparison. Two- and three-year-old females, in the opinion of these Eskimos, were also faster runners than males of the same age.

These are all generalizations, of course, but valuable pieces of information in the aggregate for distinguishing the age and sex of a wolf at a distance.

Tireless and silent, the fluid motion of the long-distance hunter.

The shading in a wolf's coat has a discernible (and purposeful) pattern. Even relatively pure black and white specimens reveal these patterns. The long, dark-tipped, or grizzled, guard hairs saddle the shoulders and extend up the neck and down the spine, fading out toward the rump, where they merge with darker hairs on the top of the tail. The underside of the tail, the insides of the legs, the belly, and the underside of the muzzle are usually light. The head is marked, particularly around the eyes and ears, in such a way as to emphasize the features of the face. The end of the tail is usually dark, with at least a few white hairs at the tip, and there is often a dark spot on the top of the tail marking the location of a scent gland.

The wolf uses a series of stereotyped body postures and facial expressions to communicate, and careful observation reveals that these signals are enhanced by shadings in the fur, making the signals more noticeable.

On Endurance

An Eskimo intent on killing a wolf for bounty but finding himself without ammunition decided to run the animal to exhaustion with a snowmobile. Referring to maps later, he determined the wolf had run for twelve miles at speeds between fifteen and thirty mph before slowing to a trot, which he kept up for another four miles, at which point he began walking. He collapsed four miles later.

Wolves are agile creatures but not as deft and quick as coyotes. Red wolves move in a more delicate manner than gray wolves, appearing to put less weight on the foot. In captivity red wolf–coyote hybrids have jumped into the lower limbs of trees, four or five feet off the ground. Red wolf/coyotes also stot when alarmed, moving off with the stiff-legged bound of a white-tailed deer.

Wolves spend an average of eight to ten hours out of every twenty-four on the move, mostly the crepuscular hours. They travel great distances and have tremendous stamina. One observer followed two wolves who broke trail through five feet of snow for 22 miles in British Columbia. The animals paused in their tracks but never lay down to rest. Taking wolves on Isle Royale as an example, they average 30 miles of travel a day in winter. A Finnish biologist reported one pack that moved 125 miles in a day. The naturalist Adolph Murie watched a pack in Alaska make a regular daily round of about 40 miles in search of food while the female was denning. Tundra wolves may run for 5 or 6 miles behind caribou before accelerating to attack.

Wolves are also good swimmers, though they rarely follow prey into the water during a chase.

The wolf's most efficient hunting tool, after its legs get it there, is its mouth. Evolved in an elongated shape, its forty-two teeth are adapted to seize (the long canines), to shear and tear (the premolars), and to crush (the molars). The incisors nibble and strip the shreds of meat from bone. The carnassial teeth (an upper premolar and a lower molar) are specially adapted to function like a set of pruning shears, slicing meat and snipping tough connective tissues and tendons. The animal can develop a crushing pressure of perhaps 1,500 lbs/in^2 compared to 750 lbs/in^2 for a German shepherd. This is enough to break open most of the bones the wolf encounters to get at the marrow.

Wolves live in packs with fairly refined social structures. Packs are typically extended families of five to eight individuals but range in size from two or three to fifteen or twenty. The largest authenticated report is of a pack of thirty-six in Alaska, though packs of more than twenty-five are rarely reported. Stories of hundreds of wolves traveling together are probably folklore. It is possible, however, from the preponderance of references in nineteenth-century magazines, to infer that packs of twenty-five to thirty animals once were rather common in northeastern Europe and central Russia.

Pack size is determined by the availability of space free of other packs and by the type and abundance of game, as well as by the personal dispositions of the various wolves involved and such factors as pup mortality and overall wolf population. Packs may break up in winter or summer, some permanently, others only for a season or a few days. An individual pack may retain an identity over a long period of time, using the same dens year after year, hunting the same territory, and outliving founding members. Murie studied a pack of wolves on the East Fork of the Toklat River in Mount McKinley National Park between 1939 and 1941. Thirty-four years later, studies by another wildlife biologist revealed a pack of similar size and habits in the same place, using the same dens. Packs develop distinct personalities, so that a good observer can tell at a distance from their behavior alone (not just from the number or pelages or in whose territory the observer might be) which pack he is watching.

Breeding normally occurs in February or March, usually every year. There is a physical tie during copulation that may last as long as thirty minutes, and some have suggested that this intimacy reinforces the monogamous bond and galvanizes the pack. As a rule, only one female becomes pregnant.

The pups are born sixty-three days later. April and May are the most common months. Mating and whelping take place later in the spring the farther north one moves. The pups are usually born in a den excavated for the purpose—in a sandy esker in northern Canada, under massive tree trunks, in cut banks, or in natural cavities around boulders or in caves in other locales. In northern Alaska, females may give birth in the open in a hastily prepared depression or "pit den," as though labor had been sudden and unexpected.

An excavated den is usually located high on a cut bank or otherwise situated in well-drained soil, and the location often provides a clear view of the surrounding area; but many dens, especially in wooded areas, have no view at all. The den is kept scrupulously clean. No bedding is used. The entrance hole is normally smaller than twenty × twenty inches; the entrance tunnel may lead back six or eight feet and then dogleg to a rounded hollow, somewhat elevated, where the pups monkeyball together for warmth. Because they have difficulty regulating their body temperature for the first few days, wolf pups require this protection from wind and weather.

Normally from four to six pups are born, but births of only one or as many as thirteen have been recorded. The pups are born deaf and blind; they can hear after a few days, will open their eyes at eleven to fifteen days, and are weaned at five weeks, by which time they are already playing at the entrance to the den. Their floppy ears stand erect at about four weeks and their first howls—the sudden sound of which often startles them—are heard at the same time. The development of a hierarchy of deference in the litter is visible by about six weeks but will change many times in the months to come.

Most of these pups die. Mortality ranges upward of 60 percent, for several reasons. Pups require perhaps three times as much protein per pound as their parents do, and food may be scarce. They sometimes wound each other during fights and a parent may kill (and eat) a severely wounded one. Distemper, listeriosis, and other diseases take a toll, as do pneumonia and hypothermia if a late winter storm hits. A pup exhibiting any untoward behavior, like epilepsy, is killed by the adults. And occasionally an eagle, lynx, or bear may snatch one.

Litter size is related to the availability of game and to the density of wolves in an area—the more wolves, the smaller the litters. Whether or not a litter is born at all, as well as who breeds, depends on social organization within the pack. One pack might even respond to pressure from a neighboring pack with a lot of surviving yearlings in it and not breed. The wolf's endocrine system may be responsible for all this, responding in some way to stress in the animal's environment—how often it sees members of another pack, how much time passes between its kills—so as to control breeding and litter size. The interesting thing is that sometimes *not* breeding—during a time of famine, for example—increases the chances for the pack to survive.

While the pups are growing up, the older wolves express strong interest in them, and the pups respond with much affection, especially toward their parents. They face-lick and nuzzle the adults, direct play at them, and huddle around them when the adults lie down. The social bond between them is so obvious that in 1576, in an age when people believed the worst of wolves, a sportsman wrote in a book on hunting: "If

Three-week-old pup, father.

the pups chance to meet their sire or dam anytime after they leave the pack they will fawn upon them and seem in their kind greatly to rejoice."

The older wolves make no effort to snatch food from the pups or, later, to keep them from feeding on a kill. Observers in the wild, in fact, have frequently commented on how benignly a pack of wolves behaves around a carcass. (In captivity, where wolves develop some level of neurosis, the reverse is sometimes true.) Because an adult will rarely use force to get food from a pup, Konrad Lorenz has wondered if such respect for "rights" might not represent a primitive sense of morality in the wolf, one that might be expected to develop only among social carnivores. The continuation of the thought is that herbivores and other gregarious animals have no food to fight over and no social structure in which to develop a sense of morals.

All this generosity and deference in caring for the pups, while less than strictly observed, is in sharp contrast of course to folk belief. As one Russian authority wrote in 1934: "Most of the prey goes to the older wolves, particularly to the males. They intimidate the yearlings and the newborn . . . and the weakest are often torn to pieces by their stronger relatives."

By the time they are five to ten months old, the mortality rate for pups has fallen off to about 45 percent. When they mature sexually (usually at two for the females, sometimes not until the next year for males), they enjoy a survival rate of about 80 percent. No animal habitually preys on the wolf and in the wild they may survive for eight or nine years. An exceptional animal may live to be thirteen or fourteen.

Wolves, of course—and it is curious how unaware we seem of this—suffer injury, disease, and violent death as part of living. Tigers kill them in India; bears kill them in North America. And although death does not normally occur as a result of strife in a pack, flight being the usual outcome, encounters between different packs do sometimes involve fatalities.

Most wolves are parasitized to some extent, internally by tapeworms and roundworms and externally by ticks, fleas, and mites, though these external parasites are rare in northern populations. Wolves sometimes endure mange and they suffer from various cancers and tumors. Rabies

and distemper are perhaps the most virulent diseases the wolf is suscep-
tible to. A wolf may cut its tongue on a bone and bleed to death. A
wind-born seed may bury itself in the inner ear and destroy the animal's
equilibrium. Porcupine quills can kill them with swelling and infection.
They get cataracts and go blind.

Wolves are sometimes injured by moose and other large animals and
these skull fractures, broken ribs, and joint injuries can precipitate arthritis (which also occurs naturally with age). Malnutrition may bring on
rickets or other diseases associated with vitamin and mineral deficiencies.
In some areas wolves are subject to endemic problems. Red wolves in
Texas are heavily parasitized by heartworm; wolves in British Columbia
suffer fatally from salmon poisoning; wolves in Spain show a high level
of trichinosis.

An examination of 110 wolves killed mostly along the Tanana River in
Alaska in 1976 showed 56 had survived one or more traumatic injuries,
principally, it was thought, in hunting moose—fractured skulls, broken
ribs, broken legs, and so on. A four-year-old male (with healed fractures
of the front left leg, two ribs on the right side and the skull) was in "fair
to good" physical condition. Others had similarly recovered.

The point of all this is that the woods is a hard place to get on, and yet
the wolf survives.

Two

SOCIAL STRUCTURE AND COMMUNICATION

THE social structure of a wolf pack is all-important. Breeding, hunting, and feeding are tied to it, as is territorial maintenance and play behavior. What evidence we have of the wolf's ability to teach its young to hunt (as well as their ability to learn) suggests that social structure plays a strong role here, too. Wolf pups raised without a pack structure adapt very poorly to life in the wild.

Generally speaking, there are three separate social structures in the pack: a hierarchy of males, a hierarchy of females, and a more seasonally related cross-sexual social structure. There is, typically, an "alpha," or primary, male that dominates the other males and an alpha female that dominates the other females. This alpha pair is thought to be the breeding pair, but there are a good many cases in captivity and in the wild where a lower-ranking male has bred with the alpha female, the alpha male expressing apparent disinterest.

Females may head packs and they always strongly influence pack activities. We often think of animals like the wolf, who appear to have so many points in common with us, in human social terms. With respect to females, who have largely a subordinate standing in Western human societies, the analogy, I think, is poor. Female wolves may not only lead packs but outlast a succession of male alpha animals. It is females, moreover, who decide where to den and thus where the pack will have to hunt for five or six weeks. In the north, where wolves are following migrating caribou, a poor guess about where caribou are going to be can be disastrous, and the possibility of failure underlines the gravity of the female's decision.

Young females, as mentioned, are thought to be slightly faster than young males and therefore better hunters under some circumstances. The male hunter–male leader image of the wolf pack is misleading but, unconsciously, I am sure, it is perpetuated by males, who dominate this field of study. For the same reason paramilitary descriptions of wolf behavior—where "lieutenant wolves" are "dispatched" to "patrol" the territory, and parents "instill discipline" in the pups—creep in and strongly color our impressions of the animal, often without our knowing it. I am certain this is part of the reason people believe that male wolves always do the killing, and why the males' weights are so often exaggerated.

Social structure in a wolf pack has been observed in greatest detail among captive wolves, which makes extrapolating to wild wolves risky. Captive animals engage in no hunting activities, are penned in areas of incomprehensible size when compared with the one-hundred-plus square miles routinely used by a pack, often lack for suitable exercise, and are constantly interfered with by human beings seeking to establish or maintain various levels of socialization. Their social displays, because they can never get away from each other, are excessive. Fieldwork has substantiated that a strong social order does exist in the wild and that there is an alpha pair at the top. It is most evident during the mating season when the alpha female asserts herself and sometimes fights to keep other females in estrus away from the alpha male, and the alpha male fights, less vigorously it seems, to keep other males away from the

Lesson

A female wolf left four or five pups alone in a rendezvous area in the Brooks Range one morning and set off down a trail away from them. When she was well out of sight, she turned around and lay flat in the path, watching her back trail. After a few moments, a pup who had left the rendezvous area trotted briskly over a rise in the trail and came face to face with her. She gave a low bark. He stopped short, looked about as though preoccupied with something else, then, with a dissembling air, began to edge back the way he had come. His mother escorted him to the rendezvous site and departed again. This time she didn't bother watching her back trail. Apparently the lesson had taken, for all the pups stayed put until she returned that evening.

---

alpha female. (These are ritualized squabbles with few physical injuries in most cases.) It is not known whether it is the alpha male that normally fathers the pups, but they are almost always whelped by the alpha female.

But the term *alpha*—evolved to describe captive animals—is still misleading. Alpha animals do not always lead the hunt, break trail in snow, or eat before the others do. An alpha animal may be alpha only at certain times for a specific reason, and, it should be noted, is alpha at the deference of the other wolves in the pack.

The wolf is a social animal; it depends for its survival on cooperation, not strife. Human beings, particularly in recent years, have grown accustomed to speaking of "dominance hierarchies" in business corporations and elsewhere, and the tendency has been to want wolf packs (or troops of chimpanzees) to conform to similar molds. The social structure of a wolf pack is dynamic—subject to change, especially during the breeding season—and may be completely reversed during periods of play. It is important during breeding, feeding, travel, and territorial maintenance, and seems to serve a purpose when wolves gather to reassure each other of the positive aspects of their life-style as reflected in this social order, one that enhances survival by collective hunting and natural population control.

To place a heavy emphasis on such supposed facets of behavior as "intimidation," "pulling rank," and games of psychological cruelty based on

Four weeks old.

social structures, however, is simply to confuse the tools of human analysis with the actual behavior of wolves.

Another factor to be considered is that wolf packs, like individual wolves, have personalities. Packs may contain autocrats, petulant individuals, or even cretins; and the personalities involved may make one pack more Prussian or austere in its organization than another.

With this to mind, the following can be taken as a "typical" pack structure: an alpha male and alpha female at the top, perhaps four or five years old; subordinate males and females, some sexually mature, in the middle, the dominant of which are called beta animals; and the pups. Deference is shown to alpha animals by subordinate animals of both sexes. Subordinates of the same sex establish their own order, usually with the yearlings at the bottom and a two- or three-year-old animal at

the top. The pups, too, have their own social order, but theirs is without regard to sex. The alpha animals and the others gradually bring the pups into the social structure as the litter stabilizes toward the end of summer. Wolf discipline is firm but not ruthless. An errant pup is typically held by the muzzle and pinned momentarily to the ground.

After the pups are weaned, the other members of the pack play an increasingly greater role in their upbringing, providing both food and recreation. The pups eat partially digested food regurgitated for them by adults. Babysitting adults play rag doll to the pups, who now have needle-sharp milk teeth and are mobbing each other, wrestling, biting, and generally grabbing reclining adults vigorously by the ruff of the neck. This behavior will later be molded into efficient hunting technique.

Daily activities center around the mouth of the den until the pups are about eight weeks old, at which time the adults move them to the first of a series of rendezvous sites where they remain while the others hunt. By late fall the pups may weigh forty-five to fifty pounds and accompany hunting adults. The knack of taking large animals like deer, moose, elk, mountain sheep, and caribou is behavior that must be taught; trapping mice with a bilateral stab of the forelimbs or surprising and catching a snowshoe hare comes more naturally.

By the time the pups are a year old they are almost full grown. Some disperse and either spend time alone or attempt to join another pack, or follow their own pack at a distance; others stay on with the pack for another year, until they reach sexual maturity.

There is probably a significant difference from year to year in the way a particular pack of wolves gets along. The loss of a good hunter, a drop or rise in the prey population, a prolonged winter, excessive social tension within the pack—all these are part of the ebb and flow of life for the wolf. Although no formal studies have been made, field studies of more than a year's duration suggest an annual cycle of individual identification with the pack that takes on unusual significance in the light of the suggestion that wolves seem to have both a sense of self and a sense of the pack and of preserving it.

Social tension increases in late winter with the evolution of a mating pair in the pack, and the level of anxiety is sometimes marked. Once two wolves have mated, however, emotions abate. The pack may split up to hunt more effectively. The pack's identity at this time may be at its loosest, with members hunting in ones and twos. The pregnant female, perhaps accompanied by her mate, selects a den site a week or more before she whelps, and the pack drifts together again to provide for her and the pups. This is undoubtedly a most difficult time in the year for the wolf. Activities center on the den site, when the most efficient kind of hunting would be one without such a locus. The pups are vulnerable and a few inevitably succumb quickly to exposure or starvation. There must be among wolves some sense of the importance of the population, as defined more by the hunting and reproductive unit (the pack) than by the individual, that leads wolves to stay together at this time in an effort to raise the pups.

With the calving of local prey species and the increased mobility that comes with moving the pups from the den to a series of sites from which the adults hunt, a climb up from this annual low point begins. The pack is given to emotional greeting, general nuzzling, and increasing horseplay as the summer goes on. They eat well. The weather is good. Their emotional peak must come in the fall and early winter. The pups are able to travel with the adults. Game is fat. The healthiest wolves have a tone of well-being, a strength of bone and mind, that will take them safely through the winter and into spring. They look to each other more often now, knowing that soon it will be impossible to get by alone as one could have done in summer. The increase in howls, their coming together frequently and wagging their tails as they orient around the alpha animals, marks the onset of winter.

After many years of work in the wild studying wolves, Adolph Murie wrote that the strongest impression he was left with was of the wolves' friendliness toward each other. Most systems of human description of animal behavior fall abysmally short in this area, which is unfortunate where wolves are concerned. Even as adults, wolves play tag with each other or romp with the pups, running about a clearing or on a snowbank with a rocking-horse gait. They scare each other by pouncing on sleeping wolves and by jumping in front of one another from hiding places. They bring things to each other, especially bits of food. They prance and parade about with sticks or bones in their mouths. I recall how one Alaska evening, the sun still bright at 11:30 P.M., we watched three wolves slip over the flanks of a hill in the Brooks Range like rafts dipping over riffles on a river. Sunlight shattered on a melt pond ahead of them. Spotting some pintail ducks there, the wolves quickly flattened out in the blueberries and heather. They squirmed slowly toward the water. At a distance of fifty feet they popped in the air like corks and charged the ducks. The pintails exploded skyward in a brilliant confusion of pounding wings, bounding wolves, and sheets of sunburst water. Breast feathers from their chests hung almost motionless in midair. They got away. The wolves cavorted in the pond, lapped some water, and were gone. It was all a game.

• • •

The social relationships of wolves are maintained through three systems of interpersonal and interpack communication: vocalization, postural signaling, and scent marking.

The wolf's howl is the social signal perhaps most familiar to everyone. It typically consists of a single note, rising sharply at the beginning or breaking abruptly at the end as the animal strains for volume. It can contain as many as twelve related harmonics. When wolves howl together they harmonize, rather than chorus on the same note, creating an impression of more animals howling than there actually are. Wolves do not have to stand to howl. They can howl lying down or sitting on their haunches. I've even seen a wolf, with an air of not wanting to miss out, howl while defecating.

There has been more speculation about the nature and function of the wolf's howl than the music, probably, of any other animal. It is a rich, captivating sound, a seductive echo that can moan on eerily and raise the hair on your head. Wolves apparently howl to assemble the pack, especially before and after the hunt; to pass on an alarm, especially at the den site; to locate each other in a storm or in unfamiliar territory; and to communicate across great distances. Some Eskimos, according to writer/naturalist Farley Mowat, claim to be able to understand what wolves are howling about and to take advantage of it when the howling reveals the approach of migrating caribou. The howl may carry six miles or more in still arctic air.

There is little evidence that wolves howl during a chase, but they may do so afterward, perhaps to celebrate a successful hunt (the presence of food), their prowess, or the fact that they are all together again, that no one has been injured. Adolph Murie, who had an eye for such things, reported a lone wolf howling while hunting mice.

There has never been any evidence that wolves howl at the moon, or howl more frequently during a full moon, though howling may be more frequent in the evening or early morning. Howling reaches a seasonal peak in the winter months, during the time of courtship and breeding; it is easy to see how the idea that wolves howl at the moon might have gained credence and played well on the imagination during these cold, clear nights when the sound carried far and a full moon lent an eerie aspect to a snowscape.

Howl

It was wild, untamed music and it
echoed from the hillsides
and filled the valleys. It sent
a queer shivering feeling along my
spine. It was not a feeling
of fear, you understand, but a sort of
tingling, as if there was hair on my back
and it was hackling.
—ALDA ORTON, *Alaskan trapper*

What emotions prompt a howl remain unknown, though field and laboratory researchers both suggest that solo howls and group howling alike are brought on by restlessness and anxiety. Loneliness is the emotion most often mentioned, but group howling has a quality of celebration and camaraderie about it, what wildlife biologist Durward Allen called "the jubilation of wolves." Murie writes of four wolves assembled on a skyline, wagging their tails and frisking together. They began to howl, and while they did so a gray female ran up from the den a hundred yards away and joined them. She was greeted with energetic tail wagging and general good feeling, then they all threw back their heads and howled. The howling, wrote Murie, floated softly across the tundra. Then, abruptly, the assembly broke up. The mother returned to the den and the pups; the others departed on the evening hunt.

Similar actions among Cape hunting dogs have been called mood-synchronizing activities by one researcher.

The wolf's other vocalizations have received less attention, though wolves seem to use these other sounds more often, to communicate more information. They are commonly divided into three categories: growls, barks, and whines or squeaks. Howls have been recorded and studied in the wild. Growls, squeaks, and barks have only rarely been heard in the field, so we must proceed here solely on the basis of information from captive animals.

Wolves only infrequently bark, and then it is a quiet "woof" more often than a dog-type bark. They do not bark continuously like dogs but woof a few times and then retreat, as for example when a stranger ap-

The wolf in the middle in the photograph on the left begins to howl in response to the others. In chorus like this, each wolf chooses a different pitch. The production of harmonics (see chart, page 42) may create the impression of fifteen or twenty wolves where there are in fact only three or four.

proaches the pen. Barks reported from the field are associated with a pack's being surprised at its den and an animal, usually the female, rising to bark a warning.

Growling is heard during food challenges and, like the bark, is associated with threat behavior or an assertion of rights in some social context. To the human ear this is perhaps the most doglike wolf sound in terms of its association with other behaviors, such as a squabble over a bone. Growling is common among pups when they're playing. Pups also growl when they jerk at the ruff of a reclining adult and comically will even try to growl adults off a piece of food. Another type of growl is a higher-pitched one that begins to sound like a whine and often precedes a snapping lunge at another wolf.

Perhaps the most interesting sounds are the whines and high-pitched social squeaks associated with greeting, feeding the pups, play, pen pac-

ing, and other situations of anxiety, curiosity, and inquiry. They are the sounds of intimacy.

Over a period of weeks one spring I observed a captive pack that included four pups. With the aid of underground microphones in the den, I was able to listen to sounds that otherwise would have been inaudible. The pups frequently wrestled down there, growling and yipping, but they would stop immediately when the mother came to the den entrance and squeaked—usually, but not always, a call for food. Sometimes it was a call to play. It was the custom with this pack for the alpha animals to take meat (chicken) from the hand of their caretaker and to then call the others—the pups and yearlings—with squeaks. They would all trot over. Then adults and young alike would engage in a twisting, supple dance—everyone squeaking, the young jabbing at the adults' muzzles—until the adults regurgitated the meat.

The mother would squeak on occasion when the pups were playing too roughly; the father would occasionally call the pups over to him with

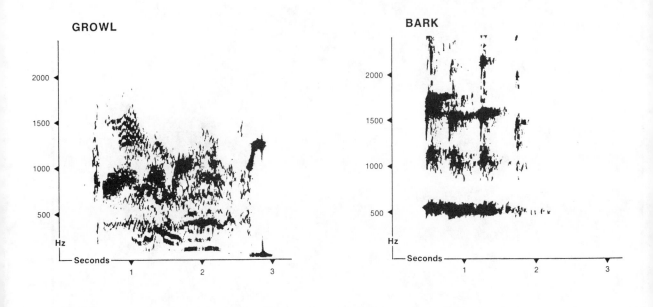

GROWL

BARK

The categories of vocal expression. There are three harmonics in this howl.

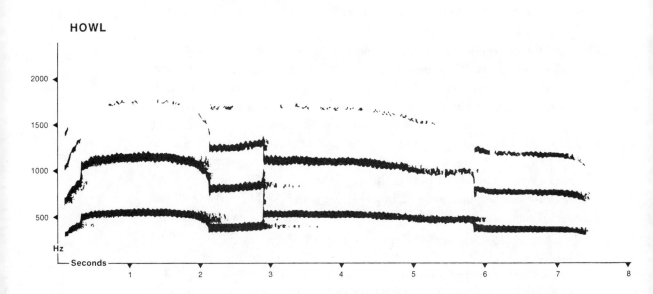

HOWL

WHINE

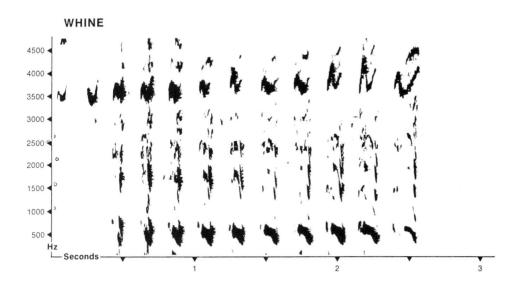

a squeak, and they would all just stand there and nuzzle. Reassurance, perhaps.

Some squeaks were repeated often enough to be recognized; these were associated with certain specific behaviors, leading one to think of them as bits of true communication.

Wolves hear well up to a frequency of 26kH. (beyond the range of human hearing, in the range where bats and porpoises produce sound), but what wolves do with high-frequency information remains a mystery. The ability to detect high-pitched sounds—wolves can distinguish between sounds a single tone apart in the range of 10–15kH.—may help them locate rodents under a snowpack. Many Russian scientists believe that wolves hunt even large game more by sound than smell and that the wolf's range of hearing and the fineness of its auditory discrimination make this its keenest sense.

Postural communication is composed of a variety of facial expressions and tail positionings, as well as such things as piloerection (raising the hackles). Lunging, chasing, body slamming and fighting, and more subtle gestures may also be considered in this category.

Rudolph Schenkel in 1947 was the first to document the great range of facial expression in the wolf and to relate it (and tail positions) to moods or feelings in the animal. These simple classifications for gestures—"suspicion," "threat," "anxiety," "submission"—later came to be understood in a more complicated fashion. Today the tendency is to treat postural gestures dynamically, as part of a complex of behaviors, augmented by vocalizations, flavored by personal idiosyncrasies.

When an alpha male encounters a low-ranking male in the same pack, he may stand erect and still, his tail horizontal in line with his spine, and stare at the other animal. The subordinate animal generally lowers his body, holds his tail down, turns slightly away from the alpha male, and lays his ears back. In a more serious encounter he might retract the corners of his mouth to reveal his teeth in what is called a submissive grin and twist his head so that he is looking up at the alpha animal. This is called passive submission. The subordinate's attempt to lick the alpha animal's muzzle would be active submission.

To a casual observer such a display appears to clearly reveal a dominant/submissive relationship; however, an observer who was with

An intense moment between a dominant ten-year-old male on the left and a yearling female on the right. The split second captured here reveals, in the body language of wolves, annoyance on the part of the older animal with a partial erection of his tail (1), the raising of his hackles (2), the forward movement of his ears (3), and the vertical retraction of his lips (4). The subordinate animal indicates acquiescence with a flattening of her ears (5), a flashing of the white of her eyes (6), an appeasement gesture called "licking intention" (7), and a general lowering of her body (8). Her raised paw (9) may be the tail end of the gesture that elicited the adult's response, or part of another appeasement gesture.

the animals regularly and was familiar with their personalities and the history of the pack—fights, matings, alliances—could tell much more. Many encounters are simple, but it would be misleading to establish simplicity of gesture as the rule. An obviously "submissive" wolf may be expressing submission, fear, and defensive aggression simultaneously. Even trained ethologists have mistaken who the submissive animal in an encounter was, thinking that an inhibited bite (a submissive gesture) was an attack (a display of dominance).

Markings on the fur already mentioned emphasize detail in postural expression, just as lipstick emphasizes the lips or eye shadow the eyes in human beings. The dark tip of the tail creates simple contrast for increased visibility and also marks the area of the tail that twitches, a sign

of excitement. A wolf's black lips are set off against white hairs on the muzzle and lower jaw to emphasize this important area of the face, and the face itself is subtly marked, especially around the eyes. The ears are lined with light hairs and rimmed with dark.

The face is the focus of silent gesture in the wolf and Schenkel and others have identified a number of facial gestures, especially in connection with movements of the eyes, ears, and lips. The terms used convey something of the range and complexity: "licking intention," "agonistic pucker," "tooth snapping," "intimidating stare." In the wild, observers are rarely close enough to see any of this. Schenkel was particularly attentive to the angle of the ears and the wrinkling of the forehead as clues to the wolf's intentions. One senses, I think, the excitement the man must have felt, sitting outside the wolf cage at the Basel Zoo, as he contemplated the slow emergence of a new kind of language, a priceless key to understanding behavior.

Nose pushing, jaw wrestling, cheek rubbing, and facial licking are common when wolves are together. One wolf mouthing another's muzzle is a friendly gesture; clamping another's muzzle between bared teeth is less friendly but not as ferocious as it appears to the human eye. "Standing over" and "riding up" are distinguished as body gestures; an animal may emphasize his dominance by standing over, or straddling, a reclining subordinate. The subordinate may respond by rolling over on his back and, in an extreme case, urinating a few drops on himself. When one wolf approaches another from the side, he may deliver a "hip slam," and after more pushing and shoving ride up on the other animal by placing his forepaws on or over the other's shoulders. This, too, is a gesture of dominance and is common among pups. Another gesture commonly seen is the stiff-legged approach of an alpha animal, which is at variance with the looser, bicycling motion of the other pack members.

It should be borne in mind that there are misunderstandings among wolves, just as there are in human relationships, and that observers occasionally glimpse amazement on the face of a wolf who catches an in-

Subtle gestures of postural and facial communication are accentuated by a set of dark lines marking the ears, eyes, muzzle, and shoulders.

timidating look meant for someone else. The idea of "submission" in a wolf pack, made visible to the human observer in ways human beings consider debasing, like rolling over on one's back, can be taken, I think, too seriously. The submissiveness is not neurotic; it is essential to the maintenance of group harmony. Submissive gestures have quite logical and very pleasant antecedents. Puppies first roll over on their backs so their parents can lick them clean. They first nuzzle adults to trigger regurgitation. Much of what is seen in a wolf pen might more profitably be viewed as "reassurance displays" aimed at group harmony rather than submissive whimpering at the feet of an ogre.

Our attempts to understand wolf language are crude and based not a little on the belief that the animal is simple-minded and therefore speaks a simple language. There are sounds we can't hear and there are signals we don't see. As we begin to put vocalizations together with a more fluid and careful description of body movement, we are bound to discover considerably more about the wolf and his language of gesture.

The third kind of communication, about which we unfortunately know very little, is the complex of olfactory cues associated with scent marking and glandular secretions.

In the wild, a traveling alpha animal either scent-marks or inspects a scent mark on the average of once every two minutes—an indication of the singular importance of the activity. It is commonly believed that the primary function of scent marking is to mark out a pack's territory and so warn off intruders; but American behavioral psychologist Roger Peters, one of the first to study the phenomenon, believes that territorial marking is a secondary function. The primary one is to mark territory on a regular basis for the benefit of the resident pack. The marks are an aid in establishing cognitive maps for the younger wolves, mental pictures of the home range, so that they know where they are with respect to certain creeks or recent kills and how to get where they wish to go. Secondly, scent marks help the pack to communicate when it is broken up. By reading scent marks one wolf can determine whether an area has been hunted recently, if a certain member of the pack is in the general area, or who has traveled through recently with whom. This, writes Peters, would ensure the efficient use of all parts of a pack's territory. An analogy would be forest dwellers leaving messages for each other, stuck in a hole in a designated oak.

Peters divides scent marks into four categories: raised-leg urination, squat urination, defecation, and ground scratching or dirt kicking. The first category is the most important. The alpha animals (primarily the males) make this kind of scent mark. They are made against objects above ground level to ensure a large evaporative surface (for a stronger odor) and to keep the mark clear of rain or snow. Squat urination and defecation probably have scent-marking as well as eliminative functions; defecation may trigger anal glands, imparting a personal scent to a scat. Dirt scratching probably functions as a visual display of dominance for the benefit of other pack members, but it may serve still another purpose if glands between the toes are stimulated and another olfactory message is left behind.

Wolves carry on a regular pattern of scent marking, visiting each section of their territory on the average of once every three weeks as they travel established routes. The area is, in effect, studded with olfactory hotspots. To ensure that a scent mark will be detected by others in a minimum of time, the marks are concentrated around trail junctions. But wolves even scent-mark when they are pursuing game cross-country, so presumably wolves can always tell whether they are in their own territory or not.

Scent marks certainly warn off intruders, but their larger role seems to be in the maintenance of a sense of spacial organization for the resident pack. They may also help wolves to find open territories, and loners of the opposite sex—the nucleus of a new pack—to find each other.

Glandular secretions form another olfactory stimulus that plays an important role in intrapack communication, but we know little about them. Anal (gland) inspection is common among male wolves, with the dominant males readily presenting their anal parts for inspection and subordinate animals withdrawing theirs or presenting them only reluctantly. Females rarely engage in anal inspection except during the breeding season when, like the males, they may be attracted to the presence of vulvar blood.

Other glands include the supracaudal gland on top of the tail, usually marked off by a dark patch of slightly stiffer hair, the glands between the toes, and glands around the cheeks. The habit dogs have of rolling in putrid substances is also found in wolves. It seems possible that odors picked up in this way and carried to other pack members have some communicative function.

Roger Peters told me once that wolves in the Superior National Forest defecate sometimes on beer cans. Like any scent mark, these scats give off both visual and olfactory signals. We should see more here than what the wolf might be telling us about our littering habits. The animals may be marking things they consider dangerous to other wolves, especially pups, for wolves also mark traps and poisoned baits by defecating on them. If Peters is correct in thinking that the olfactory information in a scat is intended for other pack members, the idea makes even better sense.

No one knows what a wolf can smell, but the guess is that he is not so highly sensitive to faint odors—the human nose is even good at that—but that he is able to distinguish among many similar odors. What to the human nose just smells like "the woods" may for the wolf be hundreds of discrete bits of information. This power to discriminate, together with an olfactory memory (analogous to the auditory memory some people develop for hundreds of bird songs, i.e., which bird, which of its songs, at what time of day, etc.), becomes another way for the wolf to fathom his universe.

It is sometimes suggested that the wolf's long nose is the result of selection for a keen sense of smell, but it is more probable that it evolved or was maintained as part of the need for large, powerful jaws.

There is another, far less obvious, kind of communication wolves employ which is perhaps extrasensory, or at least beyond our range of perception. I have noticed that captive animals at rest seem to pick up cues from each other even though there is no audible sound and they are out of visual contact. Their backs may be turned to each other or one may be off in some trees in a corner of the pen. When one animal stares intently at something, for example, it apparently creates some kind of tension. Other animals respond by lifting their heads and turning without hesitation to look at the area where the first animal is staring. In my experience it was most often the subordinate animals that responded first and the alpha animals last. Perhaps further research will establish a firmer foundation for this. It hints, of course, at much.

This may be the place to mention something that receives little attention, the fact that wolves kill each other. Recent efforts to change the bad image many people have of the wolf have led to the suggestion that while wolves may fight, the encounters aren't fatal. This is not true. Wolves do kill each other, especially in captivity. In the wild, deaths are related most often to territorial trespass, especially when pups are threatened. Strangely behaving wolves—epileptic pups, wolves caught in steel traps and thrashing about, wolves crippled by a moose or gunshot—have been killed by their pack members. Wolves in the same pack rarely square off and fight to the death, flight being the rule for the loser, and they dem-

Scent rolling, a practice that enables the wolf to transport odors wherever he goes.

onstrate an ability to work out disputes ritually, but disputes over an alpha position do sometimes come down to a bloody, eerily silent fight to the death.

It is fairly common to observe a scapegoat animal in a captive pack, typically one that has fought for or once held the alpha or beta position. If he was once dominant and abused other animals from that position, he will likely be abused in turn. If he was benevolent as an alpha animal, he will be treated kindly. Interestingly, this "omega" animal is often relegated to the area in the wolf enclosure which is directly adjacent to the area outside the pen with the greatest human traffic. In the wild an omega animal might trail the pack at a distance, feeding on leftovers, occasionally trying to join them. He might even be permitted to do so briefly—to repel an outsider from another pack, for example—and eventually he might be reintegrated.

In one captive situation I observed, the outcast, a former beta male, still enjoyed the alpha male's protection. One day the alpha male broke up a silent, serious fight between the outcast and the rest of the pack—nine animals—that left the outcast bloody and stiff with wounds for two days. One of the curious elements in this case was that the attacks were triggered by the outcast's attempts to defecate outside its assigned area. The animal seemed to be suffering from constipation and nipped at its hindquarters as though bothered by worms. It occurred to me that the ousting could have been related to this intestinal problem. It would be interesting to know whether wild wolves banished by packs in the wild suffer from infections or diseases that threaten the health of the pack.

The reader may have been tempted by now to look at wolf behavior in terms of the sorts of things domestic dogs do. It should be stressed here that this is not wise. Dogs suffer from a wide variety of emotional disorders, many of them brought on by the sort of selective breeding that destroys or radically alters their systems of communication. Tail docking (boxers), excessive facial hair (sheep dogs), ear cropping (Doberman pinschers), pendulous ears (bloodhounds), and uniform coloration (Weimaraners) all have forced dogs to seek other means of communication. Often the behavior that we see in them—scent-marking a fire hydrant, for example—is an example of frustrated communication.

Three

HUNTING AND TERRITORY

W OLVES do not get hungry in the way we normally understand hunger. Their feeding habits and digestive systems are adapted to a feast-or-famine existence and to procuring and processing massive amounts of food in a relatively short time. They are more or less always hungry. Wolves commonly go without food for three or four days and then gorge, eating as much as eighteen pounds of meat in one sitting. Then, "meat drunk," they may lay out in the sun until digestion is completed (in two or three hours), and then start again. A Russian record reports a wolf going without food for seventeen days, and it is commonly recorded that wolves may eat up to one-fifth of their body weight at one time.

53

The wolf's diet consists mostly of muscle meat and fatty tissue from various animals. Heart, lung, liver, and other internal organs are eaten. Bones are crushed to get at the marrow, and bone fragments are eaten as well; even hair and skin are sometimes consumed. The only part consistently ignored is the stomach and its contents. Some vegetable matter is taken separately, particularly berries, but *Canis lupus* does not seem to digest them very well. The red wolf commonly consumes a higher proportion of vegetable matter and subsists on smaller game, like swamp rabbit, and such things as fiddler crabs. All wolves eat grass, possibly to scour the digestive tract and remove worms. Consisting mostly of cellulose, the grass itself is never digested.

Wolves consume an average of five to ten pounds of meat a day and wash it down with large quantities of water to prevent uremic poisoning from the high production of urea associated with a meat diet. The wolf has a large liver and pancreas to aid digestion, and the feces provide an interesting example of efficiency in its large intestine. Droppings in the wild typically consist of chips and slivers of bone neatly packaged along with such items as the rubbery remains of deer hooves in a capsule of hair that moves very smoothly down the colon.

The major sources of meat in the wolf's diet are deer, moose, elk, musk ox, Dall sheep, Rocky Mountain sheep, caribou, reindeer, or beaver, depending on the area, the season, and the year—a good one or a bad one, say, for moose. Wolves also prey on buffalo (in Wood Buffalo National Park, Canada), snowshoe hares (on Ellesmere Island), flightless ducks (in the James Bay region of Canada), marmots, mice, squirrels, grouse, geese, and rabbits. Wolves fish, too, wade-herding salmon, arctic grayling, or whitefish into shallow pools where they're trapped. They also mouth-spear them in swift water from the bank with well-timed lunges. They eat carrion and occasionally insects, especially when they encounter them in epidemic populations. And they feed on domestic stock. They hunt by intent but are opportunists, too.

Many studies indicate that wolves prey largely on the aged, the diseased, and the very young. While this is the norm, it is not always true. Wolves do take animals in their prime. And they kill in excess (though excessive kills are often made at the time of denning to ensure a supply of meat while the pack is denbound). In reality, they will likely kill, or try

Surplus Killing

Wolves sometimes kill all out of proportion to their need for food. That this is also an eerie human trait is suggested by the behavior of buffalo hunters in the nineteenth century. Under peculiar circumstances, having to do with wind, perhaps—no one really knows—a herd of buffalo would remain placid while a hunter dropped animal after animal in its midst. The sight of blood and the bellowing of the wounded did nothing to disturb them. They remained oblivious until something—a gust of wind, the sight of so many carcasses—finally stampeded them. A hunter would commonly shoot until his gun barrel overheated and threatened to explode. The men who made such stands later recalled being absolutely mesmerized by the apparent oblivion, that the moment seemed utterly suspended. When the buffalo finally reacted, the almost mindless impulse to shoot abated immediately and a feeling of remorse over-came them.

---

to kill, any animal that presents itself at a disadvantage. The important thing to bear in mind is that generally wolves do not overrun the prey population and kill it out, although they have been known to do so, just as they have, extraordinary as it seems, practiced a kind of fallow-field farming by not killing deer in certain parts of their territories for four or five years, letting the prey population recover there.

In cases where wolf populations are small, or where the prey population is outstripping its food supply, wolves may kill indiscriminately across all age classes.

Just as some people would like to believe that wolves never hurt each other, so some would like to believe that wolves only kill animals that are doomed anyway—the old, the sick, the injured. But the pruning of herds attributed to predators like the wolf is, at best, crude. The question of which animals will die is also affected by severe winters, range deterioration, and human hunting, among other factors.

In a word, not enough is known.

The idea of wolves on the hunt powerfully engages the human imagi-nation. The wolf spends perhaps one-third of his life in pursuit of food. It is a task for which he evolved and to which he is well suited. With powerful jaw muscles he will clamp down on a moose's bulbous nose and hold on tenaciously while the moose swings him clear of the ground or stomps on him in a vain effort to throw him off. The wolf can course for miles behind fleeing game, and smell prey a couple of miles off. He has superb hearing and can read tracks as well.

Man admires the wolf's prowess and indefatigable pursuit, but death itself—blood, gore, and the thought of a wounded animal bellowing in its death throes—makes human beings intensely uncomfortable. There have been people throughout history who would gladly have taken a stand for the preservation of the wolf if only they could have gotten over their own revulsion at the way wolves kill. They frequently could not abide the idea of a wolf killing a creature as "beautiful" as a deer. So the hunting down of prey species warrants careful attention here.

The wolf is a marvelous hunter. Whether we care for the act (or the smelling of anal glands or rolling in decaying meat) is moot—or should be. Wolves kill the largest ungulates by running alongside them, slashing at their hams, ripping at their flanks and abdomen, tearing at the nose and head, harassing the animal until it weakens enough through loss of blood and the severing of muscles to be thrown to the ground. At this point the wolves usually rip open the abdominal cavity and begin eating, sometimes before the animal is dead. If the chase has been a hard one, the wolves may rest before eating anything.

Stories of Teutonically organized raids, where some wolves act as decoys while others wait in ambush, create a sense of hypermilitary tactics, which is misleading. Wolves are intelligent hunters, not marauders. Stories of wolves shredding each other during an attack, like a cauldron of sharks in a bloody frenzy, are spurious. But the conjecture put forth to counteract a claim of stockmen, that wolves never kill beyond their needs, is also erroneous. Wolves do sometimes kill their natural prey in excess of their need for food.

During exceptionally heavy snows in Minnesota in 1969, wolves killed almost every foundering deer they came across, leaving many of them wholly uneaten. Hans Kruuk, a Dutch biologist, studied this phenomenon among foxes in England and hyenas in Africa and gave it a name— surplus killing. He believes that a specific sequence of events leads up to an animal's death and shuts off the predator's impulse to kill. If the sequence jams—if, say a rare meteorological event like unseasonably deep snows or an excessively dark night interferes, if game animals can't, or won't, flee—the predator just keeps killing.

For the wolf, take a moose as an example of prey. The sequence (as established by the wildlife biologist L. David Mech) runs: (1) Wolf senses moose and approaches (the stalk); (2) wolf and moose sense each other (the encounter); (3) wolf charges (the rush); and (4) moose runs (the chase).

But things do not always go this smoothly. A pack of wolves may catch scent of a moose·yet ignore it. Wolves and moose may stare at each other intently—then the moose may just walk off. During a chase the moose may be surrounded, seemingly doomed, when suddenly one wolf will break off the chase in mid-stride and snap at the other wolves to drive them off—as though they had selected the wrong moose.

Out of the 160 moose that Mech saw from the air on Isle Royale and judged to be within range of hunting wolves:

> 29 were ignored,
>
> 11 discovered the wolves first and eluded detection,
>
> 24 refused to run when confronted and were left alone.

Of the 96 that ran:

> 43 got away immediately,
>
> 34 were surrounded but not harmed,
>
> 12 made successful defensive stands,
>
> 7 were attacked,
>
> 6 were killed,
>
> 1 was wounded and abandoned.

It would appear that the wolf is either inefficient or not very serious about killing moose. Or that more is going on than we understand.

There is a difference between the way wolves hunt moose and the way they hunt other animals—mice in meadows, Dall sheep on precipitous slopes, and caribou on featureless tundra. As the size of the prey increases, so does the skill and endurance required of the wolf (as well as the size of the pack) and the chance that he himself will be killed. Cursorial hunting of the moose requires a keen refinement of the wolf's skills.

And it is in such encounters with large animals that the nature of this hunter is most clearly revealed.

To illustrate, begin with a classic case that took place in Wood Buffalo National Park, Alberta, Canada, in 1951. Two buffalo bulls and two cows are lying in the grass ruminating. Three of them are in good health; one cow is lame. Wolves approach and withdraw a number of times, apparently put off by a human observer. At each approach, though, the lame cow becomes agitated and begins looking all around. Her three companions *ignore* the wolves. When one wolf comes within twenty-five feet, the lame cow gets up on shaking legs to face it alone. It seems clear that prey selection is something both animals play a role in.

Postmortem examination of moose and other large prey confirms a kind of selection. Wolves, as stated, take predominantly the very young, the old, and the injured and diseased—individuals the prey population can conveniently do without (due to senility, contagion, etc.), or ones doomed to imminent death anyway because of injury or parasitic infection. They are, after all, the easiest to catch. (It is often forgotten that wild animals like sheep, elk, moose, and deer suffer, sometimes miserably, from disease and injury, perhaps because most of us experience these animals in zoos where they are cared for. A Canadian biologist once observed a mule deer at the point of death, parasitized by an estimated seven hundred winter ticks. Moose parasitized by winter ticks leave a distinctive trail of bloody beds and showers of red on the white snow where they have shaken. Caribou can suffer terribly from warble flies and nostril flies, and moose are sometimes crippled by hydatid cysts in their lungs. Mech found one moose with fifty-seven of these golfball-sized cysts. Necrotic stomatitis, actinomycosis, and other bone and gum diseases and hoof infections are also prevalent among ungulates.)

Prey animals such as these apparently announce their poor condition to the wolf in the subtleties of a stance, a peculiarity of gait, a rankness of breath, or more obvious signs of physical incapacity, such as wounds, massive loss of hair, or visible infection. Wolves are alert to such nuances; further, by forcing a hunch, so to speak, by making a moose run or testing it, the wolf may realize that its lungs are impacted from the wheezing, labored breathing. It might know that the moose is not going to run very far before collapsing.

The testing of a prey species by a predator has been frequently ob-served in the field, especially among herd animals like caribou. It occurs so often as to be perfunctory. But hundreds of animals may be chased before a burst of speed brings one down, and the conclusion that some of these chases are not serious is at least plausible.

If the prey runs, it is almost certain to be chased. If it refuses to run, or approaches the wolves, it may be left alone. More signals, perhaps, be-tween predator and prey.

Some animals apparently set themselves up (or are set up) to be killed because they feed or travel alone. Musk oxen, practically invulnerable to attack when standing in a defensive formation together, are easy prey for wolves once they are banished. (Among gregarious species, such lone animals living away from the herd tend to be old or sick or both.)

There's a logic to all this. The injured, the aged, and the diseased have ways of announcing themselves and are subsequently removed. The young are cropped, which in turn controls the size of the population and perhaps eliminates inferior or maladaptive combinations of genes at the outset.

But there are elements of the wolf hunt that suggest there is more to it than the simple pathology of diseased prey, or behavior that might be triggered by flight and the wolf's need to eat. In fact, people make a rather curious assumption: that wolves look for moose just to kill them. Nunamiut Eskimos believe that during winter a healthy adult wolf can run down any caribou it chooses, but it doesn't always do this for reasons known only to the wolf. And perhaps the caribou.

It has long been held that wolves use various strategies when hunting, though the data are not yet clear. On occasion they do employ what seems to be conscious strategy, sending out one or two animals to herd prey into an ambush. And they vary their tactics slightly to hunt each species of prey, adapting primarily to terrain and somewhat less to the sort of prey. They prefer to attack sheep from above. They may split up to skirt both sides of an island in a frozen lake and then precipitously flush caribou or deer driven toward the island's tip. When antelope were abundant on the Great Plains, wolves reputedly lay low in the grass, switching their tails from side to side like metronomes to attract the curi-ous animals close enough to jump them. And they apparently once

Wolves expend energy carefully, taking every advantage of terrain in chasing prey, moving cross-country in trails broken through deep snow by caribou, and sleeping during the hot hours at midday. When food was scarce one year in Minnesota because of a collapse of the deer population, wolves adapted by ranging far outside their territory for food and by resting a great deal, sleeping as much as twenty hours a day.

herded buffalo onto lake ice where the huge animals lost their footing, a practice they still use to bring down elk.

Wolves hunt into the wind, and they quickly incorporate any new roads into their strategies, mostly to conserve energy and to facilitate ambushes. Wolves remain acutely conscious of their energy budgets, letting one wolf break trail in deep snow while the others follow in its footsteps, for example. An intriguing instance of this conservation of energy was observed by Robert Ahgook on March 21, 1970, on the tundra sixty-four miles northeast of Anaktuvuk Pass, Alaska. A lone wolf chased a single caribou for ten kilometers across hard-packed snow into an area of loose powder. Both animals slowed to a walk and then alternated running and walking for three kilometers, the wolf always adjusting to keep the distance between the caribou and itself constant. When the two animals emerged from the loose snow and headed down a slight incline, the wolf put on a burst of speed and brought the exhausted caribou down in a space of seventy meters.

Wolves may learn their territories well enough to take advantage of shortcuts and to know where they can drive prey into snow that will founder them; but these, like so many other observations, are being made to conform to a preconceived idea, namely, a single-minded strategy, and this could be a mistake.

Wolves halt chases for no apparent reason (to our human senses). One wolf may insist on attacking a certain individual while the rest of the pack expresses disinterest. A pack on the hunt may investigate tracks less than a minute old but pick up some subtle cue from them and not pursue.

There is no certain outcome after the prey is rushed. The chase may last only a few seconds, it may go on for miles, or it may carry on intermittently for days. With most large game successfully pursued, however, the pathology of death is similar: (1) Massive damage to the animal's hips breaks its stride; (2) crushing and tearing cause bleeding and induce trauma; (3) harassment tires the animal; (4) disembowelment causes death. With large animals like moose, one wolf may grab the nose or head while the others undercut the animal and mob it to get it off its feet. Smaller animals like sheep, deer, and caribou can be ridden down by a single wolf and killed with a neck or head hold, which appears to suffocate them. In deep, crusted snow, a single wolf may kill a moose. An animal is rarely, if ever, hamstrung.

Once the prey is wounded and has taken its death stand, one or two wolves may harass it—make it exert itself, keep it bleeding—while the others rest, play tag, or otherwise demonstrate a lack of interest. The pack may even depart, leaving one or two animals on a death watch.

Again, once one is reduced to considering those animals that are actually killed, prey selection seems in retrospect very tidy. But this does not account for the animals that are not killed, which is an equally important issue.

One of the central questions about predators and their prey is why one animal is killed and not another. Why is one chosen and another, seemingly in every way as suitable, ignored? No one knows.

The most beguiling moment in the hunt is the first moment of the encounter. Wolves and prey may remain absolutely still while staring at each other. Immediately afterward, a moose may simply turn and walk away (as we saw); or the wolves may turn and run; or the wolves may charge and kill the animal in less than a minute. An intense stare is frequently used by wolves to communicate with each other, and wolves also tend to engage strangers—wolf and human—in stares. I think what transpires in those moments of staring is an exchange of information between predator and prey that either triggers a chase or defuses the hunt right there. I call this exchange the conversation of death, and at the risk of leaving the reader hanging will discuss it further in the next section on Indians where the idea is more comfortable. For the moment let me say simply there is good evidence that signals go back and forth, and there is some other evidence to support the idea of a conversation of death. One researcher found that by arranging his fur-rimmed parka hood in a certain way, he could spook caribou at will. His observations of hunting wolves indicated that wolves seriously intent on a chase approached caribou herds with lowered heads; he deduced that it was his similarity of appearance—head buried below shoulder line in his parka hood—that was putting the caribou to flight. Other researchers have sought additional clues and have speculated that prey selection may be based on an exchange of information between predator and prey, but attempts to support such speculation have fallen short. Wolf hunts are rarely seen, even by field researchers, and when they are the observer is usually in a plane or at such a distance that picking up nuances of behavior is difficult. The best that can be done in such cases is to examine tracks in the snow carefully and to check the carcass and try to put together what happened.

There are some other elements in the wolf hunt that are intriguing, worth noting. Douglas Pimlott mentions a "bystander phenomenon." Two prey animals are pursued, and while wolves focus on one the other backtracks to watch its companion killed. Murie saw an eagle chase off a wolf that was engaged in a sheep stalk. Mech observed a "sure kill" from the air only to find when the site was examined from the ground that the prey animal had walked off.

The latter point should be well taken: in the past, it was assumed that wolves were basely motivated and bloodthirsty; then in an environmentally enlightened age, it was suddenly assumed that they were noble and wise. So, too, have we analyzed their hunting behavior in human terms, and none of it is worth more than the metaphor it's couched in. This habit indeed may eventually lead us even further from an understanding of the animal. For my own part, I mean to suggest that there is more to a wolf hunt than killing. And that wolves are wolves, not men.

Before moving on to a discussion of territory, I would like to glance quickly at something else: caching. Wolves occasionally bury parts of a kill. In the Arctic, cold helps to preserve the meat; farther south, a covering of earth and duff keeps some potential raiders at bay. The wolf digs the hole with his paws and covers it by pushing with his nose, perhaps memorizing the smell. But caching is not a very efficient system. Field researchers think that other animals—eagles, weasels, foxes, wolverines—use wolf caches as often as wolves do. Foxes seem especially adept at locating wolf caches. Murie writes about a wolf that killed a Dall lamb and carried off part of the carcass. The ground was covered with enough snow for good tracking and Murie followed him, only to find that a fox had cut the trail ahead of him and was also following. In one place the wolf backtracked for fifteen yards, jumped off the trail eight feet to one side, then wandered about in several loops. At this point the fox tracks circled around as though the fox were confused. The wolf went on across some wet tundra, stepping deliberately into shallow puddles—to destroy his scent, Murie thought. After passing through some woods, he came to a creek, and there the trail ended. The fox sniffed around for the scent before, like Murie, he discovered the tracks downstream about fifteen yards. Three hundred yards and the wolf crossed the stream and drifted into the woods. There, beside a tree, was the cache. By the time Murie got there the fox had raided it and departed.

Such incidents, it seems to me, contribute to the sense of a community of creatures in the woods which we so often lack when we examine a single species.

What land actually constitutes a wolf pack's territory is difficult to determine. Territories overlap; there are gaps between them; they are even abandoned. Tundra wolves don't really have year-round territories.

During the winter months they wander over vast areas of land in the wake of migrating caribou, centrally locating only during the denning season. Timber wolves, on the other hand, preying on species that migrate less or not at all, tend to have more recognizable territories. In an extreme case, such as on Isle Royale, where the packs are clearly defined and the landmass is exactly known, territories take on an artificial precision.

A given pack territory also changes size and shape with the season, shrinking or shifting a little during the denning period, for example. In winter the wolves may stay in one small area for weeks where a large number of deer have yarded up. Size of territory is also a function of prey density, as are the type of prey available and the number of wolves in a pack. Some wolves—loners—don't seem to have any territories.

The problem here is not simply one of definition, but one of conceptualization. "Territory" is too frequently understood to mean something rigid and well defined, like a city block. Wolf territories are highly plastic, more or less so depending on factors already mentioned. And this idea, that there is a high probability that in a certain area you will find the members of a certain pack on a regular basis, is tenable. But we are not talking about well-delineated areas patrolled in an orderly fashion by paramilitary creatures—a notion spawned by confusing the idea of territory with the idea of private property.

Wolf territories are defined, albeit rather temporarily, by scent marking and by hunting activities. We get a sense of a territory's boundaries from the way in which packs double back on themselves at various points in their wanderings. A pack at the edge of its territory might permit a wounded prey animal to escape if it flees across that border into another pack's territory. A wolf pack is repelled by the fresh scent marks of a neighboring pack. The boundary is defined from both sides of the fence; that it is not an idea to be taken lightly is evidenced by the number of trespassing wolves that are killed.

Wolf packs, everything else being equal, occupy larger territories in the north than wolves in the timbered country in the south do. Game is denser in the south; those packs need less territory to secure the same amount of food. The sheer size of a wolf pack's territory, therefore, is a relatively minor issue. More important are questions like these: Where do the lone wolves that leave packs every year go? Do they join other packs? If not, how—and where—do they define a new territory? Does a space of, say, 100 square miles suddenly open up? Which leads to the more interesting issue: How does an area where wolves are found absorb an increase in population if the loner is an unstable social entity (as he is) and the pack, as a rule, doesn't accept strangers and, furthermore, presumably controls contiguous territories? The answer, since loners do indeed find a place to live, can only be that territories are organic and not necessarily exclusive.

The idea of territory is really not very exciting in itself. Its importance lies in the fact that it precipitates such things as interpack communication through scent marking, that as a sine qua non of existence it is a major influence on the control of the wolf population, and that to violate its boundaries can result in death—sometimes.

Wolves are elusive, secretive creatures. L. David Mech, who has been studying them in the wild for twenty years, has come upon only a dozen on the ground that he didn't first see from an airplane or track down with the aid of a radio collar. Elusiveness is a defensive trait and it is conceivable that its function is to avoid detection by other wolves, so adjacent packs can overlap their territories and run little risk of fatally encountering each other. This would allow an area to "breathe" more easily as game populations fluctuated. It would also facilitate the movement of dispersing wolves.

It will be brought out in the next section that the world of the wolf and that of the Indian of North America and the Eskimo have certain things in common, but it might be mentioned here that the Pawnee and the Omaha Indians had an agreement to forget their traditional enmity and allow trespass in each other's territory in order to facilitate pursuit of migrating herds of buffalo, on which both tribes depended for maintenance. Similarly, Plains Indians moved back and forth through the territories of other tribes on various errands and cultivated the quality of elusiveness to facilitate such movement. Boundaries traditionally ebbed and flowed, and an area left unused for a period of time might be occupied by a band from a neighboring tribe.

A wolf in search of territory runs the highest risk of encountering both hostile wolves and human beings. To take such risks you must, it seems to me, be intent on something important; and to do it successfully, you must be elusive.

Most territorial fights involve the resident pack and a lone individual, though packs may also fight each other. If the encounter is fatal, it is almost always fatal to the trespassers. Four wolves killed another wolf on June 25, 1970, in Mount McKinley National Park, and the incident was witnessed by three people. They saw a black male feeding on a caribou carcass when suddenly a single gray wolf appeared, followed at some distance by three other grays. The black wolf ran, but the first gray caught up with him and pulled him down. In seconds the other three had arrived and they all began biting the black wolf. The black wolf became submissive and the grays appeared to back off. Then the black jumped up and seemed to be trying to get away. The grays attacked again and did not stop until one gray had the black by the throat. The black raised his head once and then apparently died. The grays backed off, sniffed around the area, and left.

Whether this incident was triggered by the black wolf's feeding on the caribou carcass or was simply a case of trespassing remains unclear.

There is a common belief among wolf biologists working in the field that wolves like to travel. I think they do, too, and think, further, that one reason for maintaining large territories is to have the space to travel freely and widely.

Much remains to be learned of how wolves relate to, learn about, and occupy space. Howling and scent marking are two ways they seem to have of assuring that a proper space exists between packs, thus tending to distribute food sources and ensure space for all concerned. But there are more intriguing ideas here. Research suggests that the wolves are capable of moving cross-country and intercepting herds of migrating animals that they cannot see when they set out—they appear to have an uncanny sense of where they're going to be. They certainly seem to know when caribou are coming toward them well enough to move to favorite crossings (which they must remember from times before) and set up ambushes. I remember once coming on a pack of wolves in the Nelchina Basin in south-central Alaska. One of the animals shot from the air with a tranquilizer gun went down in heavy timber; to reach her we had to land the helicopter in a clearing and wade through hip-deep snow to where she lay. As we approached I noticed how healthy she looked. It was March, a lean time of year, but she had a good layer of fat along her back. She had been eating well. When I opened her mouth, I saw her canines had been worn down to nubs. She must have been eight or nine years old. What meat she was eating she was not herself killing, and among wolves animals that don't contribute to the pack structure pass on. What did she contribute? As anthropomorphic as the notion was, I could not shake the idea that what she contributed was the experience of having done so many things. She was one, I thought, who knew where to go to find caribou.

Wolves are related in little-understood ways to animals they do not hunt. Some, like the coyote and lynx, move out of the immediate area when wolves move in. Others—the fox, the raven, the wolverine—feed off the carrion wolves provide. Wolves in turn take advantage of abandoned fox burrows and other creatures' homes for their dens, raid fox caches, and feed on an occasional bear's kill.

Wolves have a curious dependency on caribou to act as snowplows. It seems clear that tundra wolves do not follow caribou in winter solely to feed on them but because the herds open the way and pack the snow down. Wolves could not move through the deep snows of the northern forests without these highways. They also take advantage of moose trails in such snows.

The wolf seems to have few relationships with other animals that could be termed purely social, though he apparently takes pleasure in the company of ravens. The raven, with a range almost as extensive as the wolf's, one that includes even the tundra, commonly follows hunting wolves to feed on the remains of a kill. In winter, when tracks are visible from the air, ravens will follow the trail of a wolf pack in hopes of finding a carcass. They roost in neighboring trees or hop about eating bloody snow while the wolves eat, approaching the carcass when the wolves have finished. But the relationship between the two is deeper than this, as is revealed in the following incident. A traveling pack stopped to rest and four or five ravens who were tagging along began to pester them. As Mech writes in *The Wolf*:

"The birds would dive at a wolf's head or tail and the wolf would duck

The raven (Corvus corax), *who may lead wolves to their prey, who certainly feeds on their kills. Raven tag, in which ravens pester napping wolves and are in turn chased, seems to be a mutually enjoyable game.*

and then leap at them. Sometimes the ravens chased the wolves, flying just above their heads, and once, a raven waddled to a resting wolf, pecked at its tail, and jumped aside as the wolf snapped at it. When the wolf retaliated by stalking the raven, the bird allowed it within a foot before arising. Then it landed a few feet beyond the wolf, and repeated the prank.

"It appears that the wolf and the raven have reached an adjustment in their relationships such that each creature is rewarded in some way by the presence of the other and that each is fully aware of the other's capabilities. Both species are extremely social, so they must possess the psychological mechanisms necessary for forming social attachments. Perhaps in some way individuals of each species have included members of the other in their social group and have formed bonds with them."

The wolf may have similar relationships with other creatures. People have heard loons and barred owls responding to wolf howls, and vice versa.

The wolf has few satisfactory meetings with bears. In most encounters wolves snap at the bear's heels and lunge at his flanks to drive him away from a carcass or a pup, and the bear in turn swats at the wolves or tries to catch a wolf between his paws. In the end the most the wolves can hope to do is to herd a bear off in the right direction.

Wolves may kill a coyote and occasionally throttle a fox in a dispute over food. Meetings between dogs and wolves result in anything from swift death to lasting relationships. Wolves sometimes prey on dogs near villages as though they were domestic stock. (The set of steel nubs on a leather strap seen on dogs today is a gentler version of the spiked collar dogs once wore as protection against wolves.) Dispersing wolves and feral dogs may occasionally breed and establish hybrid packs. A common practice in captivity is to allow wolf pups to establish a bond with an older dog. The relationship gives humans an intermediary, and makes handling the wolves easier. Wolves will submit to dogs they have grown up with, no matter how small. I've seen a tame adult wolf act submissive before an eight-pound cairn terrier. As we shall see later, feral dogs preyed frequently on domestic stock, which precipitated massive retaliation—against wolves.

If one considers the ramifications, the wolf's most important and dangerous relationship must be his relationship with man.

It is popularly believed that there is no written record of a healthy wolf ever having killed a person in North America. Those making the claim ignore Eskimos and Indians, who have been killed, and are careful to rule out rabid wolves. The latter have attacked people several times.

Ernest Thompson Seton believed that wolves attacked and killed people before the coming of the gun and poisons, especially during the winter months when food was scarce, and native American oral history supports him. To judge from all the stories that have been told, contacts between human beings and wolves were more frequent before the massive antipredator campaigns of the nineteenth and twentieth centuries. Whether more people were attacked under these circumstances remains a matter of conjecture. In evolutionary terms, of course, wolves and men developed along similar lines as social hunters and were in competition for the same game. Undoubtedly there were encounters in prehistoric times that resulted in death, but that is going pretty far back.

Reports from Russia and Europe of wolves preying on human beings are more numerous than those from North America and there is probably some truth to them. I see no reason why under the right circumstances—a desperately hungry wolf and an unarmed man, for instance—the wolf wouldn't kill.

In a book called *Adventures in Error*, Vilhjalmer Stefansson recalls his efforts to track down virtually every report of a wolf killing a human being between 1923 and 1936. Reports from the Caucasus, the Near East, Canada, and Alaska all proved to be either fiction or gross exaggeration. Furthermore, Stefansson could not substantiate a single report of wolves traveling in packs larger than about thirty. In 1945 it was reported that no incident of wolf attack brought to the attention of the U.S. Fish and Wildlife Service in the preceding twenty-five years could be substantiated. The late James Curran, editor of the Sault Ste. Marie, Ontario, *Daily Star*, put up a standing offer of $100 for anyone who could document a wolf attack on a human being. The reward went uncollected for years and lapsed with his death. It should be noted that there are more wolves in southern Ontario than anywhere else in Canada and that there is probably a greater likelihood of a person encountering one there in the region of Algonquin Provincial Park than perhaps anywhere else in the world.

C. H. D. Clarke, a Canadian naturalist, is responsible for bringing to English readers the story of the "beasts of Gévaudan." These two animals between them killed at least sixty-four people, maybe as many as one hundred, in the Cevennes Mountains of south-central France between June 30, 1764, and June 19, 1767. The majority of the victims were small children.

The creatures were hunted down by a succession of small armies, all of whom failed until the job was finally done by a gentleman in his sixties called Antoine de Bauterne. The male of the ravening pair was killed on September 21, 1766. He weighed 130 pounds, stood 32 inches at the shoulder, and measured 5 feet, 7 inches from nose to tail. By European standards, compared to other specimens of European wolf, he was

In July 1833 a rabid white wolf wandered into two separate camps on the upper Green River in western Wyoming and attacked a number of people. Thirteen of those bitten—mountain men, traders, and Indians—died. In 1926 a rabid wolf drifted through Churchill, Manitoba. The incident, grossly exaggerated by the press, was made to sound like a siege. The wolf was run over by a car and bit no one, but in the confusion six dogs and an Indian were shot.

enormous. The female, somewhat smaller, was killed nine months later.

Clarke reviewed most of the literature bearing on human predation in southern and central Europe, and in central Asia (where the majority of stories originated) and concluded that almost every report of a wolf attacking a human being could be attributed to a rabid animal or a hybrid. The Gévaudan wolves were of such size and were so oddly colored, Clarke believed, that they must have been wolf-dog hybrids. Wolf-dog hybrids are sometimes larger than either parent and are far more likely, too, to prey on children and livestock and would probably fear men less.

Between 1740 and 1773, about two thousand wolves were killed in the region of Gévaudan, mostly in attempts to kill the Gévaudan pair.

It is the fashion today to dismiss rather glibly accounts of wolves preying on human beings. However, I think it would be foolish to maintain that no healthy wolf ever did so, or that wolves were unable to size up human beings like any other sort of domestic stock and see whether in lean times taking such a creature was worth the risk. I am sure they can. The problem is one of setting things in perspective. How many tens of thousands of encounters between wolves and unarmed individuals have passed without incident? The reality seems to be that such events are incredibly rare nowadays, in spite of stories that continue to surface even in the *New York Times,* reporting wolves descending on peasant villages in blizzards in search of human food.

While the wolf preyed rarely on man, man clearly preyed excessively on the wolf and it may be appropriate to close this chapter on the behavior and ecology of the wolf with a mention of how that predilection has affected science.

The late Adolph Murie, the first person seriously to undertake a study of the wolf, began his work in Alaska in the spring of 1939 as a game biologist in Mount McKinley National Park. It was an enormous undertaking in an age when aerial observation and radio telemetry were not available. Murie walked more than seventeen hundred miles in the six months before September 1939, examining the remains of wolf kills and observing wolves away from their dens. He returned the next year, and finished his work in the summer of 1941. The results were published by the U.S. Government Printing Office in 1944 under the title *The Wolves of Mount McKinley*. The work is a classic.

Murie was working in Mount McKinley National Park at a time when outside pressure was being brought to destroy the wolves inside its boundaries in order to protect game herds. He alludes to instances in which wolves were killed and twice makes reference to wolf dens that were raided for pups. He remarks, rather stoically, "When a den is discovered the young are destroyed and all opportunity for making further observation is lost." This in a national park where the wildlife was supposedly protected.

Thirty years later L. David Mech, also a veteran of hundreds of miles of hiking on Isle Royale and in Minnesota, and innumerable hours in foul weather in a tiny observation plane or in the back of pickup trucks listening for signals from radio-collared wolves, was confronted with similar problems. Seventeen of his radio-collared wolves were killed by human beings. In northern Michigan an experiment to establish transplanted wolves into old range where there was sufficient wild food for them came to an inconclusive end when all four animals, each wearing a plainly visible radio collar, were killed. Erkki Pulliainen's research in Finland reached a state of limbo in 1975 when the last wolf was killed there. In 1976 the state of Alaska, under pressure from hunters to reduce its wolf population, deliberately shot the radio-collared wolves in one of its own studies.

The miracle is that in such a climate of human hatred, misunderstanding, and harassment wildlife biologists have managed to bring the wolf out of the darkness of superstition at all.

In a paper presented at a conference on wolves held in Maryland in 1966, it was suggested that more could be learned about the origins of man as a social animal by studying the social structure of wolf packs than could be learned by studying primates. The suggestion was prophetic. I write now in a country and at a time when man's own brutal nature is cause for concern and when the wolf, whom man has historically accused of craven savagery, has begun to emerge as a benign creature.

Two

AND A CLOUD PASSES OVERHEAD

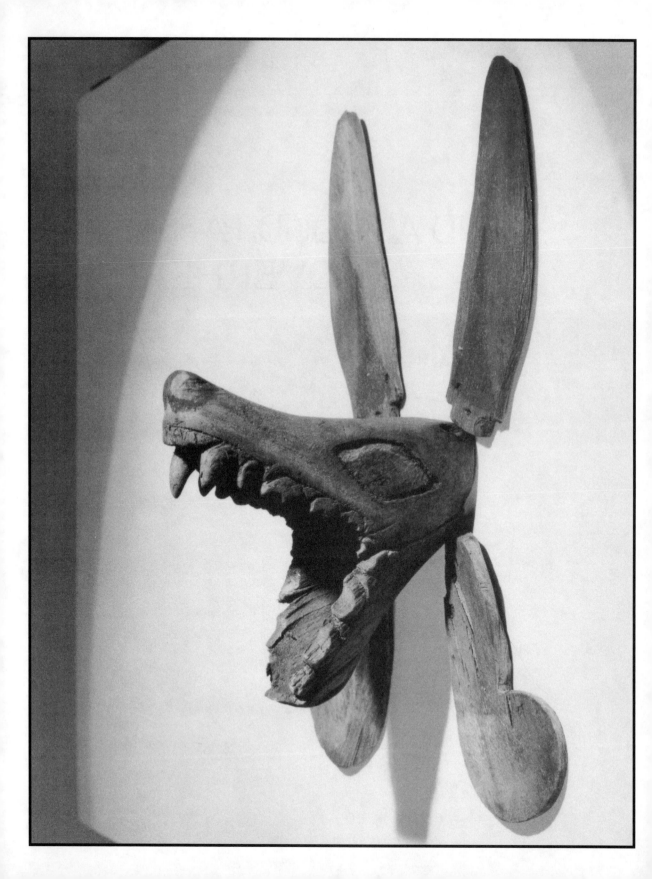

Four

AMAGUK AND SACRED MEAT

IT occurred to me early on in my association with wolves that I was distrustful of science. Not because it was unimaginative, though I think that is a charge that can be made against wildlife biology, but because it was narrow. I encountered what seemed to me eminently rational explanations for why wolves did some of the things they did, only to find wildlife biologists ignoring those ideas. True, some of the ideas were put forth by people who had only observed captive wolves; their explanations were intriguing and rational, but it was admittedly taking quite a leap to extrapolate from the behavior of captive animals to include those in the wild.

But, clearly, there was a body of evidence which seemed both rational and pertinent and which was being ignored: what people who lived in the Arctic among wolves, who had observed them for years in the wild, thought about them. Second, there was an even larger issue: what could be inferred about the behavior of wolves from the lifeways of seminomadic human hunters who faced virtually the same problems as the wolf in securing game and surviving in the Arctic?

It is difficult, and perhaps ultimately pointless, to try to keep the two ideas separated. What the arctic hunter sees in the wolf. What we see of the wolf in the arctic hunter. The Nunamiut Eskimos, the Naskapi Indians of Labrador, the tribes of the northern plains and the North Pacific coast discussed below are all, in a sense, timeless. Even those tribes we can converse with today because they happen to live in our own age are timeless; the ideas that surface in conversation with them (even inside a helicopter at two thousand feet) are ancient ideas. For the vision that guides them is not the vision that guides Western man a thousand years removed from the Age of Charlemagne. And the life they lead, you notice, tagging along behind them as they hunt, really *is* replete with examples of the ways wolves might do things. Over thousands of years Eskimos and wolves have tended to develop the same kind of efficiency in the Arctic.

It is one of the oddities of our age that much of what Eskimos know about wolves—and speak about clearly in English, in twentieth-century terms—wildlife biologists are still intent on discovering. It was this fact that made me uneasy. Later, I was made even more uneasy by how much fuller the wolf was as a creature in the mind of the modern Eskimo.

If you examine what they have to say, if you watch Eskimos hunt, you discover something about wolves; but you also discover something about men and how they envision animals. For some, the animal is only an object to be quantified; it is limited, capable of being fully understood. For others, the animal is a likeness to be compared to other animals. In the end, it is unfathomable. The view from both places—the one slightly arrogant, the other perhaps more humble—gives you an animal neither can see. When you think about it, that's quite extraordinary: a wolf that is both substance and shadow.

The hope of grasping that vision is grandiose. But that is what we are about.

• • •

In the spring of 1970, Robert Stephenson, a young wildlife biologist, went up to the small Eskimo village of Anaktuvuk in the central Brooks Range, some hundred miles north of the Arctic Circle. He was sent by the Alaska Department of Fish and Game to study wolf ecology in the region, to discover why the wolf population seemed to be in decline. He stayed for almost three years to study wolves with the Nunamiut people. He learned *Inupiatun*. He ate what the Eskimos ate. They liked him.

Stephenson had been studying arctic foxes; he knew very little about wolves when he arrived in Anaktuvuk, only some of what had been published by other wildlife biologists. It had not occurred to him then that most of their work had been done far to the south, and with only one subspecies of wolf, the Eastern timber wolf. And in a single, rather confined area: southern Ontario, adjacent northeastern Minnesota, and Isle Royale.

As Stephenson traveled around the tundra and mountain country of the Nunamiut, it dawned on him that the wolves he was watching were not like the wolves described in the literature he had read. And the Nunamiut were telling him things about wolves that no one, no biologist at least, had ever written about—not because they were odd or singular or mysterious things, but because they were things biologists were not interested in. Or never saw.

As Stephenson grew closer to the Nunamiut, as he gradually took on their sense of time and space (spending weeks during the full light of midsummer watching with powerful telescopes from foothill plateaus as wolves gamboled over sixty or seventy square miles of open tundra), his reflections on the animal led him toward a different understanding. Later, his wolf work would reflect an appreciation of the animal that was a blend of his academic knowledge and a primitive sensitivity that had been awakened, nurtured, and formed by his association with the Nunamiut. He had come among hunters to study a hunter, the one the Nunamiut called *amaguk*. Stephenson provided a bridge.

It can't be emphasized too strongly that the wolf simply goes about his business; and men select only those (few) things the wolf does that interest them to pay attention to. The biologist counts placental scars on the uterus of a dead female, something that would never occur to an Eskimo to do. An Eskimo looking for caribou is attentive to the direction of movement of wolves in various places over a period of weeks, something the biologist might regard as only anecdotal information in his reports. The mistake that is made here, with consistency, it seems, only by educated Western people, is to think that there is an ultimate wolf reality to be divined, one that can only be unearthed with microscope and radio collar. Some wolf biologists are possessed of the idea of binding the wolf up in "statistically significant" data. They want no question about the wolf not to have an answer.

This is a difficult line to hew.

The Nunamiut Eskimos are genuinely pleased by the wolf biologist's attempts to understand the animal because they, too, are very interested in the wolf. But they find the biologist's methods sometimes unfathomable—and amusing. A Nunamiut man was once shown a radio collar. The electronic principle involved was outlined. It was explained that a wolf wearing such a collar could be tracked wherever he went—he could never hide. The Eskimo said, "That's a very interesting piece of equipment. You should do that. You would learn a lot that way." He was deferring to a system of inquiry different from his own; but he did not think the biologists would learn much more about wolf movements than Eskimos already knew.

Nicholas Gubser, an anthropologist, wrote of these particular Eskimos: "The more reflective Nunamiut do not search for a primordial cause, a complete explanation or order of the nature of ultimate destiny." For the Nunamiut there is no "ultimate wolf reality." The animal is observed as a part of the universe. Some things are known, other things are hidden. Some of the wolf is known, some is not. But it is not a thing to be anxious over. Their orientation is practical: the wolf's pelt is valuable (especially to "crazy *tannik*," the white tourist, who might pay $450 for one); watching the wolf, learning his ways, will make you a better hunter—not only a caribou hunter but a wolf hunter. A feeling of integrated well-being comes to the Nunamiut who knows so much about the wolf. Studying the wolf, he gets closer to the physical world in which he lives. The lack of separation from its elements distinguishes him from the biologist.

The Nunamiut have been watching wolves for as long as they can remember. Their knowledge is precise but open-ended. For a few weeks every summer, some of the Nunamiut men watch wolves with spotting scopes from campsites in the Brooks Range where they have an enormous field of view. One day Justus Mekiana, one of the older men, saw a wolf following a grizzly bear around all day, at a distance of about twenty yards. He took his eye from the spotting scope to say "That's a new one, I haven't seen that before." Someone mentioned a family of wolves that had howled every day for two weeks during the denning season. Mekiana said he had never known wolves to do that, in forty years of watching them, but he added: "I wonder if wolves change their behavior over time, you know, different in some ways from thirty years ago?" If he is correct, then the implications for wildlife biology are staggering. It means that social animals evolve, that what you learn today may not apply tomorrow, that in striving to create a generalized static animal you have lost the real, dynamic animal. The nature of Mekiana's stake in the right answer is such that he remains open to many more possibilities. This same man admired Rudolph Schenkel's drawings and correctly identified the behavior associated with each, though he could not read a word of their English captions.

The thoroughness of the Nunamiut's observation is the result of the keen attention given to small details, and, as is the case with all oral cultures, the constant exercise of a rich memory. On a riverbank, for example, faced with a few wolf tracks headed in a certain direction, perhaps a scent mark, the Nunamiut will call on his own knowledge of this area (as well as his knowledge of wolves, what time of year it is, and so on) and on things he has heard from others and make an educated guess at what this particular cluster of clues might mean—which wolves these might have been, where they were headed, why, how long ago, and so on. His guess will be largely correct. The Eskimo's ability to do this, of course, astounds Western man.

Stephenson recalls one morning being out with Bob Ahgook, one of his Nunamiut friends, searching for a den. They were traversing a hillside when suddenly Ahgook stopped and pointed to a faint trail about four inches wide in some moss and lichen. By twisting his head to get the right angle of illumination and peering intently, Stephenson was able to make out a depression in the moss.

"Wolf trail," said Ahgook, scanning the slope above them. Suddenly a white female, who had been sleeping 150 feet up the slope, stood up and stared at them, then turned, quickly ascended an escarpment, and disappeared. In the silence that followed a bird landed on a rock near where the wolf had been, moved around a few moments, then flew away.

"She has a den up there, see that?" said Ahgook.

"See what?" asked Stephenson.

"Where that robin landed, picked up some wolf hairs, and flew away? That would be a good sleeping place, maybe very close to a den."

Stephenson recalled later that even though he had seen the bird it was so quick, so far away, he did not know it was a robin and would never have seen the wolf hairs in its beak. When they had climbed up to the spot it proved, indeed, to be a sleeping place. The female's den was a hundred feet away. Ahgook said as the wolf departed that he saw she had shed hair around her mammae, which meant she was very close to giving birth.

As Stephenson himself demonstrated, the chances were excellent that all this would have escaped the field biologist. He would not have seen the track, looked up, or guessed at the den. Edward T. Hall, the anthropologist, has called this difference of sensitivity the result of a difference in "culturally patterned sensory screens." And studies by Judith Kleinfeld have shown that Eskimos are very good at picking up visual detail, better than most whites.

Another thing that sets the Nunamiut and the biologist apart in the field is subtle, but worth noting. When the Nunamiut hunter goes out, he leaves his personal problems behind, as though they were a coat he had left on a hook. He slips, instead, into a state of concentrated, relentless attention to details: the depth of a track, the bend of grass along trails in a certain valley, the movement of ravens in the distance. It is the custom of most biologists, on the other hand, not only to bring their mental preoccupations into the field but to talk about them while they are walking along. Eskimos rarely speak when they are on the move and are inattentive to questions, giving only brief answers.

When the Nunamiut speaks, he speaks of exceptions to the rules, of the *likelihood* of something happening in a particular situation. He speaks more often of individual wolves than of the collective wolf, of "the white wolf that lives over near Chandler Lake," or "that three-legged female who had pups last year." He believes, too—and this seems quite foreign to the Western mind—that though equipped for it, the wolf is not a natural hunter. He must learn a good deal and work hard to become a good hunter.

One of the first practical things Stephenson noticed about the Nunamiuts' knowledge of wolves was their ability to determine an animal's sex and age at a distance by observing the condition and color of the pelage and fine differences in anatomy and behavior. (Some of these differences were mentioned in the first chapter.) Stephenson also learned that black wolves tend to be more high-strung than gray wolves; that two- and three-year-old females are the best caribou hunters; and that you might tell from a wolf's track alone what color it was or whether it was rabid.

Such things take a long time to learn.

The Nunamiut make these observations on the basis of thousands of encounters and, like guesses about sex and age at a distance, they are based on many small pieces of interlocking detail. When a pack of wolves lies down to sleep on a hillside, it is the black ones, usually, that take the longest time to settle down. The black wolf, too, moves differently from the light-colored wolf when he crosses the tundra. It is a very subtle thing, but over the years it begins to fit and you come to believe, if you are a Nunamiut, that the black wolf is "a little more nervous." In a caribou chase it is the sleek young females, built more like greyhounds than the males, that hunt caribou best because they are faster. As for telling a wolf's color by its tracks, a very large track, one over 5½ inches long, is most often one left by a male black wolf. It just happens to be that way. And a rabid wolf has a tension in the muscles of his feet that keeps his footpads spread when he is walking on dry ground.

These are interesting things to know, especially entertaining to the Western mind, because there is a neatness to them we appreciate: they have a graspable, definable quality that would fit nicely in a handbook. When you spend time with the Nunamiut, however, it is not such encapsulated data that fascinates you so much after a while. The wolf the Eskimo sees is a variable creature who does things because he is a certain age, or because it is a warm day, or because he is hungry. Everything

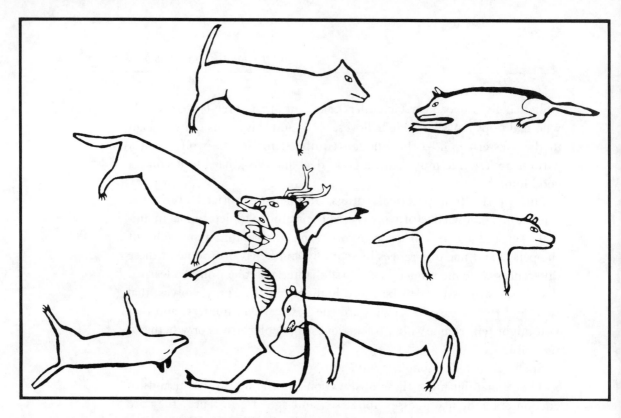

"Wolves Eating Caribou," from a contemporary Eskimo print.

depends on so many other things. *Amaguk* may be a wolf with a family who hunts with more determination than a yearling wolf who has no family to feed. He may be an old wolf alone on the tundra, tossing a piece of caribou hide up in the air and running to catch it. He may be an ill-tempered wolf who always tries to kill trespassing wolves wandering in his territory. Or he may be a wolf who toys with a red-backed mouse in the morning and kills a moose in the afternoon.

Examine some of the (until recently) basic precepts of wildlife science in the light of all this, such as that wolves kill primarily the weak, the old, and the injured. Too simple, say the Nunamiut. Temperature and humidity affect the wolf's and caribou's endurance. Terrain affects their ability to run. For caribou and moose, the nearness of deep, open water is important. With no water to get into, even the healthiest caribou may fall prey to the wolf, because no caribou can outlast the wolf. There are other things it is quite impossible to know, say the Nunamiut, but maybe the reason for some long chases is that some wolves like the taste of meat that has been run hard. Maybe, suggests one Nunamiut, *healthy* caribou are killed at times because when the wolves drive the caribou into an ambush, the healthy caribou get there first.

What about wolf territories? Depends on where the caribou are coming from, say the Nunamiut, the personalities in the pack, the season, whether there are pups, whether it's a pack of males alone.

When a Nunamiut hunter goes out to kill wolves (there is no confusion in his mind between respect and reverence), all this that he knows about the animals comes to bear. He finds the wolf by watching the sky for ravens, because ravens are frequently looking for wolf kills and following them around. When he has located wolves, he hides somewhere downwind and opens the quiet arctic silence with a howl that carries for miles. (Best, the Nunamiut reminds you, to howl in the breeding season, on a cool day when the air is still.) He waits to hear if the wolf howls back. If he is going to come to you, the wolf comes right away. His sense of direction is so good he will almost always pass within your rifle range, even starting from three or four miles away. But if he hears the click of the rifle being cocked, he may disappear like fog.

When the Nunamiut is searching for wolf dens on the tundra, he doesn't pay much attention to what yearling wolves in the vicinity are doing. He tells you yearlings are always fooling around. It is impossible to tell where a den may be by watching what they do. But older animals will show a pattern. Very subtle. Mostly it is how fast they are walking in what direction and at what time of day in June that tells you where the den might be. Subtle. Like the special way (to the Eskimo eye) the wolf holds his head when he smells caribou.

A correspondence begins to emerge.

The Nunamiut are a seminomadic hunting society, as are most of the Indian people I will consider in this section, who lead lives similar to wolves'. They eat almost the same foods—caribou, some sheep and moose, berries, not much vegetable matter. The harsh environment requires of them both the same stamina, alertness, cooperativeness, self-assurance, and, possibly, sense of humor to survive. They often hunt caribou in the same way, anticipating caribou movement patterns and waiting at likely spots to ambush them.

Hunting in this country is hard and Eskimos respect a good hunter. In all the time he spent with them, Stephenson never heard Nunamiut say anything degrading or contemptuous about a wolf. They admire his skill as a hunter because they know how hard it is to secure game. In the collective years of tribal memory there are very few stories about wolves that starved to death. The Nunamiut, on the other hand, have starved to death. Some of them alive today have gone for a month or more on only scraps of dried meat, pieces of caribou hide, and water. It is neither a mystery, nor surprising to anyone but a white man who no longer hunts for his food, that the Nunamiut admire the wolf and emulate his ways. In the land they share, hunting among the same caribou herds, hunting as the wolf does has proved to be the most reliable way to put meat in your belly.

I would like to suggest that there is a correspondence between the worlds of these two hunters about which the reader should be both open-minded and critical. I will not try to prove that primitive hunting societies were socially or psychologically organized like wolves that lived in the same environment, though this may be close to the truth. What I am saying is this: we do not know very much at all about animals. We cannot understand them except in terms of our own needs and experiences. And to approach them solely in terms of the Western imagination is, really, to deny the animal. It behooves us to visit with a people with whom we share a planet and an interest in wolves but who themselves come from a different time-space and who, so far as we know, are very much closer to the wolf than we will ever be.

What, if anything, does this correspondence mean? I think it can mean almost everything if you are trying to fathom wolves.

It became clear to me one evening in a single question.

An old Nunamiut man was asked who, at the end of his life, knew more about the mountains and foothills of the Brooks Range near Anaktuvuk, an old man or an old wolf? Where and when to hunt, how to survive a blizzard or a year when the caribou didn't come? After a pause the man said, "The same. They know the same." The remark has special meaning for what it implies about wolves. It comes from a man who has had to negotiate in polar darkness and in whiteouts, when the world surrounding him was entirely without the one thing indispensable to a

Western navigator—an edge. Anthropologist Edmund Carpenter has written of the extraordinary ability of polar Eskimos like the Aivilik to find their way about in a world that is often without horizon or actual points or objects for reference. What the Aivilik perceive is relationships, clusters of information that include what type of snow is underfoot, the direction and sound (against a parka ruff) of wind, any smells in the air, the contour of the landscape, the movement of animals, and so on. By constantly processing this information, the Aivilik knows where he is and where he is going. By implication, the Eskimo suggests that *the wolf does something similar*.

James Gibson, in a book called *The Perception of the Visual World*, wrote of not just one but thirteen kinds of depth perception. Most of us remain oblivious to such distinctions. We don't need them. The Eskimo does; if he is not aware of such things, he will not find his way home.

What Gibson and Carpenter together suggest is this: he who reads the landscape without the aid of maps as a matter of habit becomes as sophisticated of eye as it is popular to believe the bat is sophisticated of ear. The Eskimo, in other words, probably sees in a way that is more analogous to the way the wolf sees than Western man's way of seeing is.

If you are trying to fathom wolves, it is important to know how they might see. Maybe they see like Eskimos. And we can converse with Eskimos.

Recall the question asked of the old man. Who, at the end, knows more about the land—an old man or an old wolf?

Amaguk is like Nunamiut. He doesn't hunt when the weather is bad. He likes to play. He works hard to get food for his family. His hair starts to get white when he is old. Young wolves, just like Nunamiut, run around in shallow melt ponds scaring the ducks.

And Amaguk is tough, living at fifty below zero, through blizzards, for months without caribou. Like Nunamiut. Maybe tougher. And Amaguk is smart. He sets up ambushes for caribou. He sleeps high up on the ridges when there are humans around. He brings his pups to a kill but won't let them stay there alone. Grizzly bears. Young wolves do a lot of foolish things. Get killed.

Amaguk used to kill Nunamiut sometimes. Now Nunamiut can reach out and kill Amaguk from a distance with a rifle. Now Amaguk leaves Nunamiut alone.

Times change.

Amaguk and Nunamiut like caribou meat, know the good places for caribou hunting. Where ground squirrels are good. Where to get raspberries. A good place for getting away from mosquitoes. Where lupine blooms first in May. Where that big rock is that looks like achlack, the grizzly bear. Where the creeks are still running in August . . .

After a pause the old man looks up and says, "The same."

What aligns wolf and primitive hunter more strongly than anything else is that to live each must hunt and kill animals. In an area where both men and wolves hunt, they tend to hunt the same sorts of game. Given the same terrain, weather, food storage problems, and the fact that they are hunting the same prey, they tend to hunt in similar ways. The differences between them have more to do with the fact that one moves around on two feet and kills with such extensions of himself as bullets and arrows.

The Naskapi, a seminomadic hunting people of northeastern Canada, live out a hard life in a bleak and almost barren landscape. For centuries they have hunted the same caribou herds the wolves have. I would like to turn to them now to illustrate some deeper ways in which wolf and human hunters are alike.

Here is the anthropologist Georg Henriksen writing about Naskapi hunters:

"On snowshoes, the hunters quickly shuffle away from camp carrying their rifles over their shoulders. The Naskapi walk at a fast and steady pace, keeping up the same speed hour after hour. When from a hilltop the men spot caribou some miles in the distance they set off at a brisk pace alternating between putting on their snowshoes when moving in deep snow, and removing them and hanging them over their rifle barrels as soon as they reach a hard and icy surface. No words are spoken. Half running, every man takes the wind, weather and every feature of the terrain into account and relates it to the position of the caribou. Suddenly one of the men stops and crouches, whistling low to the other men. He has seen the herd. Without a word the men scatter in different directions. No strategy is verbalized, but each man has made up his mind about the way in which the herd can best be tackled. Seeing the other men choose their directions, he acts accordingly."

Approach, observation, conservation of energy, and attack—it could not be more wolflike.

It is said of the wolf that he is a deliberate hunter, that he does not wander aimlessly around the landscape but knows pretty well where prey animals are, even when he can't see them. John Kelsall, a Canadian wildlife biologist, has seen wolves shortcutting cross-country in the taiga to intercept caribou two days ahead of them with almost pinpoint accuracy.

Again, Henriksen says of the Naskapi:

"The hunting grounds of the Naskapi do not teem with caribou. The Naskapi have to search for the animals, moving their camps and hunting over a wide range of country. In this search, they use their knowledge of the country and experience with the animals and their behavior under different circumstances. They take into account features of the terrain such as how hilly it is and whether it is forested or barren. They must consider the snow and ice conditions and relate them to the feeding and moving patterns of the caribou. They have theories about how other animals and insects such as wolves and warble flies affect the behavior of caribou. For example, when no caribou are found in an area where it was reckoned there would be plenty, they explain this by the presence of wolves. They said the caribou probably fled into the forest where the deep snow would keep the wolves at a distance.

"They make use of this knowledge and do not decide randomly where to search for caribou."

It does not require two men, any more than it takes two wolves, to kill one caribou, but the Naskapi are social hunters anyway. Even when they hunt alone they are social hunters, because whatever meat they get is shared. The social fabric of the Naskapi tribe is the result of an acknowledgment of dependence on each other for food. The young, the old, the sick, they cannot hunt. The social system of the Naskapi bestows prestige on the successful hunter; that is what is exchanged for meat. Each man hunts as he chooses, calling on personal skills, but with a single, overriding goal: to secure food. The individual ego is therefore both nurtured and submerged. A man's skills are praised, his food is eaten, his pride is reinforced.

I think a similar sense of social pressure and interdependence operates to hold a wolf pack together. Old wolves and young pups can eat only because the middle-aged wolves are good hunters. During rendezvous season the wolf, hungry himself, having eaten at the kill, returns home from ten miles away with a haunch of meat in his mouth. And he is besieged with as much affection as the successful Naskapi hunter is by *his* family. In this, perhaps more than anything else, we find a basis for alpha wolves—the hunters, whose prowess is encouraged for the sake of survival. Pack survival.

We now embark on a plainly metaphysical consideration.

The focal point of the act of hunting among the Naskapi is the preparation of a ritual meal, called *Mokoshan*. Caribou meat and bones are carefully prepared and consumed by the hunters. Not a morsel of meat or a sliver of bone may touch the ground. The function of the meal for the Naskapi hunter is to ingratiate himself with the Spirit of the Caribou, to indicate respect for his food, to honor the tenuous balance that keeps him alive by asserting that there will be no waste of whatever meat is secured in the hunt.

It is not hard for Western minds to miss the seriousness of this ritual: the link between hunter and hunted (symbolized in the meal) lies at the very foundation of every hunting society. It is, literally, the most important thing in the hunter's life. To fail in the hunt is to fail to eat. To die. To be finished. The ritual preparation for the hunt, therefore, acknowledges a perpetual agreement: the game will be given to the hunter by dwellers in the spirit world as long as the hunter remains worthy. The hunt itself is but an acting out of the agreement, the bullet or arrow loosed but a symbol of the communication between hunter and hunted.

The agreement is mythic in origin, made with an Owner of the Animals. In the Naskapi world this is the Animal Master of the caribou because the caribou is the mainstay of the Naskapi diet. The Animal Master is a single animal in a great mythic herd. He is both timeless and indestructible, an archetype of the species. It is he who "gives" the hunter the animal to be killed and who has the power to keep the animals away from the hunter if he is unworthy. In the foundation myths of every hunting culture there is a story of how all this came about.

One time the people had no food—only berries and roots, no meat. A shaman steps forth and says he will go and find the food to make them strong. After a long and difficult journey he himself is on the verge of

Regurgitation. In cooperative hunting families, both human and wolf, hunters bring food back for those who do not hunt.

despair when he encounters the Owner of the Animals. The Animal Master challenges the man to show his power. He does, by bringing back to life a human being the Animal Master has struck dead. The Animal Master honors the feat by saying he will release the animals to be hunted, but under the following conditions: the hunters must treat the animals with respect, seeing that their flesh is not wasted and that their spirits are not insulted by acts of arrogance or ridicule; and the hunter must regularly perform a ceremony to commemorate this agreement. If this is done, the animals' spirits will return safely to the Animal Master and he will give them new bodies and send them out again and again. In this way there will always be enough food.

Hunting is holy. It is not viewed in the same light as an activity like berry picking. Game animals are holy. And the life of a hunting people is regarded as a sacred way of living because it grows out of this powerful, fundamental covenant.

THE SEA WOLF

One time a man found two young wolf pups on the beach. He took them home and raised them and one day after they were grown the man saw them go out into the ocean and kill a whale. They brought the whale back to shore so the man could eat. Every day it went like this. The wolves would go out and kill whales and bring back the meat. Soon there was so much meat lying around on the beach it was going bad. When the Great Above Person saw this he made a storm and brought down a fog and the wolves could not find any whales to kill. The waves were so high the wolves could not even find their way back. They had to stay out there. Those wolves became sea wolves. Whale hunters.

—A story among the Haida
of British Columbia

The killing of animals, then, entails tremendous spiritual responsibility. In the case of the Naskapi, as Frank Speck writes: "Failure in the chase, the disappearance of game from the hunter's districts, with ensuing famine, starvation, weakness, sickness and death, all are attributable to the hunter's ignorance of some hidden principles of behavior toward the animals, or his willful disregard of them. The former is ignorance. The latter is sin. The two together constitute the educational sphere of the Montagnais-Naskapi."

Two more ideas are necessary here to complete our vision of the hunter and his food: that of the strength you gained from eating sacred meat (as distinct from what was gained spiritually and physically— virtually nothing—from other meat); and that of spirit houses as dwelling places for the spirits of the game animals, where you sometimes had to go in appeal during famine.

Hunting tribes called meat "medicine." The word has two meanings. One is that meat is sacred because it comes from a sacred ceremony. The other is more literal in meaning and indicates why some native Americans did not care to eat, for example, the flesh of wolves. Hunting tribes understood the vegetable world as a pharmacopoeia; to some extent each tribe tried to cure its ills and ailments with herbs and plants. By taking the plant indirectly, concentrated in the form of meat from herbivorous animals, the hunter also indirectly partook of the plant's power to cure and soothe. One of the reasons most native Americans avoided eating wolf meat was that it was the meat of a meat eater, not a plant eater. It was still meat—you could survive on it—but it was inadequate as food. Even worse than eating wolf meat was to eat meat from a domestic herbivore, like a cow. Cattle had no Animal Master. It was not sacred to hunt them, and on *that* food you could perish. (This, of course, was not a consideration until the coming of the white man.)

When a sacred animal was killed, its spirit went to a spirit house. For the Naskapi this was Caribou House. Caribou House was a real place. It lay in a mountain range west of Ungava Bay in present-day Quebec. The mountains there were white, not from ice or snow but from centuries of caribou hair falling on the ground. The caribou entered and left this place each year, passing through a valley between two high mountains. The caribou hair on the ground was several feet deep and for miles around the cast-off caribou antlers formed a layer as high as a man's waist. The caribou paths were worn so deep a calf going along one would only show his head.

The Animal Master lived at Caribou House, together with the living caribou and the spirits of slain caribou. Animals in the surrounding area were fierce, larger than their normal counterparts, and much feared by the Naskapi. Yet in time of famine a tribe either had to conduct a ceremony of propitiation or someone had to go into this fearful land and deal directly with the Animal Master for release of the game.

That, briefly, is what hunting large game was for men. How does this touch on wolves? Can hunting be regarded as a sacred occupation among wolves? Is there a mythic contract acknowledged when wolf meets prey? Do wolves have a sense of Caribou House to which they raise mournful howls in times of famine?

We know painfully little about wolves. We can only ask the questions and guess. Communal hunting probably *is* the social activity that makes wolves hold together in packs. *Sacred* is not the right word, but hunting may have overtones for wolves that we cannot appreciate. We seem to sense them, though, when we speculate on the reasons for group howls after a successful hunt. I do not know if wolves have a sense of Caribou House. They do howl in time of anguish. The existence of Caribou

House implies a rule of conservation and, in general, wolves are not wasters of meat.

We don't know. But I am reluctant to let the idea pass unexamined. The wolf is a hunter. There is order to his world. It is not necessary that either wolf or his prey be conscious of this; a cursory examination of human hunting societies suggests that formal relationships between hunter and hunted are part of the order of the universe. It is reasonable to assume that some of these elements exist, even if they are unconscious or appear in another guise.

In the preceding section on hunting I merely touched on that moment of eye contact between wolf and prey, a moment which seemed to be visibly decisive. Here are hunting wolves doing many inexplicable things (to the human eye). They start to chase an animal and then turn and walk away. They glance at a set of moose tracks only a minute old, sniff, and go on, ignoring them. They walk on the perimeter of caribou herds seemingly giving warning of their intent to kill. And the prey signals back. The moose trots toward them and the wolves leave. The pronghorn throws up his white rump as a sign to follow. A wounded cow stands up to be seen. And the prey behave strangely. Caribou rarely use their antlers against the wolf. An ailing moose, who, as far as we know, could send wolves on their way simply by standing his ground, does what is most likely to draw an attack, what he is least capable of carrying off: he runs.

I called this exchange in which the animals appear to lock eyes and make a decision the conversation of death. It is a ceremonial exchange, the flesh of the hunted in exchange for respect for its spirit. In this way both animals, not the predator alone, choose for the encounter to end in death. There is, at least, a sacred order in this. There is nobility. And it is something that happens only between the wolf and his major prey species. It produces, for the wolf, sacred meat.

Imagine a cow in the place of the moose or white-tailed deer. The conversation of death falters noticeably with domestic stock. They have had the conversation of death bred out of them; they do not know how to encounter wolves. A horse, for example—a large animal as capable as a moose of cracking a wolf's ribs or splitting its head open with a kick—will usually panic and run.

What happens when a wolf wanders into a flock of sheep and kills twenty or thirty of them in apparent compulsion is perhaps not so much slaughter as a failure on the part of the sheep to communicate anything at all—resistance, mutual respect, appropriateness—to the wolf. The wolf has initiated a sacred ritual and met with ignorance.

This brings us to a second point. We are dealing with a different kind of death from the one men know. When the wolf "asks" for the life of another animal he is responding to something in that animal that says, "My life is strong. It is worth asking for." A moose may be biologically constrained to die because he is old or injured, but the choice is there. The death is not tragic. It has dignity.

Consider the Indian again. Native American cultures in general stressed that there was nothing wrong with dying, one should only strive to die well, that is consciously choose to die even if it is inevitable. The greatest glory accrued to a warrior who acted with this kind of self-control in the very teeth of death. The ability to see death as less than tragic was rooted in a different perception of ego: a person was simultaneously indispensable and dispensable (in an appropriate way) in the world. In the conversation of death is the striving for a death that is *appropriate*. I have lived a full life, says the prey. I am ready to die. I am willing to die because clearly I will be dying so that the others in this small herd will go on living. I am ready to die because my leg is broken or my lungs are impacted and my time is finished.

The death is mutually agreeable. The meat it produces has power, as though consecrated. (That is a good word. It strikes us as strange only because it is out of its normal context.)

I have been struck, considering these things, by the difference between captive and wild wolves, and I think that much of the difference—a difference of bearing, a dynamic tension immediately apparent in a wild wolf and lacking almost entirely in captive animals—lies in their food. The wolf in the wild subsists on his earned meat. The captive is fed on the wastes of commercial slaughterhouses and food made in factories by machines. Wolves in zoos waste away. The Naskapi, to this day, believe that the destruction of their people, the rending of their spirit, has had mainly to do with their being forced to eat the meat of domestic animals.

Plains Indians approaching buffalo.

The difference between wild meat and tame meat to a hunting culture is a matter of monumental significance. It was a fundamental principle of life that, in the case of the Indian, the white man simply never noticed and the Indians did not know how to explain. I remember the first time I gave a penned wolf a piece of chicken. And I remember the feeling in a Minnesota clearing the first time I came on a wolf kill, picked up the moose skull, and turned it in my hands.

Whether wolf and prey act according to some mutual understanding, or whether they only unconsciously participate in a fundamental drama, is something we shall probably never know. All we do know, staring up at the paintings of game animals on the cave walls at Lascaux, is that the belief that there was more to hunting than killing, and that dying was as sacred as living, was not something that one day just fell out of the sky.

This is a good place to pause and look back, because, as I said at the beginning of the chapter, the two ideas I began with—that modern hunting cultures can tell us much about wolves from their own observations, and that by examining these and older cultures and suggesting analogies with wolf behavior we can make engaging speculation—these ideas can run together.

We are basically finished at this point with the first idea, fleshing out the wolf modern biology has created by adding some observations made by Nunamiut hunters. As for the second idea, I have tried to make the point that hunting is a sacred activity among hunting peoples, the very basis of their social organization, and that it is not out of line to suggest the same for wolves. We should not be afraid—although we are, and profoundly so—to extend to the wolf and to the animals it preys on the physical and metaphysical variables we allow ourselves. It is, after all, not man but the universe that is subtle.

From here on, I will try to do two things. First, to suggest other analogies, other ways in which Eskimos and Indians led lives like wolves, in the hope that as you read them you will wonder as I do at the possibilities for the animal. And second, I will try to create a feeling for wolves that we may once have had as a people ourselves but have long since lost—one in which we do not know all the answers, but are not anxious. An appreciation of wolves, it seems to me, lies in the wider awareness that comes when answers to some questions are for the moment simply suspended.

Five

A WOLF IN THE HEART

ONE of the problems that comes with trying to take a wider view of animals is that most of us have cut ourselves off from them conceptually. We do not think of ourselves as part of the animal kingdom. Indians did. They thought of themselves as The People (that is the translation from the native tongue of most tribal names) and of animals as The Wolves, The Bears, The Mice, and so forth. From here on in this chapter, the line between Indians and wolves may fade, not because Indians did not perceive the differences but because they were preoccupied with the similarities. They were inclined to compare and contrast their way of living with, say, the weasel's way or the eagle's way. They would say, "We are like wolves in that we . . . " They were anthropomorphic—and animistic. Highly so. We aren't talking, really, about our wolf anymore. We are talking about their wolf. We are, in a sense, in a foreign country.

The question the old Nunamiut man answered was an eminently sensible one in his view. The caribou-hunting tactics of wolves in the Brooks Range and those of the Nunamiut *were* similar. And similarity in hunting technique in the same geographical area was found elsewhere. Wolves and Cree Indians in Alberta maneuvered buffalo out onto lake ice, where the big animals lost their footing and were more easily killed. Pueblo Indians and wolves in Arizona ran deer to exhaustion, though it might have taken the Pueblos a day to do it. Wolf and Shoshoni Indian lay flat on the prairie grass of Wyoming and slowly waved—the one its tail, the other a strip of hide—to attract curious but elusive antelope close enough to kill. And if we have made the right assumptions at Paleolithic sites in North America such as Folsom, early man killed mammoths in the same mobbing way wolves did, because men did not yet have extensions of themselves like the bow and arrow. They had to get in close with a spear and stab the animal to death.

The correspondence in life-styles, however, goes deeper than this. Wolves ate grass, possibly as a scour against intestinal parasites; Indians ate wild plants for medicinal reasons. Both held and used hunting territories. Both were strongly familial and social in organization. To some extent both went to specific areas to hunt certain types of game. (Two or three wolf packs today come to hunt sheep at a place called Okokmilaga on the North Slope of Alaska's Brooks Range. Various tribes, Ponca and Sioux among them, traveled to the same leks in South Dakota to hunt sage grouse.) Both wolf and Indian had a sign language. The tribe, like the pack, broke up at certain times of the year, and joined together later to hunt more efficiently. In times of scarcity, Indian hunters ate first; this also seems to be the case with wolves.

Highly intriguing is the fact that white-tailed deer in Minnesota sought security from Indian hunters by moving into the border area between warring tribes, where hunters were least likely to show up, and the fact that deer do the same with respect to wolves—seek security along the border zones between wolf territories, where wolves spend the least time hunting.

The most interesting correspondence between wolf and Indian, however, may be that involving the perception of territory.

When Indians left their own country and entered that of another tribe—a group of young Assiniboin warriors, for example, sneaking off on foot into the country of the Gros Ventre to steal horses—they moved like wolves: in small packs; at night and during the crepuscular hours; taking advantage of ground contours to observe but remain hidden; moving in and out of the foreign territory quickly. Often on foot and in unfamiliar surroundings, they had to remain invisible to the inhabitants. Elusiveness, therefore, was a quality Indians cultivated and admired. It served them as well as it served the wolf who, in a hard winter, trespasses into neighboring packs' territories to look for food, to make a kill, and to go home before anyone knows he's been there.

The definition and defense of home range was as important to the Indian as it seems to be to the wolf. The defense was mostly of food resources in general and of the physical area adjacent to the village in particular; under certain circumstances trespassers were killed. If a party of Flathead warriors was surprised in northern Idaho by a party of resident Kutenai, the Flatheads might be attacked and killed to a man. If it was bitter cold and storming, they might signal each other that it was too cold to fight (wolves probably wouldn't). If the Flathead party was reduced to one man who fought bravely and was thought, therefore, to have strong medicine, he might be let go. Fatal encounters and nonfatal encounters between trespassing and resident wolves bear a striking similarity. In Minnesota, for example, in 1975, a small pack of wolves moving through the territory of a much larger pack was suddenly surprised by the larger pack. One animal in the small pack was killed, two ran off, and the fourth, a female, held ten or eleven wolves to a standoff in a river before they all withdrew and left her.

Some tribes were stricter about boundaries and more bellicose about trespassing incidents than others, as are some wolf packs. The boundaries of most Indian territories, like those of wolves, were fluid; they changed with the movement of the game herds, the size of the tribe, the evolution of tribal divisions, and the time of year. For both wolf and Indian, where the principal game animal was nonmigratory, as deer and moose are, territorial boundaries were more important than they were in areas where principal game species were migratory, like caribou. There are instances where neighboring wolf packs have fought each other and then joined territories, just as some tribes established alliances—the five nations of the Iroquois, for example. And I mentioned earlier that the

Pawnee and Omaha, traditional enemies, had an agreement whereby each could enter the other's territory to hunt buffalo.

The Indian practice of passing family hunting territories on to succeeding generations throws even more light on this interesting correspondence of territorial spacing, hunting rights, and trespassing. Family hunting territories were most important, again, where food could be found in the same place all the time. The salmon-eating tribes on the northwest coast and the Algonkian deer eaters in the northeastern woodlands both had appropriate family and clan hunting territories that were passed from one generation to the next. Among the Tlingit, a northwest coast tribe, each family had its own place on the rivers where it fished and an area where it gathered berries. No one else would fish or berry there unless invited to do so. In the eastern woodlands, especially in northeastern Minnesota, resident wolves seem to have a strong sense of territory as defined by the major food source (white-tailed deer), at least as strong as the family hunting territories that existed in that same country when the Chippewa lived there.

Which leads to another thought, more abstract, about trespassing. It was often assumed that Plains Indians went out intending to kill their rivals. This was not true. They went out to deliberately face rivals in a very dangerous game. The danger itself, the threat of death, was the thrill, not killing; and to engage in it repeatedly was recognized as a way to prove strength of character. Analogously, it might be valuable to consider the encounters of rival wolves as a similar kind of deadly recreation. Just as intriguing is the idea that some game animals assent to a chase-without-death with wolves. Caribou and yearling wolves, for example, are often seen in harmless chases getting a taste of death. Building spirit. Training. Wolf *and* caribou.

That wolves and Neolithic hunting people in North America resembled each other as predators was not the result of conscious imitation. It was convergent evolution, the most successful way for meat eaters to live. Conscious *identification* with the wolf, on the other hand, especially among Indians on the Great Plains, was a mystical experience based on a penetrating perception of the wolf's lifeway, its gestalt. And it could, on occasion, become conscious imitation.

Native American perceptions of the wolf varied largely according to whether or not a tribe was agricultural. It was naturally among the hunting tribes that the wolf played the greater mythic-religious role because the wolf himself was a great hunter, not a great farmer. He was retained for a while in the mythology of agricultural tribes and regarded by them as an animal of great power and mystery, but his place there was slowly eclipsed by anthropomorphic gods of the harvest.

In the native American cosmology, insofar as it can be regarded as the same from tribe to tribe, the universe was perceived in six directions: the space above; that below; and the four cardinal divisions of the world horizon. Frequently on the plains the bear represented the west, the mountain lion the north, the wolf the east, and the wildcat the south. They were regarded as the creatures with the greatest power and influence in the spirit world.

It should be understood, however, that the Indian did not rank-order animals. Each creature, from deer mouse to meadowlark, was respected for the qualities it best seemed to epitomize; when those particular qualities were desired by someone, that animal was approached as one who knew much about that thing. The animals assigned the greatest cosmological significance—the bear, lion, wolf, cat, and eagle—were not regarded as the "best" animals. They were chosen primarily because they were the great hunters. The stealth of the cats, the endurance of the wolf, the strength of the bear, the vision of the eagle—these were the qualities held in high esteem by human hunters.

The Pawnee of present-day Nebraska and Kansas differed from most other tribes in that they divided their world horizon into four semicardinal points, assigning the wolf to the southeast. In the Pawnee cosmogony the wolf was also set in the sky as a star, along with the bear and the two cats, to guard the primal female presence, the Evening Star. The Wolf Star was red—the color associated with the wolf by virtually every tribe (red did not signify blood; it was simply an esteemed color).

In time, the wolf became associated among the four seasons with summer, among the trees on the plains with the willow, among the great natural forces with clouds (the others being wind, thunder, and lightning).

Like the Nunamiut, most Indians respected the wolf's prowess as a hunter, especially his ability to always secure game, his stamina, the way he moved smoothly and silently across the landscape. They were moved by his howling, which they sometimes regarded as talking with the spirit world. The wolf appears in many of their legends as a messenger in fact, a great long-distance traveler, a guide for anyone seeking the spirit world. Blind Bull, for example, a Cheyenne shaman, was highly respected among his people before his death in 1885 as one who had learned about things from the comings and goings of wolves, from listening to their howls. The wolves, for their part, took Blind Bull's messages to various places in the real and spiritual world. The wolf as oracle, as interlocutor with the dead, is an old idea.

The wolf was also held in high regard because, though he was a fiercely loyal familial animal, he was also one who took the role of provider for the larger community (for carrion eaters like the fox and raven). This was something that tribal Indians understood very well, for in

Family cohesiveness, the key to life in hunting families. A father is flanked by two generations of his family—pups to the left, yearlings to the right.

difficult times a man had the dual responsibility of feeding his own family as well as others. An Hidatsa man named Bear in the Flat acknowledged this lifeway of the wolf when he took as one of his sacred medicine songs the "Invitation Song" of the wolf—the howl the wolf used to call coyotes, foxes, and magpies to the remains of his kill. (The situation is neatly imitated among Bella Coola hunters, who sing a song to call the wolf to one of *their* kills—a bear. They would take a bear's hide but believed bears did not wish to be eaten by humans.)

The interrelationships between one's allegiance to self and household on the one hand and one's duty to the larger community on the other cannot be overemphasized; it was a primal, efficient system of survival that held both man and wolf in a similar mesh.

Consider again the Indian's perception.

Each of the animals—mosquitoes, elk, mice—belonged to a separate tribe. Each had special powers, but each was dependent on the others for certain services. When, for example, the Indian left his buffalo kill, he called out to the magpies and others to come and eat. The dead buffalo nourished the grasses; the grasses in turn fed the elk and provided the mouse with straw for a nest; the mouse, for his part, instructed the Indian in magic; and the Indian called on his magic to kill buffalo.

With such a strong sense of the interdependence among all creatures and an acute awareness of the ways in which his own life resembled the wolf's (hunting for himself, hunting for his family, defending his tribe against enemy attack as the wolf protected the den against the grizzly), the Indian naturally turned to the wolf as a paradigm—a mirror reflection. He wished directly for that power ("Hear me, Great Spirit! I wish to be like the wolf"); and he imitated him homeopathically by wearing his skin. He wished always to be as well integrated in his environment as he could *see* the wolf was in the universe. Imagine him saying: "Help me to fit, to be valuable in the world, like the wolf."

To fit into the universe, the Indian had to do two things simultaneously: be strong as an individual, and submerge his personal feelings for the good of the tribe. In the eyes of many native Americans, no other animal did this as well as the wolf.

The wolf fulfilled two roles for the Indian: he was a powerful and mysterious animal, and so perceived by most tribes; and he was a medicine animal, identified with a particular individual, tribe, or clan. In the first role he was simply an object of interest, for reasons already given. He might be marginally so in the eyes of some (most California tribes, where there were no wolves, thought little of the wolf) or of major importance to others (Cheyenne, Sioux, Pawnee).

At a *tribal* level, the attraction to the wolf was strong because the wolf lived in a way that made the tribe strong: he provided food that all, even the sick and old, could eat; he saw to the education of his children; he defended his territory against other wolves. At a *personal* level, those for whom the wolf was a medicine animal or personal totem understood the qualities that made the wolf stand out as an individual; for example, his stamina and ability to track well and go without food for long periods.

That each perception contributed to and reinforced the other—as the individual grows stronger, the tribe grows stronger, and vice versa—is what made the wolf such a significant animal in the eyes of hunting peoples. The inclination of white men to regard individual and social motivations in themselves as separate led them to misunderstand the Indian. The Indian was so well integrated in his environment that his motivation was almost hidden; his lifeway was as mysterious to white men as the wolf's.

This is obviously a complex thought, but in the light of it, the Indian's preoccupation with wolves becomes more than quaint. The wolf was the one animal that, again, did two things at once year after year: remained distinct and exemplary as an individual, yet served the tribe. There are no stories among Indians of lone wolves.

This association with, and imitation of, the wolf among American Indians was absolutely pervasive. The two great clan divisions of the northwest coast tribes were the wolf and the raven. One of the three divisions of the southern Arapaho were *Haqihana*, the wolves; one of the ten Caddo bands were *Tasha*, the wolf. A Cherokee setting out in winter on a long journey rubbed his feet with ashes and, singing a wolf song, moved a few steps in imitation of the wolf, whose feet he knew were protected from frostbite, as he wished his to be. Nez Perce warriors wore a wolf tooth pushed through the septum of their noses. Cheyenne medicine men wrapped wolf fur around the sacred arrows used to motion antelope into a trap. Arikara men wove wolf hair and buffalo hair together in small sacred blankets. Bella Coola mothers painted a wolf's gallbladder on a young child's back so he would grow up to perform religious ceremonies without making mistakes as a hunter. An Hidatsa woman experiencing a difficult birth might call on the familial power of the wolf by rubbing her belly with a wolf skin cap.

All that I have been saying about interdependence in a tribe, about individual, personal medicine power and homeopathic imitation, comes together in a famous story that Plenty Coups told many years ago about a Crow medicine man named Bird Shirt.

In a battle with Sioux, Cheyenne, and Arapaho near Pryor Creek, Montana, a Crow named Swan's Head took a large bullet square in the chest that tore through his lungs and came out his back. He held on to his horse, which turned and carried him back to the Crow village. By the time he arrived, the horse glistened red with the man's blood.

Three medicine men, Hunts to Die, Wolf Medicine, and Bird Shirt, believed he could be saved. Bird Shirt requested that a brush lodge be built next to the river which ran near the camp. After moving Swan's Head there, he asked for absolute silence. The people who gathered to watch were pushed back to keep a wide path open from the lodge to the water and told to keep any dogs away.

Bird Shirt took his medicine bundle and entered the lodge. He took a wolf skin out of the bundle. As Plenty Coups goes on:

"It was a whole wolf skin with the head stuffed. The legs of the skin were painted red to their first joints and the nostrils and a strip below the eyes were also red. I watched Bird Shirt paint himself to look like his medicine skin. His legs to the knees, his arms to their elbows, his nostrils, and strips below his eyes were made red, while he sang steadily with the beating drums. He painted his head with clay until it looked like that of the buffalo-wolf, and he made ears with the clay that I could not tell from a real wolf's ears, from where I stood. All the time he was singing his medicine song with the drums while the people scarcely breathed.

"Suddenly the drums changed their beating. They were softer and much faster. I heard Bird Shirt whine like a wolf mother that has young pups, and saw him trot, as a wolf trots, around the body of Swan's Head

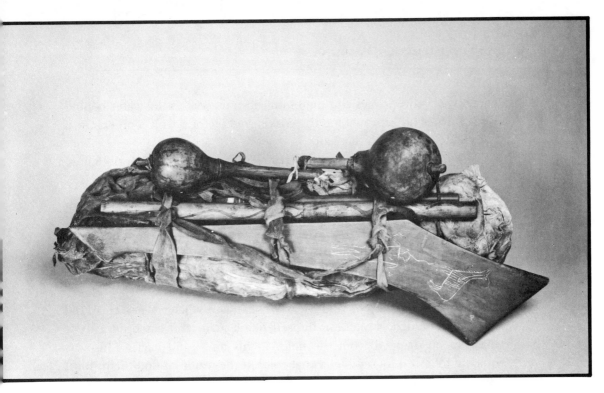

Oto Indian wolf bundle.

four times. Each time he shook his rattle in his right hand, and each time dipped the nose of the wolf skin in water and sprinkled it upon Swan's Head, whining continually as a wolf mother whines to make her pups do as she wishes.

"I was watching—everybody near enough was watching—when Swan's Head sat up. We then saw Bird Shirt sit down like a wolf, with his back to Swan's Head, and howl four times, just as a wolf howls four times when he is in trouble and needs help. I could see that Swan's Head's eyes were now open, so that he could see Bird Shirt stand and lift the medicine wolf skin above his own head four times whining like a wolf mother. I seemed myself to be lifted with the skin, and each time there was, I saw, a change in Swan's Head. The fourth time Bird Shirt lifted the wolf skin, Swan's Head stood up. He was bent, his body twisted, but his eyes were clear while Bird Shirt trotted around him like a wolf, whining still, like a wolf mother coaxing her pup to follow her.

"Bird Shirt walked out of the lodge, and when Swan's Head followed him I could scarcely hear the drums or the men's voices singing his medicine song. I felt that I was with Swan's Head when he stopped once, twice, three times and then into the open way to the water behind Bird Shirt, who kept making the coaxing whine of a wolf mother, until both had stepped into the water.

"Not once all this time had the drums stopped, or the singers, whose voices rose and fell with the drums. Everybody was watching the two men in the river.

"Bird Shirt led Swan's Head out into the stream until the water covered his wounds. Then he pawed the water as a wolf does, splashing it over the wounded man's head. Whining like a wolf, he nosed the water with the wolf skin and made the nose of the wolf skin move up and down over the bullet holes, like a wolf licking a wound.

" 'Stretch yourself,' he told Swan's Head; and when Swan's Head did as he was bidden, stretching himself like a man who has been asleep, black blood dripped from the holes in his chest and back. This was quickly followed by red blood that colored the water around them, until Bird Shirt stopped it. 'Bathe yourself now,' said Bird Shirt, and obediently Swan's Head washed his face and hands in the running water. Then he followed Bird Shirt to the brush lodge where they smoked together. I saw them. . . ."

Thus were wolf and man one.

Though the wolf was respected, he had his uses, too. Wolf fur was good for a parka ruff. A wolf pelt was powerful medicine, a good item in trade. Wolves sometimes preyed on an Indian's fish traps or meat caches or got after his horses. Indians rarely killed wolves, but when they did it was for these reasons.

The common methods for capturing and killing wolves before steel traps were available were the pit fall and the deadfall. The pit fall consisted of a deep hole, wider at the bottom to keep the wolf from running up the walls, covered over with grass and brush, and baited with meat. Some tribes put sharpened stakes at the bottom to kill the wolf when it fell in.

Deadfalls of rock, ice, and slabs of snow were more common in the north where pits were hard to dig. Pulling on a piece of bait, the wolf would trip a balanced weight that crushed or pinned him.

Rawhide snares that caught the animal around the neck were also in use. Some Eskimos coiled sharpened willow sticks or strips of baleen in frozen tallow balls, which were then left out for the wolves to eat.

Two sorts of knife trap were also used. A wolf knife consisted of a sharp blade encased in fat and frozen upright in a block of ice. The wolf licked the fat until he cut his tongue badly enough to bleed to death. The other knife trap was a baited torsion spring that stabbed the wolf in the head when triggered.

But it never was easy.

Among the Cherokee there was a belief that to kill a wolf was to invite retribution from other wolves. Many tribes felt that killing a wolf would cause game to disappear. And there was widespread belief that a weapon that had killed a wolf would never work right again. It either had to be given away, usually to a child to be used in future as a toy, or taken to a shaman to be cleansed. A Cherokee cure for a gun that had killed a wolf was to unscrew the barrel, insert small sourwood *(Oxydendrum arboreum)* sticks ritually treated in a fire, and lay it in a running stream till morning.

When the Kwakiutl of coastal British Columbia killed a wolf, they would lay the carcass out on a blanket. Small strips of meat would be cut off and each person who had participated in the killing would eat four of them, expressing his regret at the wolf's death and calling him a good friend. The remains of the carcass were wrapped in the blanket and carefully buried.

The Ahtena Indians of southern Alaska brought a wolf they'd killed into camp on their shoulders, chanting: "This is the chief, he is coming." The dead wolf was taken inside a hut, where he was propped up in a sitting position and a banquet meal was set before him by a shaman. Each family in the village contributed something. When it was felt the wolf had eaten all he wanted, the men ate what was left. No women were permitted inside.

When certain Eskimos killed a wolf, they would bring it to the edge of the village and leave it out there for four days. The man who had done the killing would walk around his house four times, expressing his feelings of regret for the wolf, and abstain from relations with his wife for four days.

Because there was such risk involved, a common practice of those who needed a wolf skin was to hire someone who knew the rites of atonement

THE WOLF AND THE INDIAN DOG

The wolf was an important part of tribal, ceremonial, and individual life but he was nevertheless regarded as Other by the Indian, distinct from man and never to be confused with a dog. Indians probably brought three or four different breeds of dog with them when they came to America, which they continued to breed to each other. Dogs were to be used: their hair for weaving, their flesh among some tribes for food. They were to pull travois and sleds, to pack food paniers and firewood, and to hunt game. They were not pets. Any that proved a nuisance by getting into food caches or digging under tipis were quickly dispatched.

Crossing wolves with dogs almost always produced hybrids that were headstrong and dangerous, so Indians rarely tried it. Dogs several generations removed from a cross might prove gentle, obedient, intelligent,

and very hardy, but few Indians were interested in this kind of special breeding. More fundamentally, dogs and wolves were poles apart in the Indian mind; it did not seem appropriate to mix them. The wolf had a soul in Nunamiut Eskimo eyes; not so their sled dogs. In the Sioux language the term for wolf was shunkmanitu tanka, *"the animal that looks like a dog (but) is a powerful spirit." The wolf was integral to many religious ceremonies; the dog was unceremoniously kicked out of any ceremonial lodge.*

There is a story that neatly summarizes native American perceptions of what wolf and dog might have thought of each other. A Crow woman was out digging roots when a wolf came by. The woman's dog ran up to the wolf and said, "Hey, what are you doing here? Go away. You only

to kill the wolf. This person then might explain to the dead wolf that he had been hired by some *other* village so the wolf would take out any revenge at the wrong place. The Chukchi Eskimo of northeastern Siberia routinely told any wolf they killed that they were Russians, not Eskimos.

The pelt was normally all that was taken from a wolf, though teeth, claws, and internal organs were needed for decorative or religious purposes. The pelt was used by shamans in curing ceremonies like the one Bird Shirt performed; to wrap sacred, usually commemorative, articles to make a "wolf bundle"; and as totemic representation of the wolf's presence. Kills in the Night, a Crow medicine woman, for example, used a wolf pelt to escape a Lakota war party that was chasing her and her daughter, Pretty Shield. After dusting their horse tracks with it, Kills in come around because you want what I have."

"What have you got?" asked the wolf.
"Your owner beats you all the time. Kids kick you out of the way. Try to steal a piece of meat and they hit you over the head with a club."

"At least I can steal the meat!" answered the dog. "You haven't got anything to steal."

"Hah! I eat whenever I want. No one bothers me."

"What do you eat? You slink around while the men butcher the buffalo and get what's left over. You're afraid to get close. You sit there with your armpits stinking, pulling dirt balls out of your tail."

"Look who's talking, with camp garbage smeared all over your face."

"Hrumph. Whenever I come into camp, my owner throws me something good to eat."

"When your owner goes out to ease himself at night you follow along to eat the droppings, that's how much you get to eat."

"That's okay! These people only eat the finest parts!"

"You're proud of it!"

"Listen, whenever they're cooking in camp, you smell the grease, you come around and howl, and I feel sorry for you. I pity you. . . ."

"When do they let you have a good time?" asked the wolf.

". . . I sleep warm, you sleep out there in the rain, they scratch my ears, you—"

Just then the woman shouldered a bundle of roots, whacked the dog on the back with a stick, and started back to camp. The dog followed along behind her, calling over his shoulder at the wolf, "You're just full of envy for a good life, that's all that's wrong with you."

Wolf went off the other way, not wanting any part of that life.

---

the Night put the wolf skin over their heads and singing a medicine song led her daughter away. The Lakota became confused in a sudden thundershower and lost the woman's trail.

The most widespread use of the wolf pelt on the plains, however, was among scouts, who used it in imitative disguise.

The Skidi Pawnee were plains scouts *extraordinaire*. The hand sign in plains sign language for *Pawnee* was the same as that for *wolf*: index and middle finger of the right hand were raised in a V next to the right ear, then brought forward. Waving the sign from side to side signified the verb *to scout*. Dressed in their wolf skin cloaks, known as the Wolf People because the wolf figured so strongly in their foundation myth, there were no others like them. The Cheyenne, Comanche, and Wichita called the Pawnee wolves because "they prowl like wolves . . . they have the endurance of wolves, and can travel all day, and dance all night, and can make long journeys, living on carcasses they find on their way, or on no food at all."

The Pawnee conceptualization of the wolf was that he was an animal who moved like liquid across the plains: silent, without effort, but with purpose. He was alert to the smallest changes in his world. He could see very far—"two looks away," they said. His hearing was so sharp he could even hear a cloud as it passed overhead. When a man went into the enemy's territory he wished to move exactly like this, to sense things like the wolf, to be Wolf.

The sense of being Wolf that came over a Pawnee scout was not the automatic result of putting on a wolf skin. The wolf skin was an accouterment, an outward sign to the man himself and others who might see him that he was calling on his wolf power. It is hard for the Western mind to grasp this and to take seriously the notion that an Indian at times could *be* Wolf, could actually participate in the animal's spirit, but this is what happened. It wasn't being *like* a wolf; it was having the mind set: Wolf.

White historians wrote off the superior tracking abilities of the Pawnee, Arikara, and Crow scouts that the army used to "native intelligence" and a "hocus-pocus" with wolf skins. What was actually present was an intimacy with the environment, a magic "going in and out," so that the line of distinction between a person and his animal helper was not always clear. The white, for the most part, was afraid of, separated from, the environment. He spent his time flailing at it and denouncing it, trying to ignore that in it which confused or intimidated him.

Pawnees wore their wolf pelts like capes during exploration of an enemy territory, the flat pelt falling across the shoulders and the wolf's head coming up over the man's head so the wolf's ears stood up erect. (Hidatsa scouts slit the pelt vertically and wore it over the shoulders, with the wolf's head lying against the chest.) A Sioux named Ghost Head wore a wolf skin tied tightly around his waist whenever he went against his enemies. In the evening he would make a small fire, smoke the skin in sweet grass (*Hierochloe odorata*), and seek to align himself with the wolf spirit represented therein, asking that the presence of his enemies be revealed to him by the (real) wolves around him, whom he considered his helpers.

It was customary for scouts returning to camp or signaling to each other to howl like wolves.

Before moving on to a deeper consideration of wolves and warriors, I would like to encourage some reflection on all these ideas by mentioning several ways in which the wolf was associated with the more or less mundane among various tribes. The number of examples is remarkable.

The wolf showed up as a child's carved, wooden toy among the Nehalem Tillamook on the Oregon coast and three thousand miles away, among the Naskapi of Labrador, in a game of lots called wolf sticks, in which the wolf stick was the long stick among several shorter ones. On the plains, children played a game of tag called wolf chase with a "rabbit" who was "it." In the north, Eskimos made an object (known to anthropologists as a bull-roarer) that made a noise when whirled overhead on the end of a tether, which they called a wolf scarer.

The Sioux called the December moon The Moon When the Wolves Run Together. The Cheyenne believed a wolf's being caught asleep at sunrise was a sign of its imminent death. In a story the Crow told, the pin-tailed grouse was created with a wolf claw for a beak. So-called wolf berries *(Symphoricarpus occidentalis)* that grew in the upper Missouri country were used in solution as a wash for inflamed eyes. And wolf moss *(Everina vulpina)* was boiled to produce a yellow dye by several tribes.

We who have largely lost contact with wild animals, have indeed gone to lengths to distinguish ourselves from them, can easily miss the significance of such a view of the human world in which the natural world is so deeply reflected. The view is fully integrated. It produces, often, an utter calm, a sense of belonging.

It is this need, I think, that people most wish to articulate when they speak of "a return to the earth."

Six

WOLF WARRIORS

THE Indian did not think of the wolf as a warrior in the same sense as he thought of himself as a warrior, but he respected the wolf's stamina and stoicism and he encouraged these qualities in himself and others. The wolf, therefore, was incorporated into the ceremonies and symbology of war. It was common practice for warriors to tie a wolf tail around the lower leg or ankle or at the back of a moccasin to signify an accomplishment in battle. Among the Mandan the practice was rather refined. A man who had never counted coup (to strike an enemy with one's hand or a stick) was entitled to wear one wolf tail on his moccasin if he was the first to count coup in a fight; two wolf tails if he counted coup twice before anyone else did; and a wolf tail with the tip disfigured if he counted coup after someone else had in the same fight.

Assiniboin warriors wore white wolf skin caps smeared with red paint into battle.

The Wolf Soldier band of the Cheyenne was one of the best known of all the wolf warrior societies on the plains and it incorporated the most wolf lore.

The Wolf Soldiers were established early in the nineteenth century by a northern Cheyenne named Owl Friend. At that time, the northern and southern bands of the Cheyenne were traveling slowly toward each other. Owl Friend set out on his own one morning to reach the southern band. He wore a red robe and deer skin leggings with a great deal of porcupine quill and beadwork in them—very dressy, but he expected clear weather. In the afternoon a thunderstorm came up which changed to sleet and, later, to snow. By dusk Owl Friend suspected he was lost. He was also distraught over his ruined clothes. But thinking he must be near the southern Cheyenne camp, he pushed on. Finally, late that night, it seemed he came to a large tipi at the edge of a creek, which he took to be the Cheyenne camp. He went up and stamped the snow off his feet and a young man came to the door and welcomed him in.

There were four or five men in the lodge and he joked with them about almost getting lost in the snowstorm. His friends put him to bed to rest, while they warmed food and went about drying and softening his clothes.

Occasionally someone would come into the lodge and say something like, "Oh, our friend is here. It's lucky he got in, he might have frozen in the storm."

Owl Friend stayed in the lodge four days, waiting out the storm. He noticed a number of unusual things, among them four pipes, four lances with red shafts and scalps tied to them, and four drums. There were also rattles decorated with feathers and weasel tails.

On the fourth day the young men asked him to look around carefully at the things in the lodge. In addition to what he had already seen, Owl Friend noticed two hawk skins, two otter skins, two swift fox skins, a bear hide, and a wolf hide. The wolf hide was slit to fit over the head and eagle feathers were tied to the middle of its back.

On the evening of the fourth day the young men began to put on some of these things and to arrange the lodge ·for a ceremony. One of

WARRIOR SONGS

The songs men sang while they traveled—short songs of encouragement or songs about a lover or in praise of past deeds—were collectively called wolf traveling songs by the Cheyenne. Such songs often came to warriors in their dreams. Francis Densmore collected this one among the Sioux:

A wolf
I considered myself

But the owls are hooting
and the night
I fear.

A warrior might also call on wolves in song to come and eat the flesh of his enemies after a battle, or, by comparing himself to a wolf, warn young men of the dangers that faced them, as in the following:

At daybreak I roam
ready to tear up the world
I roam

At daybreak I roam
shivers coming up my spine
I roam

At daybreak I roam
awake to who is following
I roam

At daybreak I roam
eyes in the back of my head
I roam.
—Santee Sioux song sung by Weasel Bear.
Translated by JIM HEYNEN

the young men went out to ask an old man to call in the Wolf Soldiers.

Another man came over to Owl Friend. "You see us, the way we are dressing and preparing things?" he said. "This is the way you will do it."

As people came in, Owl Friend could see the storm was still blowing hard, piling the snow deep.

A man named Wears His Robe Hair Out and three others began singing. The four lances were stuck in the ground. The four pipes were filled. The drums were smoked in sweet grass and one of the men struck the drum four times.

"Owl Friend," he said. "Watch closely. You will have to imitate us. Remember the songs."

Then the man looked up and said, "It will stop storming now," and began the ceremony. The dancing and singing went on all night. Between songs they would smoke the pipes and someone would go outside to see the storm. "It is clearing off nicely," they would say when they came back in. "You can see stars shining."

WOLF SONG

Music recorded for a wordless Blackfeet wolf song.

They danced late into the night. Owl Friend watched how everything was done. When the dancing was over, they had a feast and the men put their clothes away. "Now we give it all to you," they said to Owl Friend, and told him to go to bed. But before he did so he stepped outside. The sky was absolutely clear and most of the snow had melted.

When he awoke next morning before sunrise Owl Friend was surprised to find himself out on the prairie. He was surrounded by wolves, whom he recognized, howling in the dim light, as the young men he had stayed with. "Do this dance for four days and four nights," they said. "When you are through, rub this medicine [balsam root, *Balsamorrhiza sagittata*] on your body. You will be Wolf Soldiers!"

With this the wolves left. Owl Friend returned to his camp with the dance and the other particulars of his dream to inaugurate the organization.

The Wolf Soldiers was the last of the seven great Cheyenne soldier bands to be formed. The origin story contains the common elements of camaraderie, elaborate ritual, and demonstration of power (over the storm). The function of these soldier bands was to defend the camp against attack and to act as police during buffalo hunts and on moves through enemy territory.

The Cheyenne Wolf Soldier ceremony was usually held in the late spring or early summer each year. It was both a ceremony of renewal for the members and an opportunity for young men to join. Members outfitted themselves as the wolf brothers had done in Owl Friend's vision. Initiates wore only a breechcloth, and painted their hands and lower arms, feet and lower legs, and the lower portion of the face red, using crimson-colored earth or spring pussy willow buds.

At the conclusion of the ceremony each year a group of young Wolf Soldiers might elect to go raiding, as happened in the summer of 1819. Thirty Wolf Soldiers went north into Crow country, were surprised by a large Crow war party, and all killed. It was a tremendous blow to Cheyenne pride. The next year, the Wolf Soldier band having been all but wiped out, the other Cheyenne soldier bands—Dog Soldiers, Kit Fox Men, Red Shields—performed the ceremony of "Moving the Arrows Against the Crow" and attacked in revenge.

In the summer of 1837 a group of Wolf Soldiers (the society had by now gotten a name for being hot-blooded) whipped a medicine man named White Thunder until he agreed to perform the Cheyenne renewal ceremony of the Medicine Arrows early. He did so, telling them it wouldn't work; but they took no heed. Forty-two of them went against a Kiowa, Apache, and Comanche encampment on the Washita River in west-central Oklahoma and, in a moment of panic, revealed themselves when they were on foot and without cover. All of them were killed.

The next spring a man who would later be called Yellow Wolf reorganized the Wolf Soldiers, renaming them the Bowstring Men, and set out to avenge the Cheyenne nation. They and their Arapaho allies struck a Kiowa and Apache camp on Wolf Creek in northwestern Oklahoma and met one of the most famous enemy warriors in Cheyenne history, a Kiowa named Sleeping Wolf.

The Cheyenne charged across Wolf Creek into the Kiowa camp. Sleeping Wolf grabbed a war club and led a countercharge on foot, driving the mounted Cheyenne back, but not without being leveled himself three times by warriors counting coup. Racing back across the stream, Sleeping Wolf grabbed a horse and again charged the Cheyenne. The horse was shot out from under him and while he fought on, again on foot and surrounded in the water, three more warriors counted coup on him. Managing to get away to the creek bank and to grab another horse, he got halfway across before the animal was shot out from under him and another bullet broke his leg. Three more times he was struck by warriors before finally being killed.

The Cheyenne and Arapaho were absolutely awed by this show of courage. Many of them, including all nine warriors who had struck Sleeping Wolf, would name their children for him. (The man was also known as Yellow Shirt for the buckskin shirt he wore that day, and Yellow Wolf is even today a common name among the Cheyenne.)

A few Cheyenne warriors named for wolves have put on extraordinary displays of power in battle. One of them was Wolf Belly, in a fight at Beecher's Island, northeastern Colorado, on September 17, 1868. Fifty-three soldiers and civilian scouts were entrenched on the island in a dry riverbed, all of them armed with the new Spencer repeating rifle and the army's new Colt revolver. The first Indian charge was shredded in a withering fire. The second charge, led by Wolf Belly, was also stopped, but Wolf Belly himself ran completely over the trenches and, jeering at the whites, crossed them again and again. The whites thought he was insane. Not a bullet struck him.

(In a curious aftermath to this battle, Capt. Louis Carpenter, patrolling some weeks later, came upon the burial scaffolds of nine of the Cheyenne killed at Beecher's Island. He ordered his men to tear down the scaffolds so that wolves would desecrate the bodies. It was a common white belief at the time that the sole reason for elevating a body on a burial scaffold was to keep wolves from eating it. On the contrary, the Indians elevated the body out of respect. It was clearly understood that the gross body would be returned in this way to the earth from which it came, by the action of the rains and the winds, and by scavenging eagles, coyotes, and wolves.)

Another Cheyenne shaman, Wolf Man, was considered bulletproof after a fight on the Powder River in Wyoming in 1865 when, having been struck by two bullets, he simply shook them out of his vest.

WOLF MEN

Wolf Goes to Drink, Crow	Many Wolves Waiting Near the Village,
Wolf's Sleeve, Apache	Tlingit
Mad Wolf, Seminole	Wolf Walking Around a Person, Tlingit
Wolf Calf, Blackfeet	Wolf Chaser, Crow
Wolf Eyes, Hidatsa	Wolf Bear, Crow
Wolf Lying Down, Kiowa	Wolf Orphan, Blackfeet
Wolf Necklace, Palouse	Wolf Robe, Acoma
High Wolf, Lakota	Wolf Standing Alone, Kiowa
Yellow Wolf, Nez Perce	Wolf Face, Apache

The most honored warrior among the Cheyenne in the closing days of the plains wars was named Little Wolf. In September 1878, together with Dull Knife, he led 278 men, women, and children off the reservation in Oklahoma and north toward their ancestral home on the Yellowstone River in southern Montana. Their flight was arduous. Little Wolf distinguished himself in skirmish after skirmish but it all came to a tragic end, fighting in bitter cold without food or clothing that winter. The few left alive, including Little Wolf, were broken people.

The wolf name is still common among the Cheyenne: John Fire Wolf, Wolf Satchel, Blind Wolf are alive today.

Nothing has been said so far of women in connection with the wolf because where the wolf figured strongly, among shamans and warriors, there were few women. A woman's involvement with wolves was more often a matter of her rolling up the sides of her buffalo hide tipi out of reach and putting her family's belongings on a scaffold if they were going to be away for a while, to keep the wolves from getting into things. If a Cheyenne woman, for example, wanted to cure wolf hides, she had to protect herself against the consequence of touching such a powerful animal by undergoing a purification ceremony. A member of the Young Wolf Medicine Society painted her with red paint in the familiar way: the hands and feet, a circle on the chest representing the sun, and a crescent moon over the right shoulder blade, and lastly the face from the middle of the nose to the throat. A wolf hide resting on white sage *(Audibertia polystachya)* was similarly painted, but with a half moon on the right shoulder and a full circle on the back.

This ceremony was performed for a number of women at the same time. After snipping bits of hair from the wolf pelt, the women circled the camp—pausing at cardinal points to howl—and were then dusted by the master of ceremonies with white sage to signify removal of the paint, the end of the ceremony.

Women show up frequently in native American folklore and history as wives to wolves or their helpers. A Bella Coola woman who once helped a wolf with a difficult birth and helped still another wolf choking on a bone was widely known as a seer on the British Columbia coast, her shamanistic powers being a reward from the grateful wolves. Among the most moving of all these stories is one from the Sioux, about Woman Who Lived with Wolves.

The woman's husband had treated her very badly and one evening, during a storm, she left, determined never to return. She traveled all night while the snow fell and covered her tracks. When the snow stopped falling, she started to leave a trail, so she climbed up to a ridge swept clear of snow and went on. She did not want her husband or her relatives ever to find her. She burned with a deep anger.

Walking down the ridge, she came to a cave which she entered to rest. She wrapped her robe around her and went to sleep. Sometime later she felt a slight movement. Opening her eyes, she saw dark forms poised over her. They slowly began to pull the wet robe away from her. She could tell now that they were wolves. As she lay there frozen in terror, the wolves curled up next to her and she felt their warmth. She turned her head very slowly until she was looking one of them in the face. He was asleep.

That evening the wolves left to hunt, returning in the morning with deer meat for her. She was so hungry she ate the meat raw. That evening she went out on the ridge to watch the winter sky, feeling her pain and anger. The wolves sat with her; they did not say anything. When she felt the pain the most, one of the wolves walked over and stood next to her.

She lived with the wolves for a long time, making her clothes from the deer hides they brought her and sharing their food, though she cooked her meat now, in a hole where the fire would not be seen. In time she learned how the wolves spoke and was able to talk with them. They told her about the places they had been.

One afternoon when they were all asleep in the sun, she realized it was time to go. Just as this thought came into her mind, one of the wolves opened his eyes and was looking at her.

Woman Who Lived with Wolves did not want to go back to her village, even though she was now a medicine woman. Instead, she went out on the prairie to live.

One day some young Sioux men were chasing horses when they saw Woman Who Lived with Wolves running in among them. She had accidentally been swept up in their drive, and though she could keep up with the horses, she knew she could not break away without being roped.

After many miles the horses began to falter and the young men concentrated on running down the woman. They finally got some ropes on her so she couldn't move. They recognized her as the woman who had run away and returned with her to the village.

Woman Who Lived with Wolves remained distant among her people. They were kind to her, her relatives especially. She did not see her husband and no one said anything about him.

In time, in response to their questions, she told them of the time she had spent with the wolves. A man named White Bull was contemptuous of her and wanted to test her power. He was a powerful medicine man but insecure. He made people uncomfortable. White Bull told Woman Who Lived with Wolves to stand apart from him, that they would "shoot" things at each other to see whose power was strongest. White Bull went first. He shot her with bumblebees and rolled-up balls of buffalo hair. Woman Who Lived with Wolves did not flinch. Finally he shot her with "one of those small worms that comes out of the head of the elk." This staggered the woman, but she did not fall.

Then it was Woman Who Lived with Wolves's turn. She shot White Bull with a grasshopper and it was finished.

Her people believed in her and gave her her wolf name.

Wolves were not always benevolent figures in myth and legend nor strictly models for a warrior's admiration. Indians understood them in a wider context. Wolves, like grizzly bears, could, after all, kill Indians. Those who tended to fear the wolf the most were the woodland Indians, who encountered them suddenly, usually at close quarters. Those who commonly saw them out in the open, on the tundra, for example, where they could more easily appraise the wolves' motives, were much less fearful. But even they kept their distance. The nether regions of many tribes' spirit worlds were inhabited by wolves which, in this context, were enemies. Nuliayuk, a great female sea spirit of Canadian Eskimos, was guarded in her undersea house by wolves. And there were enormous mythic wolves that lived near the Naskapi's Caribou House and whose attacks hunters risked if they dared draw near.

Rabies was a real reason to fear wolves, for there were few more horrible deaths. A Blackfeet man bitten by a rabid wolf was bound with ropes and rolled in a green buffalo hide. A fire was built on and around him and he was subjected to this intense heat until the hide began to burn. The disease was believed to leave in the man's profuse sweat.

Other tribes, notably the Navajo, feared wolves as human witches in wolves' clothing. The Navajo word for wolf, *mai-coh*, is a synonym for witch. There is a good deal of witchcraft among the Navajo and belief in werewolves provides explanations for otherwise inexplicable (to them) phenomena. Witchcraft and werewolves are (the belief is current) more on the minds of some Navajos than others, specifically the more insecure, those who have many bad dreams or who suffer from a sickness or misfortune all out of proportion to those around them. Such people might be viewed by other Navajos as suffering the attention of werewolves.

A Navajo witch becomes a werewolf by donning a wolf skin. If he means to kill someone, he travels to his hogan at night, climbs up on the roof, and tosses something through the smokehole to make the fire flare, revealing where people are sleeping. He then pushes down a poison on the end of a stick, which the victim inhales. (Dirt rolling off the roof at night is a sign that a werewolf is about.)

In addition to killing people, Navajo werewolves raided graveyards and mutilated bodies. By taking the finger of a dead male or the tongue of a dead female (corresponding to the penis and the clitoris, respectively) and placing it near a living person, the werewolf ensured the vengeance of the spirit against the person, the spirit assuming that the living person had stolen the finger.

Modern Navajos are cautious around dead people and graves, and reluctant to press for the identity of a suspected human-wolf for fear of retaliation. If one is to be killed, they feel it wise to spread the task among three or four people. Most suspected werewolves are men and highly aggressive.

As a protection against witchery, Navajos even today keep gall around the house or on their person, sometimes wolf gall.

No matter who it was, whenever wolves were close everyone was a little nervous. One of the things wolves did in Indian camps that must have caused an eerie tension was to wander among the horse herds at night, drifting about in their shadowy way, lying down to rest among the animals or perhaps chewing through a rawhide picket rope. And then moving on, rarely disturbing even the high-strung horses.

Sometimes someone would bring wolf pups into a camp—a few tribes raised them for their fur—but it rarely worked out. The camp dogs killed them or they ran away or a nervous neighbor turned them loose or spirited them off. If you wanted to play with wolf puppies, you were better off going to a den. The parents would usually back off and you could dig the pups out. When Cree youngsters did this, they would sometimes paint the pups red around the nose and the lower limbs before putting them back. In their childhood game the pups were wolf warriors, just like themselves.

Once in a great while someone brought an exceptional wolf pup home and things went differently. Such a wolf one time came among the Blackfeet.

One spring two Blackfeet, Red Eagle and Nitaina, were hunting near Milk River in Montana after a heavy rainstorm. All the rivers were high; out on an island in one of them they spotted two wolves pacing anxiously back and forth. "There must be a den out there," said Nitaina. "Let's go see if there are any pups."

They had a difficult time getting the horses through the mud and water onto the island. The big wolves barked and howled at their approach and then left, swimming to the far shore. There was indeed a den Six drowned puppies floated in its entrance and one sat there in miserable silence.

Nitaina reached down and took the pup. "I will take him back," he said.

People in camp said it was no good to keep a wolf, but Nitaina insisted. The wolf stayed close to Nitaina's lodge, afraid of the camp dogs and wanting nothing to do with people. Wherever Nitaina went the wolf came along, picking up his habits. When Nitaina chased horses, the wolf chased horses. When Nitaina shot a deer that did not fall, the wolf brought it down.

When he was ten months old the wolf got in a fight with the camp dogs. He wounded several of them and people began to complain about having the wolf around. Nitaina ignored them. When the wolf greeted Nitaina he put his paws on his shoulders and mouthed his head. The man named him Laugher.

Late one spring, when the grass was high, some of the men decided to go horse raiding against the Cheyenne. Nitaina wanted to take Laugher along but the leader said no, which was his right. Many of the men felt Laugher was a strange wolf and bad luck to have around.

So Nitaina and Red Eagle and Laugher went southeast on their own, through Crow country to steal Sioux horses.

This was the first time Red Eagle had really been with Laugher. He liked the animal very much. One day Laugher killed an antelope by himself and became so excited he ran back and forth between the dead antelope and Nitaina three or four times, urging Nitaina to come see what he had done. It was good. It meant they could eat without having to fire a shot, which would have revealed their presence.

They went on for days, on foot, at night, sharing the antelope meat, until they came to the west side of the Bear Paws. Then they began traveling high on the mountains during the day, crossing Middle Creek and going up into the Little Rockies. One afternoon as they were rounding a bare rock butte Laugher stopped them suddenly. He put his nose on a rock and sniffed, and the fur on his neck stood up a little.

"Either a war party or a bear has been through here," said Nitaina.

The men could find no tracks and urged the wolf to go on. Laugher moved slowly, working his ears and looking back often at the men creeping low behind him. When they reached the top of the butte, the men raised their heads slowly to peer over. For a moment they saw nothing. Then, within shooting distance, they saw a thin pall of smoke hanging in dense timber. Laugher, exposed on the ridge, began to howl. "No! No!"

whispered Nitaina. But Laugher continued until two men were drawn out of the shadows to look around. They were Crows. They watched Laugher for a while, then went back into the trees.

Red Eagle and Nitaina slipped off the slope and ran hard until they reached a patch of cottonwoods at the foot of the butte. They had intended to walk right down the front of the butte. It would have meant their lives if Laugher hadn't sensed the Crows.

That evening two men from the Crow war party sat as lookouts on the same butte where Nitaina, Red Eagle, and Laugher had been until morning, when they were joined by about twenty others and they all left.

In another week Red Eagle and Nitaina came on a Sioux camp on Little River. Expecting raids, the Sioux kept their horses in close to the lodges at night but turned them out during the day. Waiting their chance, the two Blackfeet grabbed two good-looking horses one morning, threw war rope bridles around their jaws and, rounding up thirty or forty others, broke for home. The Sioux immediately gave chase but Red Eagle and Nitaina, by jumping from one horse to another, were able to keep fresh mounts under them and stay ahead. They rode without stopping the rest of the day, all night, and into the next day, pushing the horses ahead of them. Laugher was a great help, keeping the horses moving and together. Finally they took a short rest at sundown.

They kept moving like this, taking only short rests, until they came in two days to the mouth of the Milk River. They had not seen Sioux behind them after the second day and felt safe now taking a long sleep.

Red Eagle took the first watch but could not stay awake. When he awoke, it was with a jolt. Nitaina was yelling: "Mount! Mount! Look at what's coming!"

A war party on foot broke out of the trees at a distance and began firing. In a panic the two Blackfeet jumped on their horses and rode out, with Laugher bunching the herd and pushing behind them. One horse was killed. They didn't stop riding for two days, until they swam the horses across Milk River and north into their own camp.

Laugher, once again, had saved them. It was he who had seen the war party hiding in the trees in time to waken Nitaina.

The Blackfeet in camp came to feel differently about the wolf after hearing what he had done, but Laugher remained distant. In a medicine lodge ceremony where all the men told of the times they had counted coup, Nitaina stood up and spoke for Laugher, and the men sent up war cries and banged on their drums, very pleased at this.

Some of the older men asked Red Eagle and Nitaina to bring Laugher and go after horses with them now, but they said no. The two men preferred going alone. They went once more that summer against the Cheyenne and with Laugher's help again got twelve good pinto horses.

That winter Laugher began to disappear for days at a time. Finally he went off for three or four weeks and when he returned he was not alone. He stood on a hill near the village and appeared to be urging another wolf with him to come the rest of the way into the village. When the wolf wouldn't come, Laugher went alone to Nitaina's lodge but he did not stay long. He seemed restless, kept standing in the door and, finally, with a glance back at Nitaina, he left.

Nitaina did not see him for almost a year. Then he was with a third wolf, traveling across a valley in the Sweet Grass Hills. Two of the wolves ran off when they saw Nitaina approaching. Laugher stood watching for a few more minutes, then he, too, trotted off.

The next spring Red Eagle suggested that they go look for another wolf pup, maybe they would get lucky and find one like Laugher. But Nitaina said no.

The spirit that kept a people together through time, even as individuals passed away, was one of the most deeply felt emotions in the native American soul. Every year in small and large ways the spirit of life, of tribal identity and solidarity, of the individual's place in the tribe, was renewed. And the wolf played a role here too, in some of the Pueblo masked rituals like the Hopi Snake Dance, and in the Sun Dance ritual of the plains. I would like to close this chapter by looking at two of these ceremonials, one from the Nootka and the other from the Pawnee.

The wolf ritual of the lower Pacific northwest coast, among the Nootka, Kwakiutl, and Quillayute, was the major masked ritual in this part of the country. Usually held in the beginning of winter before a full moon, it was hosted by someone prominent in the village and served to welcome young people formally into the tribe. Tribal initiation in the wolf ceremony was central to one's sense of identity with the tribe, and participation was necessary before one could take part in any other ceremony. It also renewed a sense of tribal identity for former initiates who participated.

Although the ceremony differed slightly among the various tribes and clans, lasting five days with some, nine days with others, it derived from the same myth and was performed in essentially the same way.

The mythic basis for the initiation ceremony (as distinct from healing and puberty ceremonies like the Whirling Wolf Dance or Crawling Wolf Dance) was the stealing of a young man by a pack of wolves. The wolves tried to kill him but could not and so they became his friends. They taught him about themselves, then sent him back to his village to teach his tribe the rites of the wolf ceremony. The young man told his people that it was necessary for the strength of the tribe, for their success in war, and everything else they did, that they should be like wolves. They must be as fierce, as brave, and as determined as the one who is the greatest hunter in the woods. In this ceremony people are "stolen" by wolves, go through a terrifying confrontation, and emerge wolflike.

Among the Makah, a division of the Nootka, the ceremony begins with the gathering in the evening of the older men in the tribe, dressed in cedar and hemlock branches and blowing on small wolf whistles made of bone. They gather the young initiates quietly from their homes and take them to the house where the ceremony, the *Klukwalle*, is to be performed. On the second day messengers go through the village specifically asking each person in the tribe to come that evening to *Klukwalle*.

Toward dusk the people begin to gather and the procession winds its way to the ceremonial house.

Inside, to the accompaniment of drums and bird rattles, each member of the tribe sings his *tse-ka*, or personal medicine song, around a central ceremonial fire. The evening builds with *tse-ka* singing until someone throws back his head and the first wolf howl is heard in the lodge. Soon everyone is howling and then the howls of real wolves, responding from the woods outside the lodge, begin to be heard, louder and louder. Outside, human wolves are banging on the walls; the children are terrified. Some of the participants have already put on wolf masks and have begun to act threateningly. They are restrained with cedar bark ropes until the

Wolf mask, Kwakiutl.

evening grows tame, with a fading of the songs and a quieting of the wolves banging on the walls.

The third day begins with a ritual cutting of the flesh on the initiates' arms. Among the Makah this might have been a reenactment of a gashing that their culture hero, *Ha-sass*, subjected himself to. (*Ha-sass* wished to learn the ways of the wolves but he was afraid that if they smelled his blood they would know he was human. He had his brothers cut him with shell knives until his blood was drained away before he went to the cave where the wolves lived.)

When the gashing is completed, the initiates go outside for the first time in a procession through the village, with their wounds dripping. After noon they either go to their own homes or back to the ceremonial lodge to rest for the evening performances.

After dark the tribal members again wind in a procession past all the homes to the ceremonial house. More masks are now evident, including the raccoon mask and the honeybee mask. The *tse-ka* songs are sung, the bird rattles and drums are heard, the wolf cries go up, and for the first time there is dancing. The people in the wolf masks become more and more agitated and try to put the fire out. Restrained by the cedar ropes the wolves go into the wolf frenzy to show their power, and the initiates, many of them terrified by the howling and dancing of the wolves, begin their own dances to demonstrate a willingness to be in touch with these spirits. The frenzy of the wolves builds until they finally succeed in stamping out all the fires.

After a period of darkness the fires (for warmth and light but with spiritual overtones) are rekindled and the people eat.

The fourth day of the ceremony marks its climax, when all the members of the tribe put on their personal masks reflecting individual identity—deer, woodpecker, eagle—and costumes and proceed to the lodge to take part in the larger tribal ceremony. Waiting inside are unmasked members of the tribe who, at the appointed time, unmask each person, symbolically returning him to his human form. The unmasking of those people who are wearing the wolf masks calms the wolf frenzy. In their sudden serenity is evidence of their rebirth; the strength of their bearing shows they have internalized the strength of the wolf.

By now the young initiates have decided which animal will be their personal animal and have fashioned a mask to a likeness. The evening ends with a feast and a breaking of their fast. On the morning of the fifth day they will go down on the beach and dance with their masks on for the first time.

The Makah Wolf Ritual represents a middle ground between the sort of rituals in which the children are stolen by tribal members in wolf masks, returned after a few days of mourning, and revived by tribal members, and the more bizarre rituals of northwest coast tribes to the north, where the spirit of the wolf is replaced by the spirit of the cannibal.

However it is played out, the wolf ritual represents a personal and tribal renewal in the context of those warrior qualities that the wolf was thought to possess and that would stand tribe and individual alike in good stead.

A different aspect of tribal identification with the wolf is seen among the Pawnee, whose climatic renewal ceremony came in the spring. Called the Captive Girl Ceremony or Morning Star Sacrifice, it involved the ritual death of a young, non-Pawnee woman who was stolen in a raid. In the cosmogony of the Pawnee, Morning and Evening Star had warred and Morning Star had won; from their union the first human being was born, a girl. From time to time Morning Star revealed himself in a dream to a Pawnee warrior, telling him he wanted a girl for himself in return for the one he had put on earth.

The symbolism of the ceremony is elaborate but its focus is on death and rebirth. Since the wolf was the first animal to experience death (in the Pawnee creation legend opposite), his symbolic presence is essential. He arrives in the person of the Pawnee Wolf Man, the keeper of the sacred "wolf bundle." He takes care of the captive girl from just before the winter buffalo hunt when she is stolen until the sacrifice takes place in the spring. He treats her kindly, sees to her needs, and it is he, finally, who walks her to the sacrificial scaffolding.

The Pawnee were in some ways the most complex of the plains tribes because they were both an agricultural and a hunting people. The renewal of their corn crops and their annual buffalo hunts were two driving forces in their ceremonials and in all of them the life-death cycle—which functioned through the agreement with the Animal Master and the renewal cycle of the crops—was central. The wolf, that Red Star of Death in the southeastern sky, was associated with both corn and buffalo in the Pawnee mind; the birth and death of the Wolf Star (Sirius) each night as the earth turned was but a reflection of the wolf's coming and going from the spirit world, down the path of the Milky Way, which they called the Wolf Road.

The wolf was a symbol of renewal, just as the willow, the sacred tree of the southeast, was a symbol of death and rebirth. When the willow was cut down it grew back quickly, just as the wolf who was the first to be killed became the first to return from the dead. At that time, in the heyday of the Pawnee, anyone could look out on the prairie and know

THE PAWNEE CREATION LEGEND

It is told in the creation legend of the Pawnee that a great council was held to which all the animals were invited. For a reason no one remembers, the brightest star in the southern sky, the Wolf Star, was not invited. He watched from a distance, silent and angry, while everyone else decided how to make the earth. In the time after the great council the Wolf Star directed his resentment over this bad treatment at The Storm that Comes out of the West, who had been charged by the others with going around the earth, seeing to it that things went well. Storm carried a whirlwind bag with him as he traveled, inside of which were the first people. When he stopped to rest in the evening he would let the people out and they would set up camp and hunt buffalo.

One time the Wolf Star sent a gray wolf down to follow Storm around. Storm fell asleep and the wolf stole his whirlwind bag, thinking there might be something good to eat inside. He ran far away with it. When he opened it, all the people ran out. They set up camp but, suddenly, looking around, they saw there were no buffalo to hunt. When

they realized it was a wolf and not Storm that had let them out of the bag they were very angry. They ran the wolf down and killed him.

When The Storm that Comes out of the West located the first people and saw what they had done he was very sad. He told them that by killing the wolf they had brought death into the world. That had not been the plan, but now it was this way.

The Storm that Comes out of the West told them to skin the wolf and make a sacred bundle with the pelt, enclosing in it the things that would always bring back the memory of what had happened. Thereafter, he told them, they would be known as the wolf people, the Skidi Pawnee.

The Wolf Star watched all this from the southern sky. The Pawnee call this star Fools the Wolves, because it rises just before the morning star and tricks the wolves into howling before first light. In this way the Wolf Star continues to remind people that when it came time to build the earth, he was forgotten.

these things were true. He could hear the songs of the wolf, like the songs that took up a man's life from birth; he could see the wolf trotting, trotting, trotting, like a warrior, like people moving camp, in the great coming and going that was life.

In the latter part of the nineteenth century in preparation for the Hidatsa Sunrise Wolf Bundle Transfer Rite, an old man named Small Ankles lamented with his son that it was going to be hard to do the ceremony properly because it was hard to find a wolf around anymore. In the transfer rite the Hidatsa engaged in a kind of "historic breathing," inhaling the past and emphasizing its place in the now, the present. To lose the ceremony would be to lose the past, to be undefined, nothing, broken. The time of the Indian, Small Ankles knew, was waning, as was the time of the wolf.

One morning in Montana I sat in the home of an old man named Raven Bear, a Crow. He had made a trip to Seattle a few years before to see his family. One day he took his grandson and drove to the Olympic peninsula where he had heard there was a commercial zoo with a number of wolves. He found the place, paid six dollars and went in. In a while he was ashamed he had brought his grandson there. The wolves were all in small pens, obese animals suffering from diseases, he thought. The people running the zoo told him the wolves were the last remnants of the Great Plains wolf, *Canis lupus nubilis.* "I wanted to tell the man he didn't know what he was saying," said Raven Bear, "but I didn't know how to do that. I just took the boy and left."

It was late at night. Raven Bear was sitting on the top of a bunk bed with his stocking feet hanging over the edge. After a while he said, "It hurts like hell, you know, to see it finished."

Three

THE BEAST OF WASTE AND DESOLATION

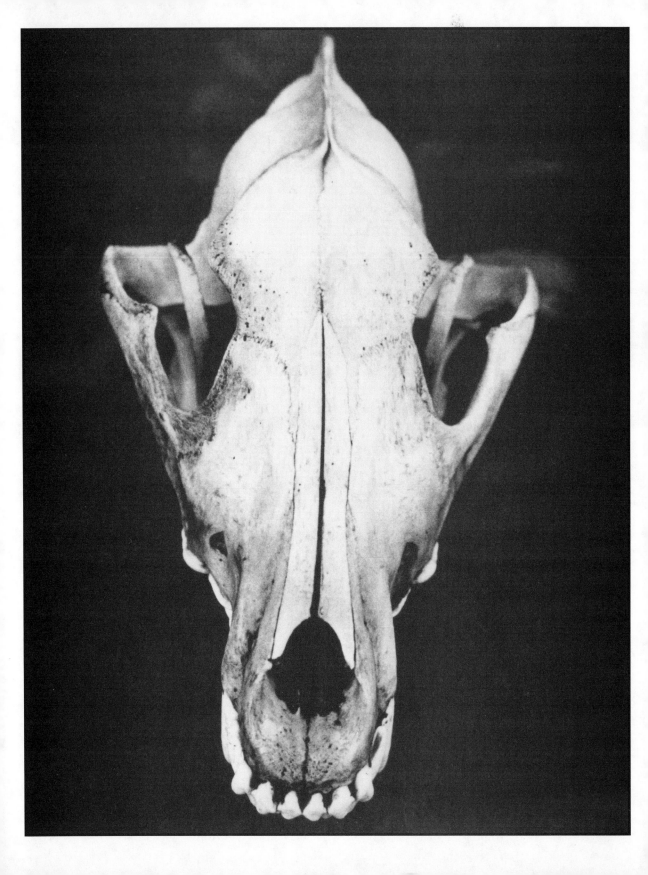

Seven

THE CLAMOR OF JUSTIFICATION

I N the course of writing this book I had a chance to talk with many
people, and to come into contact with several different points of
view about wolves. I enjoyed being in the field with biologists. I enjoyed
the range and subtlety of Indian and Eskimo ideas. My only discomfort
came when I talked with men who saw nothing wrong with killing
wolves, who felt it was basically a good thing to be doing. For the most
part, they were men who had matured in a different time and under different circumstances than I. We didn't share the same feelings toward
animals, but I could understand their positions. Some were professional
trappers. Others had lost stock to wolves. There was a larger context.

There were a few I spoke with, however, who were quite different. It
was as though these men had broken down at some point in their lives

and begun to fill with bile, and that bile had become an unreasoned hatred of many things. Of laws. Of governments. Of wolves. They hated wolves because—they would struggle to put it into words—because wolves seemed better off than they were. And that seemed perverse. They killed wolves habitually, with a trace of vengeance, with as little regret as a boy shooting rats at a dump.

They were few in number but their voices, screaming for the wolf's head, were often the loudest, the ones that set the tone at a grange meeting and precipitated the wolf's extirpation in the lower forty-eight states.

These men, and others, killed no one will ever know how many thousands of wolves in America, mostly to control predation against livestock. At the time, toward the close of the nineteenth century, it was a legitimate undertaking. Wolves, deprived of buffalo and other wild game, had turned to cattle and sheep; if you wanted to raise stock in America you had little choice but to kill wolves. But the killing was a complicated business, it was never as clearly reasoned as that. On the spur of the moment men offered ridiculous reasons—because the wolves loafed and didn't have to work for their food, they would say.

It is easy to condemn these men now, to look at what they did—destroy a national wildlife heritage—and feel a sense of loss. But they are, perhaps, too easily blamed. We forget how little, really, separates us from the times and circumstances in which we, too, would have killed wolves. Besides, blaming them for the loss is too simplistic. We are forced to a larger question: when a man cocked a rifle and aimed at a wolf's head, what was he trying to kill? And other questions. Why didn't we quit, why did we go on killing long after the need was gone? And when the craven and deranged tortured wolves, why did so many of us look the other way?

In an historical sense, we are all to blame for the loss of wolves. In the nineteenth century when the Indians on the plains were telling us that the wolf was a brother, we were preaching another gospel. Manifest Destiny. What rankles us now, I think, is that an alternative gospel still remains largely unarticulated. You want to say there never should have been a killing, but you don't know what to put in its place.

• • •

Ever since man first began to wonder about wolves—to make dogs of their descendants, to admire them as hunters—he has made a regular business of killing them. At first glance the reasons are simple enough, and justifiable. Wolves are predators. When men come into a land to "tame" it, they replace wild game with domestic animals. The wolves prey on these creatures, the men kill them in turn, and reduce the wolf population generally, as a preventive measure to secure their economic investment. The two just can't live side by side. A step removed from this, perhaps, in terms of its justification, is the action of Fish and Game departments that kill wolves to sustain or increase the yield of big game animals so human hunters can kill them. This kind of "predator control" has historically accommodated economic and political interests ahead of ecological interests. And it has acted occasionally from a basis of bar stool and barbershop biology, not wildlife science.

Wolf killing goes much beyond predator control, of course. Bounty hunters kill wolves for money; trappers kill them for pelts; scientists kill them for data; big game hunters kill them for trophies. The arguments for killing here are harder to sustain, yet many people see nothing at all wrong with these activities. Indeed, this is the way we commonly treat all predators—bobcats, bears, and mountain lions included. But the wolf is fundamentally different because the history of killing wolves shows far less restraint and far more perversity. A lot of people didn't just kill wolves; they tortured them. They set wolves on fire and tore their jaws out and cut their Achilles tendons and turned dogs loose on them. They poisoned them with strychnine, arsenic, and cyanide, on such a scale that *millions* of other animals—raccoons, black-footed ferrets, red foxes, ravens, red-tailed hawks, eagles, ground squirrels, wolverines—were killed incidentally in the process. In the thick of the wolf fever they even poisoned themselves, and burned down their own property torching the woods to get rid of wolf havens. In the United States in the period between 1865 and 1885 cattlemen killed wolves with almost pathological dedication. In the twentieth century people pulled up alongside wolves in airplanes and snowmobiles and blew them apart with shotguns for sport. In Minnesota in the 1970s people choked Eastern timber wolves to death in snares to show their contempt for the animal's designation as an endangered species.

This is not predator control, and it goes beyond the casual cruelty sociologists say manifests itself among people under stress, or where there is no perception of responsibility. It is the violent expression of a terrible assumption: that men have the right to kill other creatures not for what they do but for what we fear they may do. I almost wrote "or for no reason," but there are always reasons. Killing wolves has to do with fear based on superstitions. It has to do with "duty." It has to do with proving manhood (abstractly, perhaps, this is nothing more than wanting either to possess or to destroy the animal's soul). And sometimes, I think, because the killing is so righteously pursued and yet so entirely without conscience, killing wolves has to do with murder.

Historically, the most visible motive, and the one that best explains the excess of killing, is a type of fear: theriophobia. Fear of the beast. Fear of the beast as an irrational, violent, insatiable creature. Fear of the projected beast in oneself. The fear is composed of two parts: self-hatred; and anxiety over the human loss of inhibitions that are common to other animals who do not rape, murder, and pillage. At the heart of theriophobia is the fear of one's own nature. In its headiest manifestations theriophobia is projected onto a single animal, the animal becomes a scapegoat, and it is annihilated. That is what happened to the wolf in America. The routes that led there, however, were complex.

Those days are past. There is little to be gained now by condemning the aerial "sport" hunting of wolves (the activity is banned in the United States by federal law), or by railing against the cattle industry for the excesses of its founders. But there is something to be gained from learning where the fear and hatred originated, and where the one thing besides cruelty to the animal that sets wolf hunting apart from other kinds of hunting—the "righteousness" of it—comes from.

The hatred has religious roots: the wolf was the Devil in disguise. And it has secular roots: wolves killed stock and made men poor. At a more general level it had to do, historically, with feelings about wilderness. What men said about the one, they generally meant about the other. To celebrate wilderness was to celebrate the wolf; to want an end to wilderness and all it stood for was to want the wolf's head.

In setting down a base for our antipathy toward wilderness, the histo-

Predator-control program on the north slope of the Brooks Range, 1950s.

rian Roderick Nash has singled out religious and secular antecedents. In *Beowulf*, for example, there is an expression of the secular (i.e., non-religious) wilderness that is constituted of uninhabited forest—a region whose dank, cold depths, with its miasmic swamps and windswept crags, harbor foul creatures that prey on men. In the Bible, wilderness is defined as the place without God—a sere and barren desert. This twined sense of wilderness as a place innately dangerous and godless was something that attached itself, inevitably, to the wolf—the most feared denizen of gloomy wilderness. As civilized man matured and came to measure his own progress by his subjugation of the wilderness—both clearing trees for farms and clearing pagan minds for Christian ideas—the act of killing wolves became a symbolic act, a way to lash out at that enormous, inchoate obstacle: wilderness. Man demonstrated his own prodigious strength as well as his allegiance to God by killing wolves. I greatly oversimplify, but there is not much distinction in motive between the Christian missionaries who set fire to England's woods to deprive Druids of a place to worship and the residents of Arkansas who set fire to thousands of acres of the Ouachita National Forest in 1928 to deprive wolves of hiding places.

In America in the eighteenth century Cotton Mather and other Puritan ministers preached against wilderness as an insult to the Lord, as a challenge to man to show the proof of his religious conviction by destroying it. Mather, and others, urged the colonists to make of the "howling wilderness" a "fruitful field." In 1756 John Adams wrote that when the colonists arrived in America, "the whole continent was one continued dismal wilderness, the haunt of wolves and bears and more savage men. Now the forests are removed, the land covered with fields of corn, orchards bending with fruit and the magnificent habitations of rational and civilized people." In Europe at the same time the subjugation and ordering of shabby wilderness had reached its exaggerated apotheosis in the excessive neatness of the Versailles gardens.

The drive to tame wilderness in America never let up. The wagon-master of the 1840s "opened the road west"; he was followed by the farmer, who cleared the fields, and the logger, who "let daylight into the swamp." One hundred years after Adams wrote of dismal wilderness, the railroad barons and cattle barons were speaking of Manifest Destiny and man's right and obligation as God's steward to "make something of the land." And where they made it into towns, fields, and pastures, there was no place for the wolf. The wolf became the symbol of what you wanted to kill—memories of man's primitive origins in the wilderness, the remnant of his bestial nature which was all that held him back in America from building the greatest empire on the face of the earth. The wolf represented "a fierce, bloodsucking persecutor" (as Roger Williams called him) of everything that was high-born in man. Theodore Roosevelt, his hand on the Bible, his eye riveting the attention of men of commerce, spoke gravely of wolf predation on his ranch in North Dakota, of the threat to progress represented by the wolf. He called him "the beast of waste and desolation."

The image of wilderness as a figurative chaos out of which man had to bring order was one firmly embedded in the Western mind; but it was closely linked with a contradictory idea: that of the wilderness as holy retreat, wilderness as towering grandeur, soul-stirring and majestic. In the Exodus experience man deliberately sought wilderness to escape sinful society. Those oppressed by city living sought communion with wildlife in the countryside. The celebration of nature by Romantic poets like Wordsworth and Shelley, the landscapes of Thomas Moran, Albert Bierstadt and the Hudson River School, Rousseau's noble savage, and the later writings of John Muir and Henry David Thoreau were all in this tradition.

It was inevitable that the idea of wild land and wolves as something worthy of preservation, and wild land and wolves as obstacles to the westward course of empire, would clash. They met head on in America in the twentieth century in places like Alaska, where residents wanted to wipe out wolves to increase game herds, which would in turn attract tourist hunters to supplement a state economy inebriated with the sudden riches of oil; and environmentalists, mostly from out of state, did not want to see the wolf and the wilderness for which he was a symbol disappear in Alaska the way they had in the lower forty-eight.

The basis for conflict between these two groups becomes clearer if you recall that while people like Bierstadt and Karl Bodmer were exhibiting America's primitive beauty in European salons, American pioneers were cursing that same wilderness as the symbol of their hardships—not to mention decrying the genteel men who praised it but lived for their part in the comfort of a European city. In *Democracy in America*, de Tocqueville wrote: "In Europe people talk a great deal of the wilds of America, but the Americans themselves never think about them; they are insensible to the wonders of inanimate nature. Their eyes are fired with another sight; they march across these wilds, clearing swamps, turning the course of rivers. . . ."

The pioneer's attitude toward wilderness was hostile and utilitarian. Roderick Nash writes: "In the morality play of westward expansion, wilderness was the villain, and the pioneer, as hero, relished its destruction. The transformation of wilderness into civilization was the reward for his sacrifices, the definition of his achievement and the source of his pride."

This inheritance explains in part why a resident of modern-day Alaska, even if he is a recent arrival in the city of Fairbanks, feels he can jeer at the opinions of outsiders. He *is* on the edge of wilderness;

and he participates in a mentality that drove railroads west and thought anyone who liked wolves was "too soft" to survive in the outlands.

It is easy to criticize Western man for his wholesale destruction of the wolf and to forget the milieu in which it was effected. The men I have met who killed wolves at one time or another for a living were not barbarians. Some were likable, even humble men; others were insecure, irresponsible. But the difference was this: the ones who did it for more than a few years had no illusions about the killing and some regret; the ones who tried it only briefly seemed all but possessed by the idea that they were battling something inimicable to man, doing something terribly right. In a 1955 *Field and Stream* article entitled "Strafing Arctic Killers," an aerial hunter named Jay Hammond—later governor of Alaska—wrote that if he had not been on the scene with gun and plane in the early fifties, killing three hundred wolves a month, the local Eskimos would surely have starved. No matter that Eskimo, caribou, and wolf had got on for a thousand years before the coming of the airplane and the gun. Similarly, a trapper in northern Minnesota proudly showed me the illegal snares he used to kill Eastern timber wolves and said if he didn't go on killing wolves his livestock would be wiped out. He saw himself as a man who knew more than the "overeducated" biologists, who had the courage to stand up to them when his neighbors wouldn't. He said, "A man must stand to protect his land against the wolf when the law is wrong." (The law had made it a federal crime to kill wolves.)

A lot of people admired the forthrightness and spunk of this individual, but the sort of land ownership and stockraising and the kind of wolf threat he saw were the visions of a man a hundred years old, dreaming of a frontier farm in the wilderness of Minnesota—a time in the past.

To clear wilderness. Out of this simple conviction was spawned a war against wolves that culminated in the United States in the late nineteenth century. But the story is older, the origins of the conviction more complex.

Men first took the killing of wolves seriously when they became husbandmen, but because wolves ate the human dead on battlefields and were most often seen in the eerie twilight of dawn and dusk, they were feared not just as predators of stock but as physical and metaphysical dangers. Folklore made of the wolf a creature possessed. There was a great mystery about the wolf and a fabulous theater of images developed around him. He was the Devil, red tongued, sulfur breathed, and yellow eyed; he was the werewolf, human cannibal; he was the lust, greed, and violence that men saw in themselves. And men went like Ahab after this white whale.

Let me begin with something concrete—predation on domestic stock. Animals have been variously perceived in history: as objects for man's amusement, as slaves to do his bidding, as objects of purely symbolic interest. We smile today at the thought of putting an animal on trial for murder, but the notion of trial and punishment for murders committed by animals should not be dismissed as unenlightened farce. This was serious business in the sixteenth century, and understanding why a pig was tried, convicted, and hung for murder lends understanding to why people should seek the same fate for a wolf. It stemmed from the principle of retribution.

The scholastic mind of the time went to extreme lengths to observe principle strictly, and one of the oldest principles of justice was the law of retribution, *lex talionis*, the Judaic law of an eye for an eye. This was not simple vengeance; it preserved a cosmic order. *No act of killing was to be left unexpiated.* If such a serious transgression went unpunished, the sins of the father would fall on the son. To leave murder unpunished in the community, then, was to invite God's wrath in the form of disease and famine.

Although no longer regarded as expeditious, the law of retribution was once a powerful influence on legal thinking. And though animals were regarded by men like Thomas Aquinas as the unwitting tools of the Devil, the means by which God brought pain and anguish that would test men's mettle, it made no difference; interfere with God's plan and justice must be meted out. If a horse kicked a pestering child and the child died, the horse was to be tried and hung. Taken to its extreme, such thinking had the man who committed suicide with a knife tried, his hand cut off and punished separately, and the knife banished, thrown beyond the city walls.

• • •

Even after such trials of animals ceased, the idea that *human* murder (whether committed by another human being, the family dog, or a falling tree) had to be expiated persisted. In recent times it was preserved in the English law of deodants. The wagon that struck a man down was sold and the profits went to the state which, in theory, had lost his services as a citizen. No such reasoning was really necessary to get men to go after a wolf suspected of killing a human being, but it is important to note that men felt a moral *obligation*, not simply that they had the right, to find the wolf and kill it. It made no difference whether wolves were sentient beings or the witless tools of Satan, whether they killed deliberately or accidentally or were only suspected of having killed someone. The spirit of the deceased had to be avenged by retributive action.

This retributive stance where the slaughter of livestock was concerned—nonhuman murder—came about for two reasons. First, there was an understanding of sheep and cattle as innocent creatures unable to avenge themselves and, as such, man's wards—"Kill my sheep and you kill me." Secondly, there was a belief that domestic animals were innately good and the wolf innately evil, even that the wolf was somehow cognizant of the nature of his act, a deliberate murderer. Eventually (in the late nineteenth century in America) this defensive stance to protect innocent livestock, the righteousness of it, became a central element in the rationale for setting up bounty laws and poisoning programs to wipe out the wolf, as crucial as the issue of economic loss.

Other ideas grew out of the Middle Ages and contributed to the sense that it was morally right to kill wolves. In the popular mind, a distinction was made between animals like the dog and the cow who served man, and the wolf and the weasel who caused him grief. A distinction was made between *bestes dulces*, or sweet beasts, and *bestes puantes*, or stenchy beasts. The contrast between wolf and doe and raven and dove sufficiently conveys the idea.

Another important perception was the belief that animals were put on earth to do man's bidding, that "no life can be pleasing to God which is not useful to man." Men considered that they had dominion over animals the way they had dominion over slaves, that they could do anything they wanted with them. To clear wolves out of the forest so man could raise cattle was perfectly all right. It was not only all right, it met with the approval of various religious denominations who admired such industry, and of the state, whose aim was a subdued, pastoral, and productive countryside. It was for this reason that King Edgar the Peaceful of England let men pay their taxes in the tenth century in wolf heads and their legal fines in wolves' tongues.

One more idea born in Europe bears on the propriety of wolf killing, and that is to be found in the work of René Descartes. Descartes articulated the belief that not only were animals put on earth for man's use but they were distinctly lowborn; they were without souls and therefore man incurred no moral guilt in killing them. This was a formal denial of a "pagan" idea abhorrent to the Roman Church at the time: that animals had spirits, that they should not be wantonly killed, and that they did not belong to men. The belief that man *could* kill without moral restraint, without responsibility, because the wolf was only an animal, would take on terrifying proportions during the strychnine campaigns in nineteenth-century America. The European wolf hunter of 1650 might kill twenty to thirty wolves in his lifetime; a single American wolfer of the late 1800s could kill four or five thousand in ten years.

Additional support for wolf killing was born in America, as ideas regarding private property and the need to defend one's property against trespassers—claim jumpers, squatters, usurpers of water rights, purveyors of phony deeds—matured. It wasn't only because one owned the cow that one had the right to kill the wolf that attacked it; it was because one owned the land the cow was on and had *those* rights as a basis on which to open fire on a wolf. "Really," wrote one sheepman in 1892, "it is a stain, a foul stigma, on the civilization and enterprise of the people of Iowa that these wolves remain and are frequently seen crossing the best cultivated farms, and even near the best towns in our state."

A second idea that matured in America was that the wolf was a natural coward, not the respected hunter of the Indian and Eskimo imagination. And a disdain for cowards was especially ingrained in the frontier attitude of the pioneer. The belief in the wolf's cowardice must, I think, have grown out of several misconceptions. Once wolves had experienced gunfire they ran at the very sight of a gun, or, in the frontier mind, ran away like cowards. Another reason for calling the wolf a coward was that

In hearings before the Senate Committee on Agriculture and Forestry on S. 3483, a bill seeking a ten-year appropriation of not less than $10 million to control predatory animals, the following exchanges took place:

SEN. KENDRICK OF WYOMING. *Our fight on the ranges over which I had supervision and management at the time began in the fall of 1893. The campaign was introduced through the work of two men on horseback with guns, poison, and traps, and within the short period of two or three months they had a record of 150 wolves that they had destroyed. . . .*

Recently I've received quite a few letters from university people insisting, as I recall, on moderate action in connection with the extermination of predatory animals, but I am unable to conceive of anyone making that plea who had a personal acquaintance with either the terrific disaster wrought upon herds and flocks by wolves . . . or with the method employed by these animals in connection with the destruction of their prey. It is the most barbarous thing imaginable. No doubt the motives of these people are the best, but I believe they are uninformed. . . .

Bringing my brief statement to a close, all told on this one cattle ranch, covering territory of probably 30 or 35 miles square, we had a record when I left the ranch, and lost track of it, of about 500 gray wolves that we had killed. And the coyotes we threw in for good measure: they numbered hundreds but we had no disposition to either count them or keep track of them. . . .

SEN. THOMAS OF IDAHO. *You may proceed with your statement, Mr. Wing.*

MR. WING. *Now, gentlemen of the committee, we look at this measure, a 10-year program of predatory animal control, as meaning a saving of $10 for every dollar spent in the way of benefits to chicken raisers, to hog raisers, to turkey raisers, to cattlemen and to wool growers.*

We appreciate the difficulty that confronts this committee . . . in the matter of meeting the various necessary expenditures, but we look on this particular measure as an economy measure. If we spend this increased amount of money now, and during the next ten years, thereafter the matter of control will be a relatively simple one, and we can

he killed "defenseless" prey like deer. Man saw himself as God's agent correcting what was imperfect in nature; as he became more abstracted from his natural environment, he came to regard himself as the protector of the weak animals in nature against the designs of bullies like the wolf.

It was against a backdrop of these broad strokes—taming wilderness, the law of vengeance, protection of property, an inalienable right to decide the fate of all animals without incurring moral responsibility, and the strongly American conception of man as the protector of defenseless creatures—that the wolf became the enemy.

greatly reduce expenditures and still take care of the work without very much danger.

SEN. KENDRICK. *May I ask you a question right there?*

MR. WING. *Certainly.*

SEN. KENDRICK. *Reference has been made to those people who, with all good intentions, are protesting against the extermination of these animals. Is it not your opinion, Mr. Wing, that even with the most complete and efficient plan of extermination that may be employed by the Federal Government, the States, and the individuals interested, there will still be plenty of these animals left to breed?*

MR. WING. *There will always be.*

SEN. KENDRICK. *Now the question [of killing wolf pups in their dens] is one that might very well excite . . . the sympathy of anybody . . . who would not enjoy the punishment that the wolf undergoes in a trap. On the other hand, if anyone ever observed the way these wolves destroyed their game they would be inclined to look on it as one form of retribution. . . . The question is whether we would rather have the country overrun with these predatory animals, or*

whether we shall employ the country for higher purposes in the matter of producing meat-food animals. If you consider the question of whether we shall temporize with [wolves], you are again in deep water because the more you do that the more it will cost eventually to exterminate them.

SEN. WALCOTT. *Might I inject this one thought into your talk, Sen. Kendrick, because I know you have been a consistent conservationist in all things affecting wild life—*

SEN. KENDRICK (continuing). *And I want to say in this connection, so that there may be no mistake about it at all: My record in the State of Wyoming along the line of conserving the wild game of that State is one that at least entitles me to consideration in passing on this question.*

SEN. WALCOTT. *There is no question at all about that.*

—U.S. Senate, 71st Congress, 2nd & 3rd sessions on S. 3483, May 8, 1930, and January 28–29, 1931. Bill signed into law by President Hoover March 31, 1931.

These themes will be picked up in the next chapter.

Wolves of course were killed directly and indirectly for a diversity of reasons. Great *battues,* or drives, were organized against wolves in Europe whenever anyone suspected someone had been bitten by a wolf. Hundreds of wolves were often killed in these drives, like the one in which the beasts of Gévaudan were hunted down. Another famous outlaw wolf, a bobtailed animal named Courtaud, appeared outside the walled city of Paris in the summer of 1447. Courtaud and a pack of ten or twelve other wolves attacked small flocks of domestic animals being driven to market through the bramble woods where they lived. They chased horses, upsetting carts and frightening children. In February 1450, they supposedly entered Paris through a breach in the walls and killed forty people. As the hard winter bore on and attempts to kill the wolves in their lairs failed, they were lured into the city proper with a bloody trail of butchered livestock. Trapped in the square in front of Notre Dame, they were stoned and lanced to death.

Some wolves who killed human beings were thought to be more than mere wolves. In 1685 a wolf preying on domestic stock and supposed to have killed women and children near Ansbach, Germany, was identified as the reincarnation of a local, hated burgomaster. Hunted down and killed, the wolf was dressed up in a suit of flesh-colored cloth and fitted with a chestnut brown wig and white beard. The wolf's muzzle was cut off and a mask fashioned after the burgomaster's face was strapped on. The animal was then hung in the town square.

A generally accepted practice in Europe was an almost ritualized purging of wolves from the countryside after wars. Preying on thousands of dead bodies on the battlefields and left unmolested by a population at war, the wolf population increased and took advantage of untended flocks. Members of a victorious army, returning home elated, immediately set about killing the wolves and regarded the activity simply as a continuation of the war. Similarly, American soldiers returning after World War II to the upper Midwest began to refer to all wolves as Nazis and to hunt them down with great intensity.

Wolves were also killed as the result of being blamed for the deaths of stock and wildlife when feral dogs were at fault. In Minnesota recently, more than 100 deer were killed in separate incidents in two state parks and left uneaten. Wolves were blamed and bitter reprisals threatened by antiwolf forces until the real culprits, two dogs in each case, were found and killed.

In antiwolf campaigns in North America, wolves were killed and thrown on the steps of the state legislature well into the 1970s to garner headlines and pressure lawmakers into instituting bounties. Other angry citizens, seduced by the inflammatory language of antiwolf pamphlets, set up their own poisoned meat stations to kill wolves.

In recent years wolves have increasingly been the victims of "recreational killings," run down by snowmobiles, surprised on snowbound roads, and chased in pickup trucks, or just shot on impulse by the one in a thousand deer hunters who chanced to see one during hunting season. (In 1975 a three-year-old wolf was found during deer season at a northern Minnesota dump. He had died of internal hemorrhaging, the result of having been shot in the back with a .22. I dug old fragments of a .30-caliber bullet of undetermined age out of the same animal's skull.)

Others responsible for the death of wolves are less visible. Tourists in the Yukon demanding a wolf pelt for a den wall and willing to pay $450 or more for one are directly responsible for the deaths of hundreds of animals. In 1973 well-meaning people in New York and Los Angeles urged that the Eastern timber wolf should be classified an endangered species. The law was passed and the same people scoffed when Min-

Washington Park Zoo, Portland, Oregon.

nesota complained that it had too many Eastern timber wolves. Afforded full federal protection, the Minnesota wolf population grew larger and larger and without simultaneous control on the number of human deer hunters, the wolf's primary food source declined and many wolves died of starvation.

Wolves kept in zoos die every year as a result of poor cage design, faulty capture systems, and harassment. The failure of research institutions to isolate sexually mature animals at the correct times produces litters that have to be killed every year. Wolf pups given away to people are often put to sleep because they're more trouble to raise and keep than dogs. Lois Crisler, who wrote about her life with wolves in Alaska in a book called *Arctic Wild*, killed the wolves she raised from pups because she couldn't stand what captivity had done to them. And her.

That has been the shape of history for the wolf. Even today, in spite of a generally widespread sympathy for animals that have been persecuted through the ages, no more substantive reasons are needed to kill a wolf than the fact that someone feels like doing it. On a Saturday afternoon in Texas a few years ago, three men on horseback rode down a female red wolf and threw a lasso over her neck. When she gripped the rope with her teeth to keep the noose from closing, they dragged her around the prairie until they'd broken her teeth out. Then while two of them stretched the animal between their horses with ropes, the third man beat her to death with a pair of fence pliers. The wolf was taken around to a few bars in a pickup and finally thrown in a roadside ditch.

It is relatively easy to produce reasons why such depravity exists— because people are bored, because some men feel powerless in modern society. But this incident is, in fact, a staggering act of self-indulgence. That it is condoned by silence and goes unpunished reveals a terrible meanness in the human spirit.

Eight

WOLFING FOR SPORT

MAN has always sought to legitimize his hunting of wolves, even
when it was at the ragged edges of decency. One of the defenses he
offered was that it was simply "good sport" to hunt wolves—the wolf
was taken for the admired enemy. Even though many of these men bore
the wolf no overt hatred, their methods could not always be called sporting, however.

Theodore Roosevelt hunted wolves in Russia and North America with
dogs, sometimes on a grand scale, and he made no apology for it. (He
once set off with seventy fox hounds, sixty-seven greyhounds, sixty saddle and packhorses, and forty-four hunters, beaters, wranglers, and
journalists, all in a private train of twenty-two cars.) In Russia there was a
veneer of upper-class respectability to such hunts; in America there was

rarely legitimate claim to sport in coursing, though that was often its guise. Roosevelt was quite clear on this point. Writing of an acquaintance who hunted wolves with dogs in North Dakota, he said: "The only two requisites were that the dogs be fast and fight gamely; and in consequence they formed as wicked a hard-biting crew as ever throttled a wolf. They were usually taken out ten at a time, and by their aid Massinggale killed over two hundred wolves, including pups. Of course there was no pretense of giving them fair play. The wolves were killed for vermin, not sport. . . ."

Wolf hunting in Europe and Russia with hounds was an aristocratic amusement, popular around the turn of the century. While nobility and its guests dined and relaxed in the hunting lodge, the head huntsman and his helpers scoured the countryside for wolf sign or learned from local peasants where the wolves were. On the day of the hunt the gentlemen arrayed themselves in a line at the edge of a promising wood and the head huntsman tried to howl up a wolf. If an answering howl was heard—"commingling the lament of a dying dog with the wailing of an Irish Banshee"—the dogs began driving the woods from the far side. A beater might have as many as six dogs on leashes as he moved through the woods. Deerhounds, staghounds, and Siberian wolfhounds, the slender white borzoi, as well as smaller greyhounds and foxhounds. When he saw a wolf, he would shout: "Loup! Loup! Loup!" and slip the dogs. The idea was to trap the wolf between pursuing dogs and the hunters sitting astride their horses at the edge of the wood. Bursting from cover, the wolf would either be shot or pinned by the dogs and then speared or clubbed. Sometimes the dogs, especially the larger mastiff crossbreeds and hounds, would kill the wolf.

Wolves were also coursed, or chased, by dogs and horsemen through open prairie country where they were worried by the hounds until lassoed or shot. George Armstrong Custer was a devotee of coursing and usually traveled with a retinue of dogs. He was partial to larger greyhounds and staghounds and took two of the latter, large, white, shaggy dogs, with him into the Sioux's sacred Black Hills where he turned them loose on deer and wolves. The southern Cheyenne, who hated Custer, killed one of his favorite staghounds, Blucher, at the Battle of the Washita in Oklahoma in 1868.

A wolfer with his hounds, near Amedon, North Dakota, 1904.

A popular kind of wolf hunting in the winter in Russia was done from a flat sled drawn by horses. A butchered calf or pig or a bale of bloody straw was trailed behind, or a live pig's leg was twisted to make it squeal, until wolves fell in behind the sled. The wolves were then shot. Stories of sled hunting abound in Russia and the failure of this scheme—the horses tire or there are too many wolves or the wolves are too fast or the sled flips over in an icy turn—is a staple incident in Russian fiction. Commonly the hunters lose their driver and horses to the wolves and spend a harrowing night under the upturned sled, holding the wolves off in the manner of a wagon train surrounded by Indians until morning. The wolves drift off at first light, having killed their own wounded and eaten their own dead, and human help usually arrives in the person of distraught friends who feared the worst when the adventurers didn't return.

The most exotic sort of wolf hunting involves the use of eagles. It has been seen only occasionally in Europe; its real home is Kirgizia, in south-central Russia. The specially bred birds—a subspecies of golden eagle called a berkut—are flown by nomadic tribesmen. The birds weigh only ten or twelve pounds but can slam into a wolf's back and bind its spine with such force that the wolf is almost paralyzed. Often the bird binds the spine with one foot and, as the wolf turns its head to bite, binds its nose with the other foot, suffocating the animal or holding it down until the hunter kills it. The birds are deceptively strong; there is almost a ton of binding force in each foot and the blow of a thirty-six-inch wing can break a man's arm.

Eagles probably never attack adult wolves in the wild; wolf hunting is something they have to be trained to. A former German military officer, F. W. Remmler, hunted wolves with eagles in Finland in the 1930s and later in Europe before moving to Canada. He trained his birds by first turning them loose on children. The children were dressed in leather armor and covered with a wolf skin, and raw meat was strapped to their backs. When the eagles were used to knocking the children down for the meat, Remmler put them in an enclosure into which he loosed wolves purchased from European zoos. It might take days for the birds to learn how to kill the wolves. (Remmler doesn't say, but they were presumably muzzled.) The final step was to hunt wolves that had been turned loose on an island. Remmler and his friends would put themselves in position and the wolves would be driven toward them by dogs. When the wolves came in sight, the birds were cast off.

Writing thirty years later about one such hunt, Remmler recalled an afternoon when one of his eagles, Louhi, had killed two wolves in ten minutes. That night as Remmler and his friends sipped cognac around the fire they heard the howling of the other five wolves on the island. "First the female and then the pack stretched their noses toward the star-lit heavens," he wrote, "and both gave a howl so dreadful that my blood almost hardened in my veins. It may be that I had drunk too much that night, but the horror that filled me was very real. If I could have given the two dead wolves their lives back I would have done it immediately."

Kirgizian tribesmen still hunt wolves in Russia with eagles, on horse-back, with the aid of dogs.

Because he roamed so widely and more often than not avoided man, the wolf had to be routed out with dogs or eagles or drawn to a bait. Still hunting, where a sheep or goat was staked out, was never very success-ful, though a horse or cow might be slaughtered and its carcass dragged through the woods to leave a trail ending at a spot where the meat was hung in a tree and the hunter concealed himself. (Residents of rural northern Minnesota laughed up their sleeves when hunters from urban

Minneapolis, threatening to wipe out wolves preying on deer herds in the early 1970s, bought steaks and lunch meat at local supermarkets, set it out on frozen lakes, and waited in blinds for the wolves to show up.)

The reasoning behind hunting wolves for sport as opposed to hunting them because they were hated or considered a menace to livestock was often confused. Consider the following hunt that took place near Tamworth, New Hampshire, in 1830, described by Charles Beals in *Passaconaway in the White Mountains.*

"On the evening of Nov. 14 couriers rode furiously through Tamworth and the surrounding towns, proclaiming that 'countless numbers' of wolves had come down from the Sandwich Range mountains and had established themselves in the woods on Marston Hill. All able-bodied males, from ten years old to eighty, were therefore summoned to report at Marston Hill by daylight on the following morning.

"Marston Hill was crowned by about twenty acres of woods, entirely surrounded by cleared land. Sentinels were posted around the hill and numerous fires were lighted to prevent the wolves from effecting a return to the mountains. All through the night a continuous and hideous howling was kept up by the besieged wolves and answering howls came from the slopes of the great mountains. The shivering besiegers were regaled with food and hot coffee furnished by the women of the country-side throughout their long lonely watch.

"All night long reinforcements kept arriving. By daylight there were six hundred men and boys on the scene, armed with rifles, shotguns, pitchforks and clubs. A council of war was held and a plan of campaign agreed upon. General Quimby, of Sandwich, a war-seasoned veteran, was made commander-in-chief. The general immediately detailed a thin line of sharpshooters to surround the hill, while the main body formed a strong line ten paces in the rear of the skirmishers. The sharpshooters then were commanded to advance towards the center, that is, towards the top of the hill. The firing began. The reports of the rifles and the unearthly howling of wolves made the welkin ring. The beleaguered animals, frenzied by the ring of flame and noise, and perhaps by wounds, made repeated attempts to break through 'the thin red line,' but all in vain. They were driven back into the woods, where they unceasingly continued running, making it difficult for the marksmen to hit them. In about an hour the order was given for the main line to advance, which was done.

"Closing in on the center, the circular battle-line at last massed itself in a solid body on the hilltop, where, for the first time in sixteen hours, the troops raised their voices above a whisper, bursting out into wild hurrahs of victory. Joseph Gilman records that few of the besieged wolves escaped. But the historian of Carroll County maintains that the greater part of the frantic animals broke through the line of battle and escaped to the mountains whence they had come. Returning to the great rock on which the commander-in-chief had established headquarters, the victorious warriors laid their trophies at the feet of their leader—four immense wolves—and once more gave thrice three thundering cheers.

"The little army then formed column, with the general, in a barouche, at its head. In the barouche also reposed the bodies of the slain wolves. After a rapid march of thirty-five minutes, the triumphant volunteers entered the village and formed a hollow square in front of the hotel, the general, mounted on the top of his barouche, being in the center of the square. What a cheering and waving of handkerchiefs by the ladies, in windows and on balconies, there was! General Quimby then made a speech befitting the occasion, after which the thirsty soldiers stampeded to the bar to assuage the awful thirst engendered by twenty mortal hours of abstinence and warfare."

The paramilitary aspect, the mock nobility, and the odd air of gaiety were frequently the major themes of such hunts.

Saturday afternoon wolf killings were a popular social pastime in the Midwest at the turn of the century. Bounties collected on the dead wolves were pooled to pay for end-of-the-season parties. "In three ways," wrote one participant, "does the most popular spring enjoyment of the prairie states—the wolf hunt—originate. The farmers may desire earnestly to rid the township of 'varmints'; the men of the community may want a day of entertainment; an enterprising hardware dealer may wish to enliven the market for gunpowder and shotguns. With them all wolf hunts become increasingly numerous, not because wolves are more common, but because it is an occasion of healthful outdoor exercise and fun." These farmers more often killed a coyote than a wolf during these outings. Their casual attitude toward the hundreds of rabbits, prairie dogs, burrowing owls, gophers, and other small game killed in the process, and their habit of hanging the wolf's carcass from a pole and parading it through the streets on a Saturday night, was part of the barbarism of the times. There were few, if any, misgivings. A contemporary writer, O. W. Williams, comments: "If the lobo has any useful qualities or habits I have not yet learned of them. If it destroys any noxious animal, reptile or insect in appreciative quantity, I have no account of it. It seems to be a specialist in carnage and to have brought professional skill to the slaughter of cattle. Possibly it has its uses—but it will require a skillful man with a very high powered magnifying glass to ascertain them."

Aerial hunting for wolves in the modern age is a difficult practice to understand. It seems unfair and cruel. Wolves caught out in the open on the arctic tundra or on a frozen lake are approached with highly maneuverable aircraft and blasted with automatic shotguns. The plane lands and the trophy hunter picks up his prize. In Alaska, where the practice was widespread before it was outlawed in 1972, it was not uncommon for two men in a plane to catch ten or fifteen animals—the whole pack—in the open with no cover and methodically kill every one of them. In their defense pilots claim it was difficult to shoot a moving target from a moving plane, that in such low-level, low-speed flying it is easy to stall the aircraft, that a bad shot could blow away a wing strut, and that winter flying—in intense cold with a possibility of whiteouts and crashing in unpopulated regions—was dangerous.

The pilots were right. Planes were shot up, apparently chances to kill were missed, and people were killed when wolves turned to snap at the plane's skis and caused it to crash. But, overwhelmingly, it was a case of dead wolves, healthy hunters, and pilots exaggerating the dangers to lure still more clients—and coming to believe their own exaggerations when an outraged public tried to stop the practice. Adding to the shabbiness of the episode was the fact that the hunter-clients were usually rich, urban men who knew nothing about wolves and nothing about the Arctic. They commonly believed all wolves weighed two hundred pounds and that any movement a wounded wolf might make once they were on the ground was an attempt to attack them. The illusions were encouraged by the pilots, who took the pelt and left the carcass behind on the snow. Back in Kotzebue or Bettles or Fairbanks the story was embellished and hunter and pilot congratulated for their bravery and daring. It is both ludicrous and tragic that the death of a wolf so cheaply killed confers such enormous prestige.

There is something deep-seated in men that makes them want to "take on" the outdoors, as though it were something to be whipped, and to kill wolves because killing a wolf stands for real triumph. In view of the way most wolves are killed it is hard to see how the image is sustained, but it is. Hunting is an ingrained male activity, especially in rural America, where few male children grow up not wanting to hunt. I hunted as a boy and I remember very clearly the first time I thought there was something wrong with the men I admired, something fundamentally backward about the kind of hunting that was held out to me as what men were supposed to do in the course of things. I was reading a book about big game animals in which Jack O'Connor, then the gun editor of *Outdoor Life*, described suddenly coming on seven wolves on a river bar in the Yukon. O'Connor dismounted and opened fire. "With considerable expenditure of ammunition," he wrote, he killed four of them, and then said he was sorry he'd done it for two reasons. "For one it was August and the hides were worthless. For another, my shooting spooked an enormous grizzly bear."

I couldn't get over that.

O'Connor writes elsewhere that the greatest satisfaction he had in killing a wolf came in British Columbia while he was sheep hunting. A wolf was doggedly pursuing a sheep up a steep slope. When the wolf stopped for a breath, O'Connor leveled his gun. "It was a lovely sight to see the crosshairs in the 4x settle right behind the wolf's shoulder. Neither ram nor wolf had seen me. The wolf's mouth was open, his tongue was hanging out, and he was panting heavily. The ram, on the other hand, seemed hardly bothered by the run. When my rifle went off, the 130 grain .270 bullet cracked that wolf right through the ribs and the animal was flattened as if by a giant hammer."

O'Connor spoke for a generation of men who matured in the twenties,

Magazine illustration, 1964.

thirties, and forties in America. He shot at every wolf he ever saw, including the only one he ever saw in the lower forty-eight states. For all
he knew about guns and camping he seemed to know next to nothing
about wolves, which was also typical of his generation of hunters. He
never questioned his own role as a predator, nor his right to kill another
predator, like the wolf, in pursuit of its game. It was largely these sorts
of hunters, smug and ignorant, weaned on stories of vicious wolves, innocent deer, and poor, starving Eskimos, who became the most righteously vocal defenders of aerial hunting. As a result, at the height of the
craze its appeal was to a sense of duty (protect the defenseless herds and
help the starving Eskimo), to violence (permissible in defense of the de-

fenseless), and to a distorted sense of manhood. Argument over whether it was a sport disappeared. One hunter, promoting the activity to a sympathetic audience, wrote ecstatically of "not being more than thirty feet above the animals, so close I saw the hair fly from one of the black wolves as the hail of buckshot hit it. The wolf went down, rolling and kicking, biting at its side. Confused, the other wolves crouched, looking up at us. Tom, an enthusiastic wolf-hunter, who had once shot a cylinder off his plane trying to kill a wolf from the air, pulled the plane up into a jubilant chandelle, then let it drop off in a screaming, side-slipping dive that brought us in behind the wolves again."

This anecdote ends with embarrassing self-parody. " 'If I could afford it,' said Tex with satisfaction as we landed to pick up the pelts, 'I wouldn't do nothin' but fly around an' hunt them varmints. Every time I kill one it makes me feel good.' "

When such "hunters" stood before national television cameras in sunglasses and flightsuits and pretended to eat raw the flesh of wolves they'd just killed, they only exposed their own foolishness and the mockery they had made of traditional hunting ethics.

The sport hunter and the roustabout do-gooder came together in an interesting character in Alaska in the 1930s. During the Depression, a number of men drifted north in hopes of making a living as trappers. Most didn't. Some who did wrote about their experiences with wolves in magazines like *The Alaska Sportsman*. These men were mostly ignorant of the woods when they arrived; their stories are full of errors and cruelty to wolves and are punctuated by a righteous hatred for the animal. They believed wolves attacked and killed men in the north country, and they seemed barely able to control themselves when they told you what the wolves did to deer. "I knew what I'd find," wrote one, "deer hair and crushed bones, rent tissues and blood," as though wolves might have left something else. Stories with titles like "Wolves Killed Crist Colby," "I Match Wits with Wolves," and "I'll Get Old Club Foot Yet!" were unconscious parodies of frontier yarns in which the trappers played the role of the sheriff going for his six-shooter or shootin' iron whenever he saw a wolf.

The men who wrote these stories passionately believed they were serving humanity in the lower forty-eight states from this distant outpost. One of them, as if writing home to his family, said, "While I do my best to destroy all the wolves in the Ward Cove Game Refuge, the other animals go unmolested. On the roof of my cabin at Third Lake, the martin jump at night and the deer, unmolested, have become very tame, seeming to sense that there are few wolves and that man bears no ill will."

An Alaskan trapper named Lawrence Carson tracked a wolf that had dragged one of his traps more than twenty miles and found him hung upside down by the dragline on a steep hillside. He disentangled the wolf for the purpose of taking pictures, then shot him in the head. "Lobo died as he had lived, in defiance of all things that would dare to conquer him. His bloody career was ended, but even in death his fiery eyes and truculent jaws opened in a look of unremitting hate. Lobo, king of his domain—and rightly a king he was called—was dead."

But Carson's thoughts reveal the ambivalence in some of these men, for he continues:

"As I looked at his lifeless form, a feeling of condonation came over me. Even though he had been a wanton destroyer of wild life and ill-deserving of mercy, somehow I felt sorry that he was gone. I wondered if the great mountains and deep silent valleys that had been his range would miss him. I wondered if at night, when the moon hung low like a great ball of fire, the dark shaggy spruce trees would miss his wild, deep-throated call. Something has been taken away that would never be put back in the scheme of things. Somehow I felt as if there was an irreparable loss. The well-known axiom had again asserted itself; the sport and fun were not in the kill, but in the chase."

Those who stayed on in Alaska eventually wrote for the very same audiences of their fondness for the wolf, debunking the old stories of wolves killing people, and saying not much at all about how cute the deer were. One ended his story by saying he would like to spend his last years with wolves. He wrote, "I think I could enjoy the companionship of that magnificent creature more fully than any other creature on earth."

The O'Connor-type hunters whose hatred of wolves was gospel gave way in the 1960s to a more "enlightened" hunter, who spoke of the beneficial value of the wolf in balancing wild ecosystems, but who still wanted to kill him. The president of the Boone and Crockett Club, a national hunters' organization, said: "If more factual information can be widely disseminated to the general public as well as to sportsmen and conservationists perhaps this magnificent animal can yet attain his well-deserved status as a useful and highly important big game trophy animal." He was no longer a varmint; he was big game. The justifications are endless.

Without airplanes no one deliberately hunts wolves anymore—they are too hard to find from the ground. (Whatever sport there may be in wolf hunting, in the sense of earning a right to kill, is probably down there on the ground with the trapper who does it for a living. He works alone over long distances during a harsh season. He has to know something about wolf habits and a lot about the territory.) The wolf becomes a big game trophy animal today only when someone is lucky enough to see one while he is hunting something else. This kind of wolf hunting brings us to the present day.

Big game hunting in North America became popular after World War II. Books and articles about the romance of the sport in Alaska and Canada were suddenly everywhere. The formula for these stories was always the same: the author flew to the north country, explored widely with a guide, shot record numbers of animals, and sat around a campfire lamenting the loss of North America's best trophy animals to wolves, Indians, and Eskimos. It was agreed that if something wasn't done to thin the wolf population the herds would soon be gone.

One such book, *From Out of the Yukon* by James Bond, contains the requisite scenes and sentiments. It is worth reviewing not so much for its appeal to armchair adventurers as for the portrait it paints of the wolf and the hunting philosophy it endorses.

Around the campfire one evening Mr. Bond suggests it's not the wolves but excessive human hunting that is to blame for the depletion of the game herds. Everyone agrees. The solution they arrive at is twofold: first, increase the wolf bounty and get furriers to raise the price of wolf pelts to encourage more wolf trapping; second, "encourage all hunters to be good sportsmen and not shoot more than they need."

In his north country adventures Mr. Bond encounters wolves twice. The first time he can't get a clear shot but the guide does. "Well, I do not have to tell you," he writes, "that I badly wanted that big black devil for my trophy room, but I am glad Norman killed it, for it means one less wolf in the country."

The second wolf he meets, one howled up by the guide, he cripples and as he approaches, he thinks: "What excitement! These wolves had no conception of man." After he has killed the wolf, Mr. Bond inspects the head. "I was really amazed to find the numerous and tremendous muscles in the head and neck of this great wolf. They could only have developed through usage—ripping and tearing at our game animals. . . . It pleased me greatly to see this leader of destruction lying dead on the ground before me." The dimensions Mr. Bond reports for the wolf, typically, exceed those of any wolf on record.

I do not think men thoughtlessly kill wolves; they have reasons for doing so. Prime among them is the belief that they are doing something deeply and profoundly right. Whatever arguments are put forth—predation on big game, wolves are cowards and deserve to die—all seem rooted in the belief that the wolf is "wrong" in the scheme of things, like cancer, and has to be rooted out.

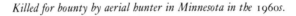

Killed for bounty by aerial hunter in Minnesota in the 1960s.

It is a convention of popular sociology that modern man leads a frustratingly inadequate life in which hunting becomes both overcompensation for a sense of impotence and an attempt to reroot oneself in the natural world. As man has matured, the traditional reason for hunting—to obtain food—has disappeared, along with the sacred relationship with the hunted. The modern hunter pays lip service to the ethics of the warrior hunter—respect for the animal, a taboo against waste, pride taken in highly developed skills like tracking—but his actions betray him. What has most emphatically not disappeared, oddly, is the almost spiritual sense of identification that comes over the hunter in the presence of a wolf.

Here is an animal capable of killing a man, an animal of legendary endurance and spirit, an animal that embodies marvelous integration with its environment. This is exactly what the frustrated modern hunter would like: the noble qualities imagined; a sense of fitting into the world. The hunter wants to be the wolf.

The first time I understood this I was talking with a man who had killed some thirty-odd wolves himself from a plane, alone, and flown hunters who had killed almost four hundred more. As he described with his hands the movement of the plane, the tack of its approach, his body began to lean into the movement and he shook his head as if to say no words could tell it. For him the thing was not the killing; it was that moment when the blast of the shotgun hit the wolf and flattened him—because the wolf's legs never stopped driving. In that same instant the animal was fighting to go on, to stay on its feet, to shake off the impact of the buckshot. The man spoke with awed respect of the animal's will to live, its bone and muscle shattered, blood streaking the snow, but refusing to fall. "When the legs stop, you know he's dead. He doesn't quit until there's nothing left." He spoke as though he himself would never be a quitter in life because he had seen this thing. Four hundred times.

It does not demean men to want to be what they imagine the wolf to be, but it demeans them to kill the animal for it.

Nine

AN AMERICAN POGROM

WHEN I was in college it was my habit to go down to West Virginia and stay with a man who, among other things, ran sheep to make ends meet. He and his wife were both in their eighties, living on an income of about twenty-five hundred dollars a year, almost all of that from the sale of mutton and wool. One winter night—I was sleeping on the second floor—I was suddenly awakened by shouts from the sheep pen. I sprang from under the down covers and ran across the bare, freezing floor to the window. The man's oldest son was out there in the snow in his underwear with a .30/30, trying to get a shot at a black bear in the sheep pens. The bear killed eleven sheep. And disappeared into the darkness. I never forgot that. The man standing there in the snow with his gun, looking at the dead sheep.

• • •

On a summer afternoon recently I sat in the shade of cottonwood trees near a trickling creek on the edge of a playa desert in southeastern Oregon, talking with an old man who had hunted wolves when he was young. He was working a cinnabar claim here now, for mercury. His nearest neighbors were a few miles away. He had no electricity in his one-room shack, no phone, no running water. But he got on from one year to the next. He was a frontier jack-of-all-trades, who'd herded cattle, been a commercial fisherman in Alaska, trapped in the Coast Range, and worked Montana oilfields. When he was nineteen he hunted wolves with a pack of dogs in the Dakotas and eastern Montana. As he spoke, he explained how he controlled the half-wild dogs and what happened when they met a wolf and how the wolves were finally killed out of that country by the late twenties.

He would turn the wolves in for an eight-dollar bounty. If the pelt was good and it was a good year, he got another fifteen or twenty dollars in trade.

"God, that was terrible big money," Dave Wallace said that afternoon. Without the ranchers' help, he told me, without meals and grain feed for his horses, he never would have made it. "It was awful work. God, the dogs, you didn't want to turn your back on them. They'd try to kill you."

When the dogs jumped a wolf, he would worry about how many dogs he was going to lose. "A wolf can't run as fast as a coyote, so he'd get in a low place like a coulee and wait for the dogs chasing him to come over the top. The first time I saw it, the wolf grabbed the first dog behind the shoulder and tore out a rib and the second one he got back of the head and crushed it. Just crushed it. Then the rest of them came in on him and I ran over the top of all of them on the horse and clubbed the wolf to death."

Wallace left Montana when he still was nineteen. He told me he never liked dogs much after that. But he did. As is the way, oddly, with such men, he was quite fond of animals, and he imagined himself, in his later years, something like them. Lonely. Looked down on.

Dave Wallace died a few months after I spoke with him. One afternoon in the spring he had a heart attack while he was driving his pickup down the road. It drifted off into the sagebrush and coasted to a stop in some cheat grass. From where the truck came to rest, out the windshield, you could see most of a thirty-thousand-acre cattle ranch. It was in the interest of that industry, ironically, that Wallace had killed fifty-nine wolves for bounty.

One evening before he died, Wallace told me how cold it would get in the Dakotas in the winter, and that he would bundle himself up in wolf furs to keep warm at forty and fifty below. "A wolf will live through that kind of cold, walk around in it. Jesus they're a tough animal." We talked about dying and I told him that as part of an Aztec ritual of last rites a man's breast was pricked with the sharpened bone of a wolf. Wallace looked across the room at me and said nothing. It was as though he understood exactly the kind of meaning this had, the sort of encouragement it was to a dying man. Uneducated, alone in a shack in the desert, dying of old age, Wallace smiled for a moment, as serene in his comprehension of the mystery of life as Buddha.

No other wolf killing ever achieved either in geographic scope or economic or emotional scale the predator-control war waged against wolves in the nineteenth and early twentieth centuries in the United States and Canada, on the tail end of which Dave Wallace found himself. Eric Zimen, a German wolf biologist, once remarked that he was utterly unable to fathom the relentless carnage. "We killed the wolf in Europe," he said, "and we hated the wolf, but it was not anything like what you have done in America." Even speaking as a prejudiced European he was correct.

The immigrant newly arrived in North America in the seventeenth century faced certain hardship. Starting almost literally from scratch he had to clear timber, build a home, secure food, and deal with a host of adverse conditions, many of which were dangerous and some of which he had never heard of, like poison ivy and rattlesnakes. In addition he had to effect some sort of understanding with native Americans, a people whose language he did not speak, whose customs he did not understand, and whose power was mysterious. The Indians came and went like fog; they survived well in an environment that seemed to him intractable.

They were like the wolves who came at night and snatched a pig, a small enough thing in itself but not to a man who had brought the pig thousands of miles to a place where there were no domestic pigs. The Indian came in the middle of the night and took an ax and disappeared. Wolves and Indians stared at him from the edge of his fields for hours and made him uneasy; he wrote that the wolves were not as ferocious as European wolves but were more numerous. In the colonist's mind Indian and wolf often fused into a symbol of the land's hostility, of the dangers that lay ahead. In more sober moments he recognized that both Indian and wolf were simply curious; but he did not deal well at all with curiosity. He built walls around his villages to keep wolves and Indians out. He began to shoot wolves and Indians. He wrote in his bounty ordinances of "wolf scalps," and said of Indians that they attacked his villages "like a pack of wolves." A Massachusetts law of 1638 stated, "Whoever shall [within the town] shoot off a gun on any unnecessary occasion, or at any game except an Indian or a wolf, shall forfeit 5 shillings for every shot."

Newly arrived Protestant ministers drew parallels between the savage paganism of the Indian and the wolf. Both, they preached, tried the souls of men with their depredations, and the ministers urged colonists to give in to neither. They didn't. By the end of the nineteenth century the primary food resources of Indian and wolf were gone—both had been deliberately poisoned—and both had been reduced to living on reservations. Insofar as the Indian became a Christian and lived like a white man he was accepted; insofar as the wolf became a dog, a pet, or a draft animal in someone's sledge harness he, too, was accepted. But by 1900 there wasn't much point in being either a wolf or an Indian in the United States.

The colonist had no experience in dealing with Indians and knew little more about killing wolves. But since the two seemed so alike, he fell to dealing with them in similar ways. He set out poisoned meat for the wolf and gave the Indian blankets infected with smallpox. He raided the wolf's den to dig out and destroy the pups, and stole the Indian's children and sent them to missionary schools to be rehabilitated. When he was accused of butchery for killing wolves and Indians, he spun tales of Mohawk cruelty and of wolves who ate fawns while they were still alive, invoking the ancient law of literal equivalents. By the late nineteenth century the argot of the Indian wars was the argot of the wolf wars. General Sheridan said: "The only good Indians I ever saw were dead," and the wolfer said, "The only good wolf is a dead one." Indians and wolves who later came into areas where there were no more of either were called renegades. Wolves that lay around among the buffalo herds were called loafer wolves and Indians that hung around the forts were called loafer Indians.

In the aftermath of this persecution, America came to beat its breast over the murder of Indians. But most people never knew, and few cared, what had happened to wolves. Insofar as both were exterminated for similar reasons, that is interesting. Insofar as the wolf, unlike the whooping crane and the buffalo we almost killed out, led a life similar to our own, it is odd that no one ever asked why.

The European colonist was not much troubled by wolves until he began raising stock. The first livestock came to Jamestown, Virginia, in 1609—swine, cattle, and horses. By 1625 these animals were common in colonial settlements and how to stop the wolves who preyed on these beasts was a topic to galvanize community discussion. While the European farmer might have dealt with predation by himself, in America, where people were forced to band together for a variety of reasons, wolf control was a community problem. Together with his neighbors a man dug wolf pits and erected palisades. He conducted *battues* and paid salaries of professional wolf hunters, as he had done in Europe. And he passed bounty laws. Wolf bounties had been a means of effecting wolf control for thousands of years and were current in Europe and the British Isles at the time of immigration. A system both biologically ineffective and wide open to fraud, it was nevertheless popular because raising the bounty payment and exchanging it for a dead wolf was tangible, daily evidence that something was being done.

The first wolf bounty law in America was passed in Massachusetts on November 9, 1630. Further bounty laws were soon passed in Virginia at Jamestown (on September 4, 1632) and in the other colonies. Payments were made in cash, tobacco, wine, corn, and, for Indians, blankets and trinkets. A New Jersey law of 1697 states: "Whatsoever Christian shall kill and bring the head of a wolf . . . to any magistrate . . . shall be paid a bounty of twenty shillings. . . ." Only half that much was to be paid to Indians and blacks who killed wolves; it also became the custom to require Indians to produce without compensation one or two wolf pelts a year. A Virginia law passed in 1668 broke down the requirement of tribute in wolves to be paid according to the number of hunters in each tribe, asking 725 hunters to produce 145 wolves annually. (A hundred and fifty years later at Fort Union, Montana, trading companies were buying wolf pelts they didn't need in order "not to create any dissatisfaction" among the Indians.)

In 1717 residents on Cape Cod tried to build a six-foot-high, eight-mile-long fence across the peninsula between Plymouth and Barnstable counties to keep the wolves from knocking off an occasional cow, but the project proved too expensive. Someone else discovered spring-loaded tallow balls. A steel fishhook was rolled back on itself like a spring, bound with thread, and covered with tallow. The balls were scattered around a wolf kill and the wolves who ate them died of internal hemorrhaging. Iron shipments from England and the production of local bog iron resulted in a variety of traps being produced, but they were too heavy and unwieldy to be popular. Some towns bought their own wolfhounds and appointed a hound master. (The huge Irish wolfhounds, 36 inches at the shoulder and weighing 120 pounds, were hard to come by. Oliver Cromwell in 1652 had issued an order that the popular dogs were not to be exported as they were too much needed in Ireland.)

By the first part of the eighteenth century the colonies were striving for self-sufficiency and the need for a sheep industry was clear. One of those concerned with wool production was Gen. George Washington. In a series of letters he exchanged with Arthur Young, president of the Agricultural Society of Great Britain, with Thomas Jefferson, and with Richard Peters, of the Philadelphia Agricultural Society, Washington lamented the attacks of feral dogs and wolves, which "retarded the growth of the sheep industry." Young couldn't understand why, since there were wolves in Europe and sheep raising flourished there. It was one of the last times America went to England for advice.

Two points had eluded Young: first, that there were a lot more wolves and wild dogs in America; and second, that the tendency in the States was not, as it was in Europe, to subdivide more or less settled land but to expand into decidedly *unsettled* land. Under those conditions more than a couple of shepherds and a hedgerow were required to guarantee a sheep industry.

The extent of predation on sheep by feral dogs that the Washington– Young correspondence alludes to has largely been ignored by historians of the period, who were content, as were the colonists, to ascribe all canine predation to the wolf. Since the wolf, not the dog, wore the cloak of evil and few could tell the difference between their tracks, wolves were blamed for the death of any animal if a canine print was close by. If a sheep died of natural causes—and sheep diseases were another thing that worried Washington—and its carcass was scavenged by dogs, it was often reported as a wolf kill. This error was far from innocuous. Long after the wolf ceased to be important as a predator on New England livestock, he was still bountied and blamed for predation caused by feral dogs.

Compounding the issue was the indiscriminate killing of wolves when only one or two were actually doing the damage in a region where twenty or thirty lived.

Under such continued pressure and harassment, the wolf had begun to disappear in the Northeast before the end of the eighteenth century. What few wolves were left lived in remote areas and avoided men. Some may have emigrated over the Alleghenies like the Indians, ahead of westward expansion.

The New England experience with the wolf was repeated as settlers moved west through the eastern hardwood forests of Pennsylvania, Ohio, Indiana, and Kentucky. Bounties were enacted, wolf drives took place, pits were dug, poison and traps were set out. To the north in

"Moonlight, Wolf" by Frederic Remington.

Michigan and Wisconsin and to the south in Tennessee and Missouri the wolf held out longer. By the time the settlers reached the edge of the Great Plains, they could turn and see behind them a virtually wolfless track, hundreds of miles wide, that stretched all the way back to the Atlantic seaboard.

The prairie expanse of rich grasslands they now faced was a different kind of wilderness for the settlers. De Smet had called it a desert, but farmers whose fathers and grandfathers had cleared the rocky soil of New England and the pine forests of Virginia looked with disbelief at the square miles of open space, dotted here and there with oak groves, and at the richness of the black soil.

The wolf hunted the buffalo herds out here. (Meriwether Lewis had referred to him in his journal as "the shepherd of the buffalo.") The compulsive attitude of extirpation toward the wolf (but not the fear) eased for a while at the edge of the Great Plains as the pioneers emerged from the dark forests.

Canis lupus nubilus, the Great Plains wolf, was as different from the Eastern timber wolf, perhaps, as woodland Indians like the Delaware were from buffalo Indians like the Sioux, but like the Sioux, he soon came to stand for all his kind. He showed up frequently in the writings of early explorers and pioneers, in ways both good and bad. The greatest attention was paid to the wolf's howl and then to imaginings about his nature. What to us may seem visions bordering on fantasy were recorded. The German explorer Maximilian of Wied, for example, writes of great white wolves drifting over distant hills one evening with the fireball of the sun setting behind them. Maximilian was unusual in that like many foreign visitors he found the wolf's howl pleasing and he was "long amused" by the gambols of wolves on the open prairie. He wrote of wolves sitting at the edge of the firelight, "gazing at us without appearing to be at all afraid."

Out West most people were unnerved by wolves staring at them, and shot at them. A more typical description of the wolf's howl was this one by James Capen Adams, a self-styled mountaineer and grizzly bear hunter from California: "It is indeed a horrible noise, the most hateful a man alone in the wilderness at night can hear. To a person anywise low-spirited, it suggests the most awful fancies, and it is altogether doleful in the extreme . . . the lugubrious howl of a pack of wolves is more than I like; and I was glad to put the cowardly rascals to flight by sending a ball after them."

As for prairie visions of the wolf, few had Maximilian's appreciation. More common was this buffalo hunter's description of the wolves: "Each [was] the very incarnation of destruction, with his powerful jaws of shark teeth . . . and the cunning of man."

After its howl—it is arresting how often the wolf's voice is mentioned, as though it were a bell tolling, reminding the traveler of his loneliness in the new land, that he didn't fit, of Indians, that he was vulnerable—after its howl and stare, it was the wolf's cowardly nature that was most often mentioned. Wrote one traveler: "Large, gaunt, and fierce as it looks, it is one of the greatest cowards known, even when assembled in numbers, and seldom has the courage to face even a boy. . . . I have actually kicked them and pelted them with stones and dried buffalo chips, but I never knew them to display any more dangerous characteristics than to howl fearfully, or grin with pain as they trotted away."

Francis Parkman told prospective pioneers in *The Oregon Trail*, "There is not the slightest danger from them, for they are the greatest cowards of the prairie."

The wolf's having learned to be wary of the reach of guns led some people to charge that he was a coward. Others confused being shy with being timid. In view of the war to come, these words of Col. Richard Dodge's, written in 1878, are strange: "All these wolves are exceedingly cowardly, one alone not possessing courage enough even to attack a sheep. When in packs and exceedingly hungry they have been known to muster up resolution enough to attack an ox or cow if the latter be entirely alone." Ten years later cattlemen would throw such writing in the fireplace. Dodge, by the way, went on to say that the wolf "of all the carnivorous animals of equal size and strength, [is] the most harmless to beast and least dangerous to man."

Dodge, like Maximilian, was the exception. A Canadian hunter named Billings wrote in 1856 that the wolf "is a cruel, savage, cowardly animal, with such a disposition that he will kill a whole flock of sheep merely for the sake of gratifying his thirst for blood, when one or two would have been sufficient for his wants. I have found them the most cowardly of animals—when caught in a trap or wounded by a gun, or when cornered up so they could not escape, I invariably killed them with a club or tomahawk, and I never met with any resistance. It is true I have seen them show some boldness if a number of them had run down a deer when I attempted to drive them away, yet have always seen them give way if a shot was fired amongst them."

In *Pattie's Personal Narrative, 1824–30*, what I take for a common exaggeration of the times shows up. James O. Pattie tells of breaking up a wolf pack along the Santa Fe Trail. "We judged there were at least a thousand. They were large and white as sheep." Of all the likely tall tales of wolf attack at the time, one of the best is C. W. Webber's account in *Romance of Sporting; or, Wild Scenes and Wild Hunters*, in which Capt. Dan Henrie of the Texas Rangers is attacked by a pack of wolves. They eat his horse out from under him as he scrambles into a tree, where he holds them off with rifle fire. In a bloody frenzy the wolves tear each other apart and chew the stock off Henrie's rifle when it falls among them before they realize what it is. Just when all seems lost, a lone buffalo at-

They tell a story about Jim Bridger, the mountain man, who was setting beaver traps along a creek in the Bitterroot Mountains in 1829 when he was jumped by wolves. Bridger ran for the nearest tree and was able to climb out of reach before the wolves could get to him. After milling around for a while, all the wolves but one, who was left behind to guard, departed. A half hour later the other wolves returned with a beaver whom they set to chewing the tree down.

tracts the wolves' attention and off they go. Captain Henrie climbs out of the tree, builds a fire, and begins roasting wolf flesh to regain his strength.

As one might guess from these stories, the relating of such scenes lent an aura of importance to the lives of those involved. For that reason the storyteller did not often hew the mark of truth.

The wolves of the plains were, of course, whatever one wanted to make of them. Thus the howling wolf was the Pawnee's spirit talker, the missionary's banshee, Maximilian's music, and the lone traveler's sleepless nightmare.

The first people to express any interest in killing wolves on the plains were trappers, who came into the West on the heels of the Lewis and Clark expedition, looking for beaver. They incidentally killed wolves that raided their food caches and trap lines, and when the beaver were trapped out in the 1850s they began killing wolves specifically for their pelts. In the 1830s a wolf pelt was worth only about a dollar; by 1850 the price was up to two. Records of the upper Missouri outfit of the American Fur Trading Company indicate that in 1850 they shipped twenty wolf pelts downriver, but by 1853 the total had jumped to 3,000. Yet this was still primarily incidental killing. The class of men who had wiped out beaver turned now to buffalo, and between 1850 and 1880 they killed over 75 million of these animals, mostly for hides. This incredible slaughter provided wolves with a virtually unlimited supply of meat. As wolves got in the habit of following around after the buffalo hunters to scavenge the carcasses, the hunters began increasingly to shoot them for sport; they took the time to skin them only after they were finished with the buffalo.

With the gold rushes of the 1840s, 1850s, and 1860s there came teamsters, bullwhackers, and mule skinners to transport ore and supplies. In winter when the wagons couldn't move easily these idled men turned to wolfing. It was easier than buffalo hunting, which required moving around looking for the animals and wrestling with large carcasses. All a wolfer had to do was set out strychnine and gather in the dead at two dollars a hide.

By 1860, then, a large number of men were out on the plains looking for quick money—in minerals, transportation, land, anything—looking to make a killing. Few did. The thousands who didn't rode herd on other men's cattle, built other men's railroads, fenced other men's land, processed the ore from other men's mines. It was mostly these men who took up wolfing as a formal occupation to make their grubstake. First the money came from the wolf hides alone, then it was for the bounty, too. In the thirty years after 1865 they killed virtually every wolf from Texas to the Dakotas, from Missouri to Colorado. But most of them stayed poor, drifting on to other jobs on the frontier.

It cost a wolfer about $150 to outfit himself for the winter season when pelts were prime. This included food and clothing plus a wagon, horses, cooking gear, rifle, skinning knife, and the essential supply of strychnine, usually in crystalline sulfate form. From this investment he might expect to make anywhere from one to three thousand dollars for three or four months' work. As in the case of the gold miner and the land speculator, he had no concept of prior or inherent rights; the wolves, like the gold and the land and buffalo, were there for the taking.

A wolfer spent each day in the same routine. In the afternoon he would ride out and shoot two or three buffalo and lace the carcasses with strychnine. The next morning he would return to dress out the ten or twenty victims. One wolfer, Robert Peck, left a record of his days in a journal that was later turned into a book, *The Wolf Hunters*, by George Bird Grinnell. Peck mustered out of the army in 1861, and he and two friends set up a wolf camp about twenty-five miles north of Fort Larned, Kansas. Over the winter they killed 3,000 animals: 800 wolves, more than 2,000 coyotes, and about 100 foxes. Wildlife was so plentiful (biological historians think the fauna of the Great Plains at this time was as rich as it had ever been anywhere in the world) that they never had to go more than ten miles from camp to shoot whooping crane, deer, antelope, and small game for food or buffalo for baits. The wolf pelts brought $1.25 each, the coyotes $.75, and the foxes $.25 at Fort Larned in the spring of 1862. The three men split about $2,500.

Hundreds of similar outfits in succeeding years killed an unfathomable number of animals: buffalo, the last few beaver, antelope (the strip of backstrap meat brought $.25), and all the animals that fed on the poisoned meat—ferrets, skunks, badgers, weasels, eagles, ravens, and bears. "The Indians have an especial antipathy to the wolfer," wrote J. H. Taylor in *Twenty Years on the Trapline*. "Poisoned wolves and foxes in their dying fits often slobber upon the grass, which becoming sun dried holds its poisonous properties a long time, often causing the death months or even years after of the pony, antelope, buffalo and other animals feeding upon it. The Indians losing their stock in this way feel like making reprisals, and often did."

Overlapping the period of wolfing for pelts—most of them were shipped to Russia and Europe for coats—was the development of the livestock industry that would seal the wolf's doom. In the spring of 1858 a herd of oxen that had been abandoned to shift for itself on the high pastures of Colorado the previous fall was found fat and healthy. The commercial value of America's great interior grasslands was suddenly recognized, and the industry that would be the most important economic activity in the West in the 1880s began laying its foundation. Enterprising cattlemen bought up vast areas of cheap grazing land. The indigenous browsers and grazers were replaced with cattle. By 1870 most of the commercial wolfers were working for cattlemen, killing wolves that could no longer find buffalo to eat and were turning to domestic stock.

It was during this period, 1875 to 1895, that the slaughter of wolves on the plains reached its peak. Spurred by the promises of substantial state and local, as well as stockmen's associations, bounties, a market value for the pelts, and the possibility of hiring on somewhere as a wolfer for wages, thousands of men bought up enormous quantities of strychnine and rode out pell-mell on the range. They lay down poisoned meat everywhere, in lines as long as 150 miles. The more demented among them shot small birds, carefully painted a thin paste of strychnine solution under the skin at the breast bone, and then scattered these about the prairie. Ranch dogs died. Children died. Everything that ate meat died. The greed, the ready availability of poison, and a refusal to consider the consequences generated a holocaust.

Stanley Young, an historian of the period, writes: "Destruction by this strychnine campaign . . . has hardly been exceeded in North America, unless by the slaughter of the passenger pigeon, the buffalo and the antelope. There was a sort of unwritten law of the range that no cowman would knowingly pass by a carcass of any kind without inserting in it a goodly dose of strychnine sulfate, in the hope of killing one more wolf."

There is some irony in the fact that the first strychnine to reach the West came on a boat that was bound for South America—until its crew learned of the California gold strike.

No one knows how many animals were killed on the plains from, say, 1850 to 1900. If you count the buffalo for hides and the antelope for backstraps and the passenger pigeons for target practice and the Indian ponies (by whites, to keep the Indian poor), it is conceivable that 500 million creatures died. Perhaps 1 million wolves; 2 million. The numbers no longer have meaning.

As elusive is an answer to the question of how many wolves were left on the prairies by the time cattle ranching became big business. A nation that wanted beef had to control wolf predation—had to kill wolves—there was no way around that—but it didn't have to, as it did, kill every last wolf. I remember once asking some Eskimos what they would do about wolves if they were raising reindeer. Would they wipe them out? No, they said. You would have to live with a little predation. The way they put it, speaking of it as they spoke of all things that were subject to natural forces, was, "We know it wouldn't go one hundred percent for us."

The wolf was not the cattleman's only problem. There was weather to contend with, disease, rustling, fluctuating beef prices, the hazards of trail drives, the cost of running such enormous operations. But more and more the cattlemen blamed any economic shortfall on the wolf. You couldn't control storms or beef prices or prevent hoof and mouth disease, but you could kill wolves. Since nobody cared for wolves, no one thought to put a limit on it; and, in the way angry men pound desks, the wolf was pounded until there was nothing left.

Edward Curnow, in a history of the development of the cattle industry and wolf eradication in Montana, remarks that before about 1878 cattlemen were more worried about Indians killing their cattle than they were about wolves. As the land filled up with other ranchers, as water rights became an issue, and as the Indians were removed to reservations, however, the wolf became, in Curnow's phrase, "an object of pathological hatred."

Montana was the center of the cattle-raising industry in the northern plains in the late nineteenth century and what the wolf got there is what he got in the Dakotas, Wyoming, and Colorado.

The first wolf bounty law passed in Montana was in 1884. It offered one dollar for a dead wolf. The first year, 5,450 wolves were turned in for bounty; in 1885, 2,224 were turned in, and 2,587 the next year. Cattlemen, fat on profits from a high beef market in those years and

Wolf-killed Hereford cattle, near Douglas, Arizona.

cushioned by a tremendous influx of investor money from the East, were convinced the wolf problem would fade to insignificance. The harsh winter of 1886/87 wiped out 95 percent of some herds and changed the investors' minds swiftly. Free grazing on public lands ended; speculative money dried up. Suddenly cattlemen who had never before bothered to go out on the range to see their cattle began to count every cow and steer. In 1887 a legislature dominated by mining interests repealed the expensive wolf bounty program. Enraged, conceivably panicked, cattlemen immediately mounted a propaganda campaign to have the law reinstated. The wolf population had thinned out; no one was willing to kill wolves just for the pelt anymore. Bounty money was needed as an incentive. The heart of the campaign was a series of newspaper editorials and widely circulated pamphlets that stressed the dollar damage done to the state economy by wolves. The longer the legislature held out, the more outrageous the claims became. By 1893, when the legislature finally gave in, the desperate stockmen were reporting losses that were mathematical impossibilities.

The effect of this exaggeration was contagious. The Montana sheep industry, which up to this time had lost more animals to bears and mountain lions than to wolves, began to blame its every downward economic trend on the wolf. The 1899 legislature raised the wolf bounty to $5. People went out and killed wolves far and wide, wolves up in the Bitterroot Mountains that had never even seen sheep and cattle. The wolf population declined sharply in the 1890s. Many stockmen, stretching their own credulity to document wolf damage, finally soured on the slaughter. Where before a rancher didn't dare not support claims of wolf damage, despite any personal feelings to the contrary, for fear he would be without help at roundup time, now men openly declared it was enough. In 1902 the legislature, for the first time, assessed a tax on cattlemen to help defray the mounting cost of wolf bounty payments, which in that year were about $160,000. That turned more cattlemen off. In 1903 the bounty fell to $3 and it looked as though it was over.

But the most bizarre chapter was yet to unfold.

By 1905 wolf predation in Montana was light, but a small cadre of bitter stockmen, unable to stand *any* loss, obsessed with the idea that the wolf was taking money out of their pockets—what actually galled them was that someone was living for free on their land—not only got the bounty back up to ten dollars but had passed an outrageous law requiring the state veterinarian to inoculate wolves with scarcoptic mange and then turn them loose. Cattlemen were to get fifteen dollars from the legislature for every wolf they trapped for the program. In spite of the ethical outrage, in spite of the fact that it didn't work, in spite of the fact that a similar disease spread to domestic stock and the federal government forbade human consumption of cattle from some counties, this program was continued for eleven years.

An increased bounty of fifteen dollars in 1911 failed, as had the ten-dollar bounty of 1905, to produce any more bountied wolves. The animal was virtually wiped out, and in 1933 the bounty law in Montana was repealed.

It is hard to look back on this period in American history and understand what motivated men to do what they did, to kill so thoroughly, so far in excess of what was necessary. In Montana in the period from 1883 to 1918, 80,730 wolves were bountied for $342,764.

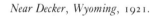

Near Decker, Wyoming, 1921.

Of all the wild creatures of North America, none are more despicable than wolves. There is no depth of meanness, treachery or cruelty to which they do not cheerfully descend. They are the only animals on earth which make a regular practice of killing and devouring their wounded companions, and eating their own dead. I once knew a male wolf to kill and half devour his female cage-mate, with whom he had lived a year.

In captivity, no matter how well yarded, *well fed or comfortable, a wolf will watch and coax for hours to induce a neighbor in the next cage to thrust through tail or paw, so that he may instantly seize and chew it off, without mercy. But in the face of foes capable of defence, even gray wolves are rank cowards, and unless cornered in a den, will not even stop to fight for their own cubs.*

—WILLIAM T. HORNADAY
The American Natural History

Men in a speculative business like cattle ranching singled out one scapegoat for their financial losses. Hired hands were readily available and anxious to do the killing. There was a feeling that as long as someone was out killing wolves, things were bound to get better. And the wolf had few sympathizers. The history of economic expansion in the West was characterized by the change or destruction of much that lay in its way. Dead wolves were what Manifest Destiny cost.

By and large, the kinds of men who did the killing in the 1880s and 1890s were drifters who gave strong lip service to Progress, the mandate to subdue the earth, and the ghoulish nature of the wolf. Ben Corbin, a frontier roustabout who at one point killed wolves for a living, left his wolf-hunting wisdom behind in the pages of a privately printed booklet called *The Wolf Hunter's Guide* (1901). It is typical of hundreds of other such memoirs in that it has very little to say about how to actually kill wolves but a great deal to say about the Bible, free trade, the privilege of living in a democracy, and the foulness of the wolf's ways. It expresses the sentiments of the day and is full of bad biology and fantastic calculations. Corbin notes, for example, that for the two-year period 1897/98, 15,211 wolves were turned in for bounty in North Dakota. He proceeds to argue: "There being 1,207,500 wolves in North Dakota, and allowing two pounds of beef per day at 5 cents per pound, to feed them will take for one year 881,475 steers of 1000 pounds each, worth $44,070,750. The wolves will outnumber all other stock after July 4, 1900.

"If there should be no future increase in wolves in three years they would eat meals at the above figures, to the value of $132,212,250, considerably more than the total evaluation of the state ($114,334,428).

"If each man kills a hundred wolves it would take 12,075 men to kill the present wolf crop in one year. During the three months after May 1, 1900, 862,500 wolves are born, or 9,583 per day.

"If 50,000 wolves are killed this summer, next year (1901) at their rate of increase, there will be 5,208,750 wolves at large in North Dakota."

Corbin's naïveté would be amusing if such reasoning had not been taken seriously by so many people, including state legislators.

Corbin advises his readers that wolf farming—or raising wolves for bounty—is a good way to supplement income, and readily admits to the common bounty hunter's practice of raiding dens for wolf pups but leaving the mother to breed the next year.

The author describes himself as a man "with eighty wolf scalps hanging to his belt" when he arrived in Dakota Territory in 1883. He speaks of the wolf as "the enemy of the state . . . for what greater enemy can the state have than one that is able to wage war on the state's chief industry both day and night?" For Corbin everything had to be assigned an economic value. Though he tells you no more of the techniques of wolf killing than was common knowledge to be heard at the general store, he says, "I have devoted my life to it, have studied it, have practiced it, till I have it down fine, and believe I should be paid for telling others what it took me so long to learn."

Perhaps the most revealing statement in Corbin's long, rambling autobiography is this: "When I drove with my hunting outfit through the city of Bismarck and showed the staring citizens of that metropolis the fruits of my industry I received such marked attention as a politician with a bag of gold in one hand and the constitution in the other might have been proud of."

Corbin was an eccentric, of course, but he was also a wolf killer. With no social or legal controls on what he could do with wolves, and with stockmen eager to put him to work, he could kill to his heart's content. If one is looking for villains, however, I think one has also to look beyond

Corbin to the ranchers who paid him to do what they were ashamed to do themselves, because they knew men like Corbin wouldn't quit until there was nothing left to kill.

The wolfer came to regard himself after the turn of the century as a folk hero, as a man of deliverance. Without him the nation, hungry for beef and in need of wool, could not carry on. As his services became less and less required, he billed the wolf more and more as a sagacious and vicious enemy that only he could track down and kill. To this end he supported the outrageous claims of the stockmen who employed him, even when he knew it was all nonsense.

A lot of men were attracted to bounty hunting wolves. It offered money and respectability. An article in *Field and Stream* in 1886 extolled the adventure to be had, noting that one man "with not much on his hands but idle time, practiced a week at the business in Yellowstone county [Montana], and the result was nine wolf skins and twenty-six coyote skins." For this the man received in bounty and in payment for the pelts $118.50. The activity was described as "lots of fun," and the cost "about $5 for strychnine and time. Bait was to be had in one dead animal picked up on the range."

The appeal of this life was mostly to men with little formal education, at a loss for something to do in life. Many fancied themselves knowledgeable outdoorsmen. Some were; most knew as much about animals as they did about the pyramids. In a pamphlet on wolf trapping one of this fraternity warned that live pups "should never be handled with bare hands, as blood poisoning is likely to result from a bite," and suggested wearing a brown corduroy suit when working in order to blend into the local vegetation.

Their lack of biological knowledge made them vulnerable to criticism from anyone who knew better and so as a group they developed the habit of bluffing when stockmen questioned them too closely about wolves, and cultivated the aplomb and insouciance of Owen Wister's Virginian. Over the years their keenest antipathy was reserved for college-educated biologists fresh in the field, for whom they had nothing but contempt. Part of the tragedy—and it was a tragedy—was that wolves who bothered no cattle were hunted down by men who largely wanted to prove to other men that they were no fools.

The situation changed, rather radically in part, when the federal government passed a law in 1915 providing for the extermination of wolves on federal lands. Stockmen for years had been grazing their animals for a pittance on public land and hounding the government to provide them with wolf hunters at government expense. With an appropriation of $125,000, the government hired its first government hunters on July 1, 1915. Between then and June 30, 1942, when the program was terminated, these hunters killed 24,132 wolves, mostly in Colorado, Wyoming, Montana, and the western Dakotas. The extermination program even included wolves in the country's national parks.

The government hunters were a different breed from the previous generation of get-rich-quick bounty hunters. They were federal employees who took their work soberly and seriously. They had to; by the time they went to work, the wolves left to be caught were mostly so trap-wise and man-shy that it sometimes took a man six months to catch one animal.

As early as 1910, however, these dwindling wolf populations had created some well-paying jobs for good wolfers. The two- and three-dollar bounties of the 1880s were now as high as $150—the price paid for an adult wolf by the Piceance Creek Stock Growers' Association of north-central Colorado in 1912. A good trapper working out of a large ranch might expect $200 a month in salary plus his board. In addition he might get as much as $50 from his employer for each adult wolf he killed and $20 for each pup. To that might be added another $5 or $10 from the county and state plus stock association bounty money. One of the trappers of this era, Bill Caywood, made $7,000 over the winter of 1912/13 in stock association bounties alone on the 140 wolves he killed.

Caywood was widely respected among outdoorsmen of the time. He was one of the first hired by the federal government for its program, and he went on to become the best-known government hunter working for the Biological Survey (the forerunner of the Department of the Interior). "Big Bill Caywood," said a blurb in a 1939 issue of *Outdoor Life*, "wise in the ways of the savage, cattle-killing lobos, was so good at his job that there's almost no job left." Caywood was credited with killing some of the most famous outlaw wolves, all in Colorado: Rags the Digger, the Butcher Wolf, the Cuerno Verde Gray, and the Keystone Pack. But what made the man such a hero in the eyes of those who admired him was that he'd invested all his bounty earnings in land and become a successful rancher in the Horatio Alger tradition. It was a marvelously right, thoroughly American success story. Lost in the telling was Caywood's habit of sending his son down into wolf dens in the spring to get the wolf pups. And any mention of bounty fraud, which even a man like Caywood was supposed to countenance as harmless fun.

Getting away with bounty fraud, especially duping a game warden, was considered part of wolfing, it being the conviction of many bounty hunters from the beginning that they provided a service to all mankind for which the compensation was inadequate. A sign hanging in a State Fish and Game office in Pierre, South Dakota, read as follows:

> We, *the willing*
> *Led by the unknowing*
> *are doing the impossible*
> *for the ungrateful.*
> *We have done so much*
> *for so long*
> *with so little*
> *we are now qualified*
> *to do anything*
> *with nothing.*
>
> —THE TRAPPER

If the wolf's ears were required as proof for bounty payment, dog, fox, coyote, or bobcat ears might be turned in. The ears might be turned in in one county and the nose in another, so the bounty was paid twice. What was turned in was taken out the back door and turned in somewhere else—or back at the same place. Road kills were turned in. Badger noses were turned in. Attempts to control the cheating became as varied as the methods of infraction: oaths that one was not knowingly preserving the life of a female wolf in order to turn her pups in for bounty each spring, or ears or nose or tail having to be removed in the presence of the person paying the bounty. In Washington State the whole wolf had to be turned in and the bone of the right foreleg was to be burned in the presence of two court officials before the pelt was released to the trapper for subsequent sale. Nothing prevented one, of course, from taking those ears over to Idaho or sending the pelt to a friend in Oregon, where it would be stamped, bounty paid, and released again for sale to a furrier. In 1909 the federal government took pity on states whose treasuries were being looted of hundreds of thousands of dollars every year and published a booklet by government hunter Vernon Bailey entitled *Key to Animals on which Wolf and Coyote Bounties are Paid*, which helped the state officials to differentiate between legitimate and illegitimate claims.

Government hunters who couldn't apply for bounties were less likely to condone this sort of thing and also less prone to exaggerate the wolf's role in stock predation. With the entry of the federal government into the picture, therefore, the incidence of fraud was reduced and much of the hysteria over wolves abated. In a speech before the Montana Stock Growers' Association in 1916, Wallis Huidekoper finally said what ranchers had known for a long time: "It is a well-known fact that stock-killing individuals among wolves are only a small portion of their kind inhabiting a given area." But by then the point was academic. The wolves were gone. In the nine months since this particular program began, Montana's nine government hunters had found and killed exactly six wolves.

The government hunter went about his business with methodical, bureaucratic dedication. He used poisons to kill the last of the easy ones, then resorted to steel traps and exotic ploys to get the rest. The traps he used were the ones originally designed in 1843 by Sewell Newhouse and manufactured by the Oneida Community in New York, of which Newhouse was a member. Newhouse himself was preoccupied with the trap as a symbol of civilization and recommended that it be incorporated in state seals. In his *Trapper's Guide* he says the trap goes before the ax and the plow, forming "the prow with which iron-clad civilization is

Newhouse #14 wolf trap.

pushing back barbaric solitude" and causing the wolf to give way "to the wheatfield, the library, and the piano."

Whatever they may have thought of his rhetoric, government trappers had nothing but praise for his traps. The Newhouse #4½ steel wolf trap weighed 5¼ pounds and had smooth jaws. It was the standard wolf trap until the turn of the century, when it was replaced by the Newhouse #14, a toothed trap that held the wolf more securely. A #114 trap was later developed to accommodate the longer foot of Alaskan wolves. All three traps came with a six-foot length of steel chain to which a drag hook was attached. The trap was set in a hole just below the surface of the ground and carefully covered with earth until it was completely concealed. Set in a trail where wolves were likely to step, it was called a blind set; placed near rotting meat, it was a bait set; a scent set was one by a rock or bush on which a pungent homemade mixture had been carefully dripped. Underwater or tidewater sets were also occasionally used, but they could ruin a pelt if not checked frequently.

Strychnine was by 1900 considered too dangerous to use and setting traps was harder than shooting a buffalo and stuffing a fistful of poison in it. You had to find the right place and make a set that would more likely catch a wolf than a badger and not be sprung by range cattle or ruined by rainfall. Understandably, the ranks of professional wolfers thinned out with these requirements.

When he wasn't tending to traps, the government hunter was looking for dens. The pups were dug out and strangled in the spring. Although the knack for finding dens was much praised, the killing of pups made most men sick. "I have done it many times and since," wrote one, "but I have never had to do anything that goes against the grain more than to kill the pups at this stage. Potential murderers they may be, but at this time they are just plump, friendly little things that nuzzle you and whine little pleased whines.

"We both felt somewhat ashamed and guilty," he said, speaking for his partner, "but it was duty."

The widest public interest in the wolf wars was generated by government hunters' attempts to capture the last "outlaw wolves." The stock associations ballyhooed their existence as though they were criminal geniuses that demanded a nation's attention, when, in fact, many of them were simply the last wolves left in areas where everything to eat but cattle had been wiped out. Others really deserved that reputation. Apparently some wolves spent years in a careful, methodical pattern of destruction that seemed almost designed to enrage ranchers. Certain animals were credited with destroying ten and twenty thousand dollars' worth of stock in their lifetimes. And they all proved exceedingly difficult to catch.

Curiously, many of these outlaw wolves were white wolves. The Sycan Wolf of Sycan Marsh, Oregon; the Snowdrift Wolf of Judith Basin and the Ghost Wolf of the Little Rockies, both in Montana; the Pine Ridge Wolf and the Custer Wolf from South Dakota; Old Whitey of Bear Springs Mesa, Colorado. And it was said that many of them were born and lived on Indian reservations—the Pryor Creek Wolf on the Crow Reservation, the Ghost Wolf of the Little Rockies on the Fort Belknap Reservation, the Pine Ridge Wolf on the Pine Ridge Reservation. Many of them had toes missing, pulled off in a trap, and one of them, Old Lefty of Burns Hole, Colorado, ran around on three legs.

Of them all, Three Toes of Harding County, South Dakota, was perhaps the most famous. According to Stanley Young, 150 men over a period of thirteen years tried to capture the wolf before a government hunter finally caught him in the summer of 1925. Stockmen credited him with having destroyed fifty thousand dollars' worth of stock.

The death of one of these animals occasioned parades, banquets, speeches, and the awarding of engraved gold watches.

One of the more poignant stories about an outlaw or renegade wolf concerns the Currumpaw Wolf of northern New Mexico and his mate Blanca, who were killed in 1894 by the naturalist Ernest Thompson Seton.

Seton, called in by a concerned rancher who was a friend, tried every sort of set he could devise, to no avail. Each time, the Currumpaw Wolf would dig up and spring the traps or pointedly ignore them.

One evening Seton set out to concoct the be-all-and-end-all of baits:

"Acting on the hint of an old trapper, I melted some cheese together with the kidney fat of a freshly killed heifer, stewing it in a china dish, and cutting it with a bone knife to avoid the taint of metal. When the mixture was cool, I cut it into lumps, and making a hole in the side of each lump I inserted a large dose of strychnine and cyanide, contained in a capsule that was impermeable by any odor; finally I sealed the holes with pieces of the cheese itself. During the whole process, I wore a pair of gloves steeped in the hot blood of the heifer, and even avoided breathing on the baits. When all was ready, I put them in a raw-hide bag rubbed all over with blood, and rode forth dragging the liver and kidneys of the beef at the end of a rope. With this I made a ten mile circuit, dropping a bait at each quarter mile, and taking the utmost care, always, not to touch any with my hands."

Seton's caution and arcane science were techniques much praised by wolfers of the time. The Currumpaw Wolf, for his part, carefully gathered four of the baits in a pile and defecated on them.

The female wolf, Blanca, was finally caught in a steel trap in the spring of 1894. Seton and a companion approached the wolf on horseback. "Then followed the inevitable tragedy, the idea of which I shrank from afterward more than at the time. We each threw a lasso over the neck of the doomed wolf, and strained our horses in opposite directions

OUTLAWS

Three Toes of Harding County, South
  Dakota
Old Whitey, Bear Springs Mesa, Colorado
Big Foot, Lane County, Colorado
The Truxton Wolf, Arizona
Lobo, King of Currumpaw, northern
  New Mexico
White Wolf, Pine Ridge, South Dakota
Rags the Digger, Cathedral Bluffs, Colorado
The Traveler, west-central Arkansas
Virden Wolf, Virden, Manitoba
Old Lefty, Burns Hole, Colorado
Custer Wolf, Custer, South Dakota
Aquila Wolf, western Arizona
Cody's Captive, Cheyenne, Wyoming

Mountain Billy, Medora, North Dakota
Sycan Wolf, Sycan Marsh, Oregon
Queen Wolf, Unaweep Canyon, Colorado
Black Buffalorunner, Carberry, Manitoba
The Greenhorn Wolf, southern Colorado
Three Toes of the Apishapa, Colorado
Werewolf of Nut Lake, Ft. Qu'Appelle,
  Saskatchewan
Split Rock Wolf, west-central Wyoming
Snowdrift Wolf, Judith Basin, Montana
Pryor Creek Wolf, southeastern Montana
Pine Ridge Wolf, southeastern
  South Dakota
Ghost Wolf of the Little Rockies,
  north-central Montana

until the blood burst from her mouth, her eyes glazed, her limbs stiffened and then fell limp."

The dead female was taken back to the ranch. The male, abandoning all his former caution, followed her and the next day stepped into a nest of traps set around the ranch buildings. He was chained up and left for the night but was found dead in the morning, without a wound or any sign of a struggle. Seton, deeply moved by what had happened, placed his dead body in the shed next to Blanca's.

The price offered to the man who would kill the Currumpaw Wolf was one thousand dollars. Seton never says whether he took it. (In a long short story called "Wolf Tracker" by Zane Grey, which appeared in *The Ladies' Home Journal* in 1924, the hero, Brink, walks a wolf to exhaustion and strangles him. Offered the five-thousand-dollar reward, he says a few words about the nobility of wolves and the poorness of human spirits and rides off.)

After the outlaw wolves were caught, government hunters turned to other predators. No one knows the dates when the last wolves disappeared, but by 1945 there were only stragglers. A few Mexican wolves drifting north into southern Arizona and New Mexico. A few British Columbia wolves moving south into northern Washington and Idaho. Some northern Rocky Mountain wolves coming into Glacier National Park in Montana and, rarely, down into the Bitterroot Mountains. But for a single pocket in northern Minnesota, a few on Isle Royale in Lake Superior, there were no more gray wolves in the lower forty-eight states.

There had never been a killing like it.

The final act of the wolf war in North America was staged in Canada in the 1950s.

The section of Ontario adjacent to the United States and southern sections of the prairie provinces had been involved in America's wolf war early on. Ontario established a wolf bounty in 1793, Alberta not until 1899, and British Columbia in 1909. Canadian wolf populations began to decline steadily west of Manitoba after 1900 under increased bounty pressure. By 1948 attention had shifted north to the Northwest Territories, where the herds of barren ground caribou were declining. Almost in a panic, the Crown and provincial governments set in motion the most intensively organized wolf-control program ever mounted.

It was never argued that there was any other cause than excessive human hunting for the caribou decline, but it was decided to remove substantial numbers of wolves anyway because the situation was critical. Between 1951 and 1961, 17,500 wolves were poisoned. In 1955, when most of the wolf range in northern Canada was covered with poison bait stations (some of them poisoned wolf carcasses) served by airplane, the take reached 2,000 animals a year. Some attempt was made to keep the baits in areas where they would not harm other wildlife. Nevertheless, in one area, from 1955 to 1959, 496 red fox, 105 arctic fox, and 385 wolverines were killed, along with 3,417 wolves.

The caribou herds recovered and the program was terminated.

When the herds first began to thin in the north in 1948, some wolves apparently drifted south into Alberta, Saskatchewan, and Manitoba, and Alberta's Veterinary Services Branch claimed an antirabies campaign was needed to protect people against possibly rabid wolves. Behind the prop of a public health program an astonishing arsenal of poison was distributed: 39,960 cyanide guns, 106,100 cyanide cartridges, and 628,000 strychnine pellets. Sodium fluoroacetate (1080) poison bait stations were increased from 25 in 1951 to 800 by 1956. There is no record of the number of wolves that were killed, along with 246,800 coyotes, but in all that time exactly one rabid wolf was diagnosed, in 1952.

British Columbia established a Predator Control Division, ostensibly to assist cattle ranchers in the south, but under pressure from professional guides and outfitters it concentrated its efforts in the north where wolves preyed on big game.

Wolf bounties were dropped in the western provinces in the mid-fifties in favor of using provincial hunters in certified problem areas. Ontario struck its bounty on wolves in 1972, Quebec in 1971. Between 1935 and 1955, about twenty thousand wolves were bountied in British Columbia; between 1942 and 1955, about twelve thousand in Alberta; and between 1947 and 1971, about thirty-three thousand in Ontario.

Recently in the 1970s a declining deer population in Quebec triggered a vigorous antiwolf campaign. Antiwolf sentiment is also still strong in coastal British Columbia, another deer hunting area. In the Yukon, complaints from guides and outfitters that wolves bother their horses (grazing free on Crown lands) and elk (artificially introduced) have resulted in a wolf-control program there. In northeastern British Columbia guides apparently have kept up a private wolf-poisoning program to protect trophy Dall sheep for their clients.

At present, however, the wolf population of Canada seems fairly healthy. Canada got into and out of unlimited warfare on wolves rather quickly. Major portions of Canada are still only thinly settled, and in these areas wolf populations have recovered from the effects of the poisoning campaigns.

The state of Alaska established a wolf bounty in 1915, but the number of wolves killed there in the past sixty years has not seemed to affect the overall population, which remains somewhere between five and ten thousand. The Mexican wolf population, on the other hand, has declined precipitously in the last thirty years. Livestock interests have expanded into former wolf ranges and human hunters have reduced the wild game populations of deer, bighorn sheep, and antelope that wolves feed on. The owners of large ranchos pay no attention to Mexico's wolf protection statutes, and there is little hope that the Mexican wolf *(Canis lupus baileyi)* will survive except in isolated pockets. (One such region is in southern Durango, where the wolves are protected by the Tepehuanan Indians.)

Incredibly, the unrestrained savagery that was once a part of wolf killing in the United States continues with efforts in America to control "brush wolves," or coyotes. These animals are hunted down by ranchers from helicopters with shotguns. Their dens are dynamited. Their mouths are wired shut and they are left to starve. They are strung up in trees and picked apart with pistol fire. They are doused with gasoline and ignited.

All this was done to the wolf—and more. One of the cowhand's favorite ruses was to stake out a dog in heat in hopes of attracting a male wolf. During a copulatory tie the animals cannot break apart. Thus trapped, the wolf was clubbed to death.

It seems to me that somewhere in our history we should have attempted to answer to ourselves for all this. As I have tried to make clear, the motive for wiping out wolves (as opposed to controlling them) proceeded from misunderstanding, from illusions of what constituted sport, from strident attachment to private property, from ignorance and irrational hatred. But the scope, the casual irresponsibility, and the cruelty of wolf killing is something else. I do not think it comes from some base, atavistic urge, though that may be a part of it. I think it is that we simply do not understand our place in the universe and have not the courage to admit it.

I would like to close this chapter with a few observations on some of the people I spoke with while I was writing this book: Dave Wallace, who lived out on the Oregon desert; a retired wolf trapper in Minnesota; a government hunter from North Dakota; and an aerial hunter from Alaska.

These men were not barbarians. They all liked wolves and were sorry for the killing. They grew up in hard times and today they are not rich. There is cause in their lives for bitterness, but they are not bitter. They are patient men. They have cultivated patience. It fills a human need, I suppose, to believe that the wolf is an incredibly intelligent animal, very difficult to trap. Stories like that about the Currumpaw Wolf and the other outlaws tend to support the idea but, really, the wolf wasn't all that hard to trap. What it took more than anything else was patience. To make a good set and just wait till a wolf stepped in it.

Each of these men hunted wolves for bounty in a different way. They were not particularly vain men, but they knew what they did was done well. They smile whenever you mention the equipment fetishes of some of the old trappers, the wolf tail used to dust off the ground after the trap was set, or the concoctions of store-bought, sure-fire wolf scent advertised in trapper magazines in the twenties. They knew in the end it all came down to work and to being careful and to knowing the wolf and the land he lived in. One of these old men knew as much about wolves as some of the biologists I'd spoken with, but without a formal education, a good suit of clothes, and a set of teeth he was hard pressed to communicate it to anyone.

They'd been in a grim business but they had not thought much about it at the time. It was, as the man who killed the pups said, duty. They would tell you stories of horror, and struggle to find their own reasons and end up silent, beaten by history, by something they couldn't understand.

They remembered some tight times. The Minnesota trapper was attacked by a wolf in a trap and bitten. The government hunter was threatened with losing his job when he refused to kill a wolf that wasn't killing stock but which local cattle ranchers, well connected politically, claimed was.

They remembered things that made you laugh. An inexperienced man who tried to kill wolf pups underground with a .45 and broke both eardrums with the first shot. A North Dakota rancher who admitted one day he didn't really know how to tell a coyote from a wolf but he was pretty sure it was wolves that were running his horses around the corrals at night. It turned out to be his own dog and two feral Irish setters.

They remembered when the last wolf around them was killed. "The last gray wolf killed in eastern Montana was in June 1927, over in the Lone Pine Hills, over east of Ekalaka in what is now Carter County." They remembered it that well, staring now out the window of a battered trailer house at the vision, as though they wished they might have gone then, too.

They'd been on the bad side of the law. The aerial hunter and his son had been fined for illegally hunting wolves from the air. The trapper had been fined for bounty fraud.

You could not blame these men, at least I could not, for what they had done, as though it had all happened in a vacuum. The aerial hunter, trapping on the ground one year, caught a large male black wolf in one of his traps. As he approached, the wolf lifted his trapped foot, extended it toward him, and whined softly. "I would have let him go if I didn't need the money awful bad," he said quietly.

The old trapper I met in Minnesota I think is a tragic figure. There was, at the time I spoke with him, an argument over the status of the wolf in Minnesota. He, and others, claimed there were too many in the northeastern corner and that they were killing all the deer and should be trapped out. Others, particularly people outside the state, thought the wolf should be federally protected as an endangered species. The old man had a stake in this argument, and for him it was larger than the fate of the wolf. It was his own. He was staring at the end of his life.

He told me stories of wolf predation that were clearly exaggerations, and admitted freely that they were. But he persisted in telling the stories, and as the statewide controversy wore on, he became more and more insistent on the truth of his silly stories about bloodthirsty wolves and wanton slaughter. He wanted, more than anything else, a reinstatement of the wolf bounty program. I could not understand what he was thinking about until one day I drove him over to a friend's house, a man in his eighties with whom he'd once trapped.

As these two men talked with each other about the early days with wolves, they were saying to anyone listening that they wanted to be needed. If no one needed wolves trapped anymore there wasn't any reason for them to be around. They were useless. So they talked each other up about what a killer the wolf was, and how hard he was to trap, because that's what they wanted their neighbors to believe. They wanted the attention and respect they used to get in a township, young boys tagging after them, men their own age cheering their shenanigans with the game wardens. It was all slipping away from them now.

That afternoon the old man had shown me three wolves hanging up in his garage. Under the provisions of the Endangered Species Act he could have been fined twenty thousand dollars for each one. He told me he didn't give a damn. He'd gotten a call from the owner of a cattle ranch north of his place to come up and trap out wolves that were "bothering stock." He had not asked, as he would have done in the old days, to see the tracks, to see a kill, to see evidence. He just set his traps. And he got three wolves.

As the three of us sat in the small, overheated house that afternoon in Minnesota, looking at sepia-toned prints from years ago, I felt very bad for the old men. They had little left but these pictures in their lap, nothing but the yellow newspaper clippings crumbling in their weathered hands, even as they showed them to me.

We killed hundreds of thousands of wolves. Sometimes with cause, sometimes with none. In the end, I think we are going to have to go back and look at the stories we made up when we had no reason to kill, and find some way to look the animal in the face again.

Four

AND A WOLF SHALL
DEVOUR THE SUN

Ten

OUT OF A MEDIEVAL MIND

U P to this point I have been considering wolves from three fairly distinct viewpoints: as objects of scientific inquiry, as objects of interest to people bound up in the natural world with them, and as objects of hatred for livestock raisers. But the points of view are not quite so distinct. And the intimation that the wolf can be objectified is one that must ultimately break down, even for science.

We create wolves. The methodology of science creates a wolf just as surely as does the metaphysical vision of a native American, or the enmity of a cattle baron of the nineteenth century. It is only by convention that the first is considered enlightened observation, the second fanciful anthropomorphism, and the third agricultural necessity.

Each of these visions flows, historically, from man's never-ending struggle to come to grips with the nature of the universe. That struggle has produced at different times in history different places for the wolf to fit; and at the same moment in history different ideas of the wolf's place in the universe have existed side by side, even in the same culture. So, in the wolf we have not so much an animal that we have always known as one that we have consistently *imagined*. To the human imagination the wolf has proved at various times the appropriate symbol for greed or savagery, the exactly proper guise for the Devil, or fitting as a patron of warrior clans.

How did people arrive at all these notions? The wish, of course, is to uncover some underlying theme that synthesizes all perceptions of the wolf, all allusions to him, in one grand animal. I will suggest some themes below, some ways to organize the visions so that when a human being suddenly confronts a wolf there can be both a sense of the richness of ideas associated with the animal and a sense that an orderly mind has been at work. But I am not hopeful that a feeling of integration will be forthcoming. And even if it is, I don't think it should be trusted. It seems important to be kept slightly off-balance through all this. Otherwise the temptation is to think that, although what we are examining may be complex, it is in the end reducible. I cannot, in the light of his effect on man, conceive of the wolf as reducible.

We embark then on an observation of an imaginary creature, not in the pejorative sense but in the enlightened sense—a wolf from which all other wolves are derived.

The entrance to the Pierpont Morgan Library in New York is shaded by London plane trees. On a cool autumn afternoon, with the stiff, sycamorelike leaves scraping the sidewalk in the wind and their dying yellows offset against the lush green of well-kept lawns, the building seems surrealistically isolated. It is not the wrought-iron gates through which you pass to the grounds or the oak doors by which you enter the building that sustain the illusion of being slightly out of time. It is the knowledge of what information rests on the shelves of this library, contrasted with the noise and impatience of the modern city streets outside.

Most of the scholars at work here in quiet rooms have come to read original sources, often in dead languages. They turn, or have turned for them, the leaves of manuscripts in one of the most extraordinary collections in the Western world. Among the many treasures are a twelfth-century bestiary; a life of an obscure English saint, Saint Edmund; a copy of Dante's *Divina commedia*, published on August 30, 1481, in Florence; and a fifteenth-century edition of Pliny's *Historia naturalis*.

I chose these books out of the thousands carefully preserved here because there are wolves in all of them, and because the Middle Ages, during which these very manuscripts were being either written or eagerly read, was a time when the wolf was distinctly present in folklore, in Church matters, and in the literature of the educated classes.

As one's fingers brush the crinkled vellum and parchment of the oversized folios, there is a stunning, almost electric sense of immediate communication with another age. The people who wrote or printed these texts were people who sat down to dinner like you and me, who marveled at the universe, who stood up and stretched at the end of the day. These people have long since turned to dust, but what they wrote remains behind, complete with grammatical errors and notes in Latin in the margin, made by some unknown Renaissance readers. Here, too, is the sense that even we in a more modern age are bound to this heritage.

In bestiaries like the one mentioned you will frequently find a woodcut of the wolf with his foot in his mouth—an allusion to the belief that if the wolf broke a twig and thereby alerted the shepherd's dogs to his presence, he would turn around and snap at his own foot to punish it.

In the history of Saint Edmund, a ninth-century king of England, appears the story of his murder and decapitation by invading Danes, and the statement that his head was guarded against further desecration by a great gray wolf, until it was retrieved by his friends a year later and properly buried.

In the first canto of Dante's Inferno in the *Commedia* the wolf appears in one of the oldest and most durable associations in its history, as a symbol of greed and fraud. In the eighth circle of Hell, Dante finds those condemned for "the sins of the wolf": seducers and hypocrites, magicians, thieves, and liars.

And in Pliny's *Historia naturalis* there is an account of werewolfry, one of the earliest, which Pliny himself passes on with skepticism. About a family called Anthus in Arcadia, Greece, one of whose members is chosen by lot every nine years *"abire in deserta transfigurarique in lupum"*—to go away into a deserted place and be transformed into a wolf.

You cannot examine any of these books without sensing that you have hardly touched in them the body of human ideas concerning the wolf. The wolf seems to move just beneath the pages of these volumes, loping along with that bicycling gait, through all of human history, appraised by all sorts of men but uttering itself not a word. Contact with this mystery seems as tenuous as the delicate movement of one's fingers over the vellum pages. Also in this library are copies of the story of Little Red Riding Hood hundreds of years old; the *Malleus Maleficarum* or *Hammer of Witches*, the authority used by the Inquisition to condemn hundreds of alleged werewolves to burn at the stake; and fourteenth-century encyclopedias with their collections of folk beliefs about wolves.

There is a record in this library of men's wolf thoughts, from the time of Aesop and before, from the age of Fenris and the other giant wolves of Teutonic myth, through the years of the werewolf trials, to the time of belief in wolf children in the modern era. There is no proper name for all this. It is one long haunting story of the human psyche wrestling with the wolf, alternately attracted to it and repelled by it. It is a story preserved with an almost eerie aura in a collection of medieval volumes like those at the Morgan.

All these ideas came to the fore at a particular time in history, in the Middle Ages—a time of growing enlightenment and of crushing ignorance and superstition. The medieval mind, more than any other mind in history, was obsessed with images of wolves. A belief in werewolves was widespread and strong. Pagan festivals in which wild men, mythic relatives of wolves, played the central roles were popular. Peasants were in revolt against their feudal lords, and the hated nobles were represented by wolves in the proletarian literature. Medieval peasants called famine "the wolf." Avaricious landlords were "wolves." Anything that threatened a peasant's precarious existence was "the wolf."

The wolf who stood guard over Saint Edmund's head.

Fear of real wolves occasionally bordered on hysteria. Wolves did kill travelers and they did occasionally transmit a terrible disease, always fatal, for which there was no cure: rabies. The wolf threatened a peasant's spiritual world by exhuming bodies, and hungry wolves standing in stark tableaus on piles of the dead during the Black Plague were a chilling reminder of what little separated peasants from a life of scavenging. A family's goats, sheep, cows, pigs, and poultry represented both sustenance and income to them—and it could all be wiped out in a single night by a pack of wolves.

The Roman Church, which dominated medieval life in Europe, exploited the sinister image of wolves in order to create a sense of real devils prowling in a real world. During the years of the Inquisition, the Church sought to smother social and political unrest and to maintain secular control by flushing out "werewolves" in the community and putting them to death. In so doing it deepened fears about the wolf, in whatever form.

In the dim woods that lay beyond the plowed fields of medieval villages there grew a sun spurge called wolf's milk (*Euphorbia helioscopia*), and wolf's fist (*Lycoperdon bovista*), and wolf's claw (*Lycopodium* sp.) and wolf's thistle (*Carlina acaulis*), and the small yellow flowers of the poisonous wolf's bane (*Aconitum lycoctonum*). On the perilous roads of these same dark woods travelers feared being waylaid by either highwaymen or wolves, and the two often fused in the medieval mind: the wolf and the outlaw were one, creatures who lived beyond the laws of human propriety. To call for "the wolf's head" was to pronounce death on a man accused of wrongdoing. He could then be killed by anyone without fear of legal recrimination. A belief in the transmigration of souls held that the soul of a highway robber would be enclosed after death in the body of a wolf. Edgar, the tenth-century English king, accepted in lieu of incarceration a set number of wolves' tongues from a convicted criminal according to the crime, as though one were turning state's evidence.

The medieval mind was one caught between the ignorance of the Dark Ages and the illumination of the Renaissance. In terms of the most potent architectural metaphor of the age, it was moving from a dimly lit Roman cathedral into a soaring Gothic church filled with windows and light.

*Among the animals named for their wolfish ways are the predatory wolf spiders (*Lycosidae *is the family) and wolf fish (in the genus* Anarrachichas), *and the wolf moth (*Tinea granella), *whose larvae used to destroy the contents of granaries. Pike fishes in the genus* Esox *are called freshwater wolves and the killer whale,* Orcinus orca, *has been called a sea wolf by both Indians and whites. There are also an African wolf snake (*Cryptolycus nanus) *and a wolf wasp (*Philanthus triangulum).*

It is perhaps not an accident that the wolf, a creature of the twilight hours, came and went so frequently in the expressions of a people emerging from the Dark Ages. From classical times he had been a symbol of things in transit. He was a twilight hunter, seen at dawn and dusk. From the common perception that his way of life bore some resemblance to that of primitive man came the idea that wolves themselves had taken form halfway between man and the other animals.

The link between the wolf and a period of halflight—either dawn or dusk, though dawn is more widely known as the hour of the wolf— suggests two apparently contradictory images. The first is the wolf as a creature of dawn, representing an emergence from darkness into enlightenment, intelligence, civilization. The second is a creature of dusk, representing a return to ignorance and bestiality, a passage back into the world of dark forces. Thus, in the Middle Ages, the wolf was companion to saints and the Devil alike. His howl in the morning elevated the spirit. Like the crow of the cock it signaled the dawn, the end of night and the hours of the wolf. His howl at night terrified the soul: the hours of the wolf (famine, witchery, carnage) were coming on.

The association is old enough to have been the basis for the Latin idiom for dawn, *inter lupum et canem*, between the wolf and the dog. Darkness and savagery are symbolized in the wolf, while enlightenment and civilization are symbolized in the tame wolf, the dog. Another Latin idiom expresses it a bit more abstractly: *Hac urget lupus, hac canis*, literally, "The wolf presses here, the dog (light) there," a reference to the dimly lit area between two fires in a Roman military camp.

The Greek for wolf, *lukos*, is so close to the word for light, *leukos*, that the one was sometimes mistaken for the other in translation. Some schol-

ars have argued that Apollo only came down to us as both the god of
dawn and a god associated with wolves because of this etymological confusion. But the association between wolf and twilight is found among too
many of the world's cultures to be so simply dismissed. One can turn,
for example, to the Icelandic *Eddas* or the Pawnee legend of the Wolf Star
and find the association among two vastly different peoples. In Latin,
again, the word for wolf, *lupus*, and that for light, *lucis*, are as close and
suggest a third association: that with the Devil. Lucifer (a contraction of
lucem ferre, literally, "to bear light") was called the Son of the Morning
by both the poet John Milton and the prophet Isaiah, and the wolf of the
Middle Ages was, of course, "the devil devourer of man's soul." Loki, the
Teutonic god of dawn, provides a second example of the link between
wolves, light, and the Devil, for the Christians recast him as the Evil
One when they proselytized among the Saxons. Long before this, however, Loki fathered Fenris, the huge wolf of Teutonic myth whose prog-
eny would devour the sun at the end of the world and precipitate *Götterdämmerung*, the twilight of the gods. There is a German folk rhyme
invented to help children learn the hours of the day that preserves this
fourth association between wolves and a return to darkness. It ends: *"um
elfe kommen die wolfe, um zwolfe bricht das gewölbe"*—at eleven come the
wolves, at twelve the tombs of the dead open.

If twilight is the time of the wolf, it is interesting to note that Mars,
before he became the Roman god of war, was the agricultural god of the
lands that separated cultivated fields from wild woods. The twilight
image of the wolf begins to resonate here with the sort of truth the mind
both generates and delights in, because Mars' special animal was no
other than the wolf.

The wolf as a symbol of war and lust, two very common associations
throughout Western history (and psychoanalysis), became an appropriate metaphor for Shakespeare in *Troilus and Cressida*. There the parallel
themes of violence and sex end in self-annihilation. The wolf is dead; the
beast in man is dead. There is promise in a fresh dawn.

The medieval mind was straining toward this dawn, toward dead
beasts, but it adhered to a prejudice against wolves at every level. Indeed, it fixed that prejudice in the human imagination so solidly that it

was not until the twentieth century that the human imagination could produce a new wolf, one that was no longer a projection of the confusion, superstition, depression, and anger that characterized the Middle Ages. In considering the roots of wolf imagery—from which all the wolves we know today spring—that age is pivotal. The chapters that follow, therefore, are loosely anchored in those years.

Eleven

THE REACH OF SCIENCE

T HERE is an old story about a wolf in Gubbio, Italy, involving Saint
Francis. The wolf had been threatening the villagers and Saint
Francis was trying to get the animal to desist. He and the wolf met one
day outside the city walls and made the following agreement, witnessed
by a notary: the residents of Gubbio would feed the wolf and let him
wander at will through the town and the wolf, for his part, would never
harm man nor beast there.

Beneath the popular, anecdotal appeal of this story is a common allegory: the bestial, uncontrolled nature of the wolf is transformed by sanc-
tity, and by extension those identified with the wolf—thieves, heretics,
and outlaws—are redeemed by Saint Francis's all-embracing compassion and courtesy.

Medieval men believed that they saw in wolves a reflection of their own bestial nature; man's longing to make peace with the beast in himself is what makes this tale of the Wolf of Gubbio one of the more poignant stories of the Middle Ages. To have compassion for the wolf, whom man saw as enslaved by the same base drives as himself, was to yearn for self-forgiveness.

Men came to such philosophical points chiefly through dialogue with the doctrines of the Roman Church, which preached both compassion and hatred for sinners, for the bestial, for the wolf in man. And yet when laymen came to ask, in effect, "What is this animal, *alone,* and how does he get on in the universe?" the Church responded less than compassionately. When laymen said, "Let's consider the wolf as a biological entity, quite apart from the Devil and pagan worship and evil and the symbolism of man's bestial nature," the Church, the seat of appeal for such inquiries in the Middle Ages, replied, "No, it would be inappropriate even to consider such a thing."

It was, in fact, an idea that only a handful of people in the long climb from Aristotle to Francis Bacon could have been expected to formulate.

If, at the moment when Saint Francis was accepting the wolf's promise outside the walls of Gubbio you had entered the shop of the local apothecary, you would have found many of that wolf's relatives laid up in jars and boxes. There would be wolf dung to treat colic and cataract, powdered wolf's liver to ease birth pains, and the right front paws of wolves to treat swelling in the throat. You'd find wolf teeth for teething, and, if the proprietor were open-minded and had had a visitor from the East, there might even be dried wolf's flesh stored away, after a Bedouin belief that it was good for aches in the shins.

Had you stepped into the street and gone to inquire of local learned men the contents of their library, they would likely have eagerly shown you, along with copies of the *Psalter* and the *Apocalypse,* a *Physiologus,* for these were the most popular illuminated books of the time. The *Physiologus* was a moralizing, didactic work in which elements of natural history—animals, vegetables, and minerals—were allegorically presented as reflections of the moral order in God's universe. A naturalist's curiosity about animals hardly existed. Animals were worth thinking on

The wolf of Gubbio, with Saint Francis.

only as food and clothing, as a source of economic gain, as beasts of burden, or as symbols. There was little concern for separating fact from folklore. Since the animal was an object, like a stone, there seemed no point in it.

The imaginative, often fabulous, entry on each animal in the *Physiologus* was preceded by a quote from Scripture and followed by a moral lesson. Accompanying illustrations, which had little to do with the natural world, were fanciful interpretations of the entry, which itself was contrived to fit the Scripture and produce a moral lesson as needed.

You might have asked yourself, standing in some library in Gubbio with a *Physiologus* in your hand, why human inquiry was stalled in such a curious place as this, a thousand years after Aristotle. The entry on wolves, staring up at you in Latin, would bear as accurately on the natural history of the wolf as his paw would compare with penicillin as treatment for goiter in a modern hospital.

I hesitate to single out the Church as the lone culprit to bear responsibility for such ignorance. Clearly, this was not so. But it is inescapable that the Church, because it largely controlled both the publication of books and the institutions of learning, profoundly affected the progress of natural history by subjecting it to theological constraint, by making it conform to preconceived ideas. What the Church supported, survived. What it regarded as in error—and a secular interest in animals smacked of paganism—did not.

Books like the *Physiologus*, in which zoology had been reduced to a search for edifying symbols, where wolves were important because they were the Devil's hounds, was almost the best a learned man could offer you in the way of natural history in the twelfth century.

To return to the apothecary's shop, here would be not only powdered wolf's liver but the gonads, entrails, excrement, and saliva of hundreds of other animals. The medical authority of record would be Galen, a second-century Greek physician. The science—as opposed to magic—of healing the human body began with Hippocrates and entered a limbo with Galen, through no fault of Galen's. He was taking monkeys and pigs apart and extrapolating from their anatomy to make statements about human anatomy. (Neither the Church nor the state at the time looked favorably on human dissection.) Galen was a Christian and the enormous encyclopedia of medical knowledge he wrote endorses a God-ordained balance between illness and its treatment by a physician, a mirror image of the treatment of the sinful soul by a priest. Because of its Christian bias, the book found favor with the Church and superseded the knowledge of other men for nearly a thousand years.

Galen and his errors (he endorsed many folk treatments involving the use of animal parts) were perpetuated, incredibly, until the sixteenth century, when Andreas Vesalius, William Harvey, and Anton van Leeuwenhoek reintroduced the use of reason, observation, and experiment as means to furthering medical knowledge. The fate of natural history in the Middle Ages was closely tied to what physicians thought of animals. Animals were a source of medicaments and useful as anatomical analogs, but how they lived was of little interest.

Natural history can be said to have begun formally with Aristotle. He wrote with some accuracy about wolves, in his *Historia animalium*, giving the period of gestation as from fifty-nine to sixty-three days, noting that

THE WOLF DISEASE

Seventeenth-century Europeans commonly referred to a lump that might announce breast cancer as a wolf. They similarly called open sores and knobs on their legs (and on the legs of their animals) wolves. In nineteenth-century medicine a type of general skin disorder characterized by ulcerative lesions and tubercules was called lupus vulgaris, *the common wolf. A related disorder was* lupus erythematosus unquium mutilans, *literally "the mutilated red talons of the wolf," a disease that attacks the hands and so disfigures the skin and nails that they look like the paws of a wolf. The notion is medieval and the hint of werewolves is hardly concealed. Today, systemic* lupus erythematosus *is recognized as one of the most puzzling disorders in medicine. An autoimmune or connective tissue disease like rheumatoid arthritis, its cause is unknown. The body simply produces antibodies that continue to attack healthy tissues. Eight out of ten victims are women, mostly in their child-bearing years. It remains incurable.*

females came into heat but once a year, that the pups were born blind, and that the wolves of Arabia were smaller than European wolves. He showed open skepticism about folklore as a basis for scientific fact, being very much in favor of personal observation. This is not to say he never passed on fancy for fact. Later in the same volume he writes, "The fleeces and wool of sheep that have been killed by wolves, as also the clothes made from them, are exceptionally infested with lice."

The scientific tradition of Aristotle was carried on by the Roman naturalist Pliny the Elder, in his *Historia naturalis,* and later by Solinus in his *Collectanea rerum memorabilium,* or *Polyhistor,* which repeats much of Pliny and Aristotle. And there, except for the redundant work of the encyclopedists—Aelian in the second century, Isidore in the seventh, Neckham in the twelfth, Bartholomew in the thirteenth—scientific interest in the lives of animals ends. Four hundred years after Aristotle, Plutarch was writing: "Wolves give birth to their young when acorn-bearing trees shed their blossoms because, when she-wolves eat these blossoms, their wombs are opened. When the blossoms are not available, the embryo dies in their body and cannot be expelled; for that reason those regions where there are no oaks or mast-trees cannot be troubled by wolves."

What replaced science was the folklore of the *Physiologus,* which, by the twelfth century, had expanded into the better known "bestiary."

• • •

The first *Physiologus*—the word is Greek for "the naturalist"—may have appeared in Syria in the fourth century B.C., but it does not turn up in the Western world for another five hundred years. A collection of popular stories about animals, plants, and gem stones, it is likely the product of many authors representing an amalgamation of the oral literature of the ancient world. Unlike Aristotle's contemporary *Historia animalium*, it made no pretense to scientific objectivity. Its authors were more intrigued by folklore, myth, and mysticism. The *Physiologus* was a book of wide popular appeal, probably as well known as Aesop, with which it soon came to share common features. Because of its popularity, it became an appropriate vehicle for didactic instruction. By the second and third centuries the stories in the *Physiologus* were being restructured to reflect Christian morals and world view. What was once entertaining pseudoscience had now become moral allegory.

This should not be construed so much as conscious plot on the part of the Church as a reflection of the intellectual climate of the times. Flor-

Twelfth-century bestiary, from England.

ence McCulloch, in a history of medieval Latin and French bestiaries, writes: "A characteristic of scholarship at this period was its preference for allegorical exegesis of the Scriptures and in like manner nature was interpreted mystically. Creatures of nature were to be explored for what they revealed of the hidden power and wisdom of God." Accordingly, the *Physiologus* that began to appear at this time soon incorporated Scripture and moral lessons into its format.

It is important to understand that most men of learning did not take the contents of the *Physiologus* for science. As McCulloch points out, "Illustrations used by the Church Fathers to render subtle theological concepts more intelligible and vivid to the unlettered people [cannot] be presumed to prove that medieval man actually believed such examples as were perpetuated in the *Physiologus* and later the bestiary."

The *Physiologus* did not come into its own until the seventh century, when it was expanded to include the work of Isidore of Seville, a Spanish bishop and encyclopedist. Isidore's *Etymologiae* was an attempt to set down all the knowledge of man in twenty books, the twelfth of which, *De animalibus*, was the source for material for a new *Physiologus*. Isidore's work is derivative. He borrowed heavily from Pliny and Solinus, and in some places drew ludicrous conclusions or passed on, unquestioning, the ignorance of those he drew from. But this is, nevertheless, one of the most important works from the early Middle Ages. (Of the wolf he tells us, erroneously, that the word *lupus* is derived from two words, *leo*, "lion," and *pes*, "foot," and means "lion-footed.")

By the ninth century the excessively nonsecular character of the *Physiologus* begins to show a secular influence, with the inclusion of chapters without Scripture or morals; but it is still the anonymous authors' intent to show that the natural world is but a reflection of the moral order of God's universe. By the twelfth century the *Physiologus* includes fanciful chapters on the dragon, the basilisk, the manticore, and the centaur, and is richly illustrated and widely enjoyed.

With natural curiosity about animals in a state of suspension and the natural world itself valuable only for the practical use to which it could be put, it is not *Canis lupus* we find in these bestiaries but the unabashed imagination of the times. The wolf does not appear in the earliest *Physiologi;* he does not show up consistently, in fact, until some time in the seventh century. After that we find a record in the section on wolves of most of the superstition that had come down from the time of the Greeks.

A thirteenth-century bestiary from the library of the monastery of Saint Victor in Paris, for example, tells (in the twentieth chapter of its second book, *De luporum natura*) of the association between wolves and light. The bestiarist also says it is appropriate that the Latin words for whore *(lupa)* and female wolf *(lupa)* should be the same, because both "plunder a man's goods." In the same bestiary the author cites Solinus as an authority for asserting that there is a tuft of hair on the wolf's tail with the power of an aphrodisiac, which the wolf bites off if capture is imminent.

The wolf of the *Physiologi* and the bestiaries could strike a man dumb with his gaze, though if the man saw the wolf first he could put the wolf to flight. (The *Malleus Maleficarum*, written by two Franciscans as philosophical underpinning for the excesses of the Inquisition, says that the sorcerer can bewitch "by a mere look or glance from the eyes." This and the above, I suspect, explains the origin of the French idiom *elle a vu le loup*, "She's seen the wolf," meaning she's lost her virginity.) A common illustration in these books was that of a man standing on his shirt and clacking two rocks together, a method offered for curing dumbness. The wolf of the bestiary was reputed to have only one cervical vertebra; thus he was unable to turn his head and look behind him. Some said the backbone was so stiff that a wolf taken by the tail could be held under water, stiff as a board, until drowned. Aristotle and Pliny are cited as authorities here and, to be sure, both say the wolf has only one, not seven, cervical vertebrae.

The wolf was also thought to eat earth in times of great famine. Drawing on information in the bestiaries, Albertus Magnus wrote in the thirteenth century:

"It is said the wolves eat the mud called *glis*, not for the sake of getting nourishment but to make themselves heavier. Having eaten it the wolf preys on very strong animals—the ox or stag or horse—by leaping at them, straight on, and clinging to them. If he were light he would readily be shaken off, but when he is weighed down by *glis*, he weighs so much that he can neither be shaken off nor gotten rid of. Presently when

In French to be known by everyone is to be as well known as the white wolf, il est connu comme le loup blanc. To sneak along is to walk with the step of a wolf, marcher à pas le loup. Speak of the wolf and he appears, quand on parle du loup, on en voit la queue (literally, one speaks of the wolf and one sees his tail). The word loup *can mean* wolf *or, in different contexts, a flaw in cabinetmaking, an error in calculation, or a blown entrance in the theatre. A black velvet mask worn at a costume ball, a device used to pull nails, and a machine used to break apart bales of wool are also "wolves."*

In the fields of France the wolf is a spirit of the crops. When the wind blows in waves across the fields the peasants say "the wolf is going through." When young children go to pick the blue cornflowers the parents warn of the wolf that sits in the corn. If a wolf is seen out in the fields they look to see if it carries its tail high or low. If the tail hangs straight down it is the crop spirit himself, and they salute him.

At harvest time the wolf moves through the fields of grain just ahead of the reapers. If a man stumbles or cuts himself with a scythe they say, "The wolf got him." When they come to the last sheaf in the field, that is called the wolf sheaf and the person who cuts it (who kills the wolf in doing so) is called the wolf until spring. The sheaf is called the rye wolf or the wheat wolf or the corn wolf, accordingly. In some areas it is burned, in others taken home and destroyed in the spring.

In the farm country around Bordeaux a wether, or castrated sheep, was led around the fields, its horns dressed with flowers and small harvest sheaves, its body wound with garlands and bright ribbons. Its sacrifice signaled the death of the wolf corn spirit.

---

his prey is worn out and collapses, he tears at their throats and windpipes and so kills them. Then he vomits out the *glis* and feasts on the flesh of the animal he has slain."

Other beliefs endorsed by the bestiarists were that the wolf was repelled by squill, or sea onion; that a horse that stepped in a wolf print would be crippled; that a pregnant mare who kicked a wolf would miscarry; that wolf-bitten mutton is sweeter; and that wolves are repulsed by music. The bulb of the squill (*Urginea maritima* and other species) was hung around the neck of sheep in a flock to ward off wolves and carried as a protection by travelers. (Red squill is still used today in Europe as a rat poison.) That the wolf should be considered the bane of the horse, a principal domesticated beast of burden with more nobility than the ass, the ox, or the cow, is evidence of the moral structuring of the bestiaries. The Devil seeks the saintliest to bring down. For the same reason a sheep picked out of the flock and killed by wolves took on special significance. That the meat would taste sweeter might be an opinion derived from Plutarch, who wrote that the breath of the wolf was so hot it softened and cooked the meat it devoured. Others felt, very strongly, that wolf-bitten meat was poisonous. Jacob Grimm writes in *Teutonic Mythology* of the belief that any woman who ate wolf-bitten lamb or goat would give birth to a child that showed the wolf bite in its flesh.

Aelian, the third-century Roman, tells in *De natura animalium* the story of Pythochares, a flute player who drove off a pack of wolves with his music. This is an early reference to the widespread and persistent belief that wolves hate music. An analogous belief is that a drum with a wolf skin head will drown out any number of drums with sheepskin heads, or that a string of wolf gut will dominate strings of sheep gut. In music today a discordant note on the violin is still called a wolf, as are the harsh, howling sounds of some chords on the organ.

It is apparently not the music of clacking stones, in the case of the man struck dumb, that frightens the wolf off and returns speech, however. Wolves, writes one sixteenth-century writer, hate stones and avoid them wherever they go because the bruises they cause breed worms. Richard Lupton, a medieval English writer, puts it quaintly: "When he is constrained to go by stony places, the wolf treads very demurely. For being hurt with a very little stroke of a stone, it breeds worms, whereof at length he is consumed and brought to his death."

T. H. White, in a modern translation of a twelfth-century bestiary, gives us the moralizing on this point: "For what can we mean by the Wolf but the Devil . . . and what by the stones but the Apostles or the saints or the Lord Himself? All the prophets have been called stones of adamant. And He Himself, Our Lord Jesus Christ, has been called in the Law 'a stumbling block and a rock of scandal.' "

Who could argue that it was in the nature of wolves to hate stones?

There is a third group of books, after the natural histories of Aristotle and Pliny and the bestiaries and *Physiologi*, that sought to reveal the wolf and those are the encyclopedias of such men as Alexander Neckham, Albertus Magnus, and Bartholomew of England. They wrote in the tradition of Isidore but much later—Neckham in the twelfth century, and Magnus and Bartholomew along with Vincent of Beauvais in the thirteenth. In the work of the encyclopedists one finds more political and social allegory than moral allegory, and a good deal of folklore. Bartholomew tells us that wolves eat marjoram to whet their appetites and sharpen their teeth before leaving for the evening hunt, and that they are fond of fish. In fact, he tells us, if wolves find a fisherman's nets on the beach and see no fish around they will tear the nets in anger, a story Aristotle perhaps told first about wolves near Lake Maeotis in Greece. Albertus Magnus writes that any man who binds a wolf's right eye to his right sleeve will be protected against men and dogs alike.

Lupton in his *Notable Things* catalogues the habits of hanging up a wolf's head to keep sorcerers at bay and of burying a wolf's tail at the entrance to a village to keep off other wolves. The grease rendered from a wolf's body, he says, will protect the hands from the worst cold, and wolf dung buried in the barnyard to keep off wolves will drive sheep and cattle crazy until it is removed.

And an English writer of the sixteenth century, Edward Topsell, in *A Historie of Foure-footed Beastes*, fascinates us with the following:

"The brains of a wolf do decrease and increase with the moon. The neck of a wolf is short which argueth a treacherous nature. If the heart of a wolf be kept dry, it rendereth a most pleasant or sweet-smelling savor. They will go into the water two-by-two, every one hanging upon another's tail, which they take in their mouths. . . . Their manner is when they fall upon a goat or a hog, not to kill them, but to lead them by the ear and with all the speed they can drive them to their fellow-wolves; and if the beast be stubborn, and will not run with them, then he beateth his hinder parts with his tail, holding his ear fast in his mouth. But if it be a swine that is so gotten, then they lead him to the waters, and there kill him, for if they eat him not out of cold water, their teeth doth burn with an intolerable heat. . . . If any labouring or travelling man doth wear the skin of a wolf about his feet, his shoes shall never pain or trouble him. He which doth eat the skin of a wolf well tempered and sodden will keep him from all evil dreams, and cause him to take his rest quietly. The teeth of a wolf being rubbed upon the gums of the young infants doth open them whereby the teeth may the easier come forth."

• • •

On the twenty-third of April, Eastern
Europeans celebrate the feast of Saint George,
a patron of cattle, horses, and wolves. On the
morning of the feast day, provided various
taboos have been observed, Saint George
rings the wolves' snouts and puts them on
leashes so the herds can be taken out to spring
pasture for the first time without fear. Wolf
dung is sometimes burned—or asafetida
(devil's dung)—and the cattle are herded
through the smoke to absorb its scent.

It was believed that if you sewed anything
together on Saint George's morning, wolves
born that spring would lose their sight, as
though their eyes had been sewn shut. A
peasant who wished to know which of his
sheep would fall prey to wolves in the months
following set eggs on the ground before the
barn. Those that stepped on the eggs would be
killed before the year was out by wolves. To
salvage the meat, a peasant might slaughter
the sheep right there.

In Russia the same feast is that of Saint
Yury, and the wolf is known as Saint Yury's
dog. During the year wolf-killed sheep and
cattle are not disturbed. They are considered
the animals Saint George has set aside for the
wolves.

It was an urge to inform that motivated writers like Topsell, just as it
was an urge to teach that saw the Christianization of the *Physiologus*. The
wolf did not come off well in either effort. Even Renaissance veneries
like *Tuberville's Booke of Hunting* (1577), which explain knowledgeably
how to lure wolves to a blind and praise the devotion of young wolves to
their parents, still have them eating snakes and killing each other "for
spite."

Secular inquiry into the lives of animals, inquiry for the sake of *learning* rather than for the sake of edifying moral lessons or entertainment,
did not begin again until the sixteenth century. At that point we find
Konrad Genser's *Historia animalium*, published in 1551, and the animal
encyclopedias of Aldorvandi. But it is not until the eighteenth and
nineteenth centuries—when Carolus Linnaeus provides a system of organization, Charles Darwin writes of finches in the Galapagos, and John
James Audubon draws birds in Florida—that the system of knowledge
that had taken natural history for little more than symbology or a source
of literary entertainment begins to break up. And for the wolf, astound-
ingly, the tradition continues almost unbroken until 1945, when *The
Wolves of North America* by Stanley Young and Edward Goldman was
published. A mixture of science and folklore, it passed as the only au-

thoritative general work on wolves in America and Europe until the 1960s. Aside from Adolph Murie's *The Wolves of Mount McKinley*—the first unbiased ecological treatise on wolves, published in 1944—and a couple of popular books, there was nothing else around.

It is hard to conceive of another animal—I don't think there is one— that has suffered such prejudice as an object of our scientific curiosity.

I recall one afternoon, sitting in a university library, reading in the *Journal of Mammalogy* about a biologist named Eugene Johnson who was in Alaska observing wolves. He was able to approach a wolf pup in his canoe without being seen. In his lap he had a small shotgun loaded with buckshot. Each time the pup, who was walking along the riverbank, looked up, Johnson put the paddle down and raised his gun. "There was not the slightest chance," he wrote, "that two buckshot might find a vital spot at that distance, but I felt we ought not to deny ourselves what satisfaction we might get out of frightening the beast to the utmost of our ability."

That was written in 1921. It is, of course, an isolated incident, but it properly belies the sometimes arrogant claims of science to objectivity. It was just such biologists as this whom stockmen sought out in the twentieth century to support with "scientific testimony" ideas about wolves that they might as well have gotten from Edward Topsell.

That some scientists obliged them is one of the sadder facts of man's association with wild animals, and of the politics of science.

Twelve

SEARCHING FOR THE BEAST

Y OU do not have to explain to anyone that wolves and sheep
don't get along. When Lord Byron wrote in *The Destruction of
Sennacherib* that "the Assyrian came down like a wolf on the fold," he did
not leave his readers struggling for his meaning, and when Chaucer
wrote in The Parson's Tale of "the devil's wolves that strangle the sheep
of Jesus Christ," his Christian audience did not wonder that it should be
wolves who do the Devil's work. War correspondents writing of German
wolfpacks prowling the North Atlantic clearly conveyed the Allied perception of the Third Reich as a creature of abominable cruelty and greed
preying on Europe. And people reading of The Wolf Lair, a fanciful Allied name for the Führer's military retreat in eastern Prussia, found it
very apt. Had someone noted, further, that the name Adolf was a con-

traction of *Edel-wolf*, the noble wolf, the reader would have understood.

The human mind entertains itself with such symbols and metaphors, sorting out the universe in an internal monologue, and I think it delights in wolves. The wolf is a sometime symbol of evil, and the mind dotes on distinctions between good and evil. He is a symbol of the warrior, and we are privately concerned with our own courage and nobility. The wolf's is also a terrifying image, and the human mind likes to frighten itself.

The symbolism and metaphor of wolf imagery is not vast, but it is potent. It is rooted in the bedrock of the soul. The tradition of the wolf as warrior-hero is older than recorded history. The legends of Romulus and Remus and other wolf children point up another ancient image, that of the benevolent wolf-mother. The deaths of those taken for werewolves and burned alive in the Middle Ages represent yet another, focusing negative feelings about the wolf. As old as these, though not as widespread outside Europe, is the sexual imagery associated with wolves, the Latin *lupa* for whore and female wolf, the wolf whistle, and the French idiom *elle a vu le loup*. On the walls of a Roman catacomb the story of the compromising of the voluptuous Susanna by two elders is depicted as a sheep crowded by two wolves.

I wrote above of the wolf as a symbol for twilight. Other writers have suggested, and I agree with them, that the wolf was a symbol reflecting two human alternatives at war: instinctual urges and rational behavior. In *Hesitant Wolf and Scrupulous Fox*, Karen Kennerly says the wolf is the creature who is most like us in animal fable. "Out of phase with himself," she says, "he is defeated alternately by hubris and naivete. . . . He becomes the irreconcilability between instinct and rational thought." His attempt to live a rational life is defeated by his urge to behave basely. Thus, the human and bestial natures.

Throughout history man has externalized his bestial nature, finding a scapegoat upon which he could heap his sins and whose sacrificial death would be his atonement. He has put his sins of greed, lust, and deception on the wolf and put the wolf to death—in literature, in folklore, and in real life.

The central conflict between man's good and evil natures is revealed in his twin images of the wolf as ravening killer and (something we have not examined before) as nurturing mother. The former was the werewolf; the latter the mother to children who founded nations.

Today we, like most people in history, are favorably inclined toward surrogate wolf-mothers, even if we consider such things folklore. But we have lost track of werewolves in the twentieth century. Werewolves were a stark reality in the Middle Ages. Their physical presence was not doubted; at a symbolic level the werewolf represented all that was base in man, especially savagery and lust. If, as Kennerly and others suggest, to love what was good in the wolf was really to express self-love, and to hate what was evil in the wolf was to express self-hate, then the hunting down of werewolves was simply the age-old attempt to isolate and annihilate man's base nature. That it went on for so many hundreds of years indicates an abiding self-hatred in man.

Reflection on what happened in the Great Plains in America during the wolf wars reveals a certain amount of self-hatred, but we are drawn back inevitably to the Middle Ages. At a time when no one knew anything about genetics, the idea that a child suffering from Down's syndrome—small ears, a broad forehead, a flat nose, prominent teeth—was the offspring of a wench and a werewolf was perfectly plausible. The Middle Ages were a melancholy time, accurately reflected I think in the surreal and grotesque imagery of painters like Heironymus Bosch and Pieter Brueghel the Younger; a time of famine, of endless wars, of epidemic disease, of social upheaval. Civilization was not as precious as it is to us today. The temptation to strike back at a painful world must have been strong. There were herbs to be purchased. There were Faustian pacts that could be made. Wanting to *be* a werewolf, in other words, was somehow understandable. In a history of witchcraft in the Middle Ages, Jeffrey Russell has written that some peasants were moved by "the Promethean urge to bend both nature and other people to their own ends . . . to obtain the objects of their pecuniary or amatory desire or to exact revenge on those whom they feared or hated."

Given a depressed populace, a belief in werewolves, and the intimidation practiced by the court of the Inquisition, it is not surprising that people panicked and confessed precipitously to being werewolves, to having committed crimes against nature. And it wasn't just werewolves;

in 1275 a deranged woman named Angela de la Barthe confessed to the Inquisition at Toulouse that she had given birth to a creature that was half wolf, half snake, and that she had kept it alive by feeding it human babies she stole. In 1425 in Neider-Hauenstein near modern Basel a woman was sentenced to death for consorting with wolves, on whom, it was alleged, she had ridden across the night sky.

The Middle Ages were years of very deep frustration for human beings, caught in the twilight between the Dark Ages and the Renaissance. It was the time of the wolf. And anger that men felt over their circumstances, they heaped on wolves.

But before the story of the werewolf can begin, another story must be told. There is a character in the bestiaries, *L'homme sauvage*, the wild man of the woods, whose path intersected the werewolf's. The wild man was the product of an evolutionary synthesis of Pan and Dionysius, Roman

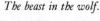

The beast in the wolf.

gods of the pasture and the harvest respectively. Dressed in a suit of bright, tattered cloth, he was a central figure throughout the Middle Ages in the ancient pagan midwinter celebrations. In that same tattered suit he later became the harlequin figure in the commedia dell'arte and also Shakespeare's Caliban in *The Tempest*. A carnal, frivolous, somewhat slow-witted prankster most of the time, he was also thought of as a somber, almost ascetic loner, wandering the vast stretches of thick forests that lay between medieval settlements, eating berries, roots, and wild game. He shared the dank, dismal woods with religious and social outcasts and with the wolf, who stood as symbol for them all. Most importantly for our interest, the wild man was associated with acts of depravity and sexual indulgence. As his image began to diffuse in the 1400s and 1500s, these qualities were impressed on the werewolf.

The wild man, depicted in scenes such as the Rape of Proserpine (where he appears as Pluto), was widely popular. The art historian Richard Bernheimer, speculating on the vigor of the wild man's survival through the ages, writes: "It appears that the notion of the wild man must respond and be due to a persistent psychological urge. We may define this urge as the need to give external expression and symbolically valid form to the impulses of reckless physical assertion which are hidden in all of us but are normally kept under control."

And the historian Jeffrey Russell says in his *Witchcraft in the Middle Ages:* "The wild man, both brutal and erotic, was a perfect projection of the repressed libidinous impulses of medieval man. His counterpart, the wild woman, who was a murderess, child-eater, bloodsucker and occasionally a sex nymph, was a prototype of the witch." The latter recalls the vargamors in Scandinavia, women who procured human victims for their wolf companions, frequently by promising sexual favors. Bernheimer's and Russell's statements both reflect the beast in search of a violent sexual connection. And indeed it is not surprising to find as a common theme, especially in the later Middle Ages (and still later more violently in pulp novels), men who became werewolves solely to avenge rejection by a lover. (It is rare that women become werewolves. When they do, it is almost always as a means to an end—to steal a child victim for a sabbat, for example.)

There are other places where the paths of the wild man and the werewolf cross. The Twelve Days between Christmas and Epiphany were the days of the wild man rituals in Europe and also the time when werewolves were supposed to be on a rampage. The men who dressed up to portray wild men during the celebrations were expected to drink to excess, to abuse women, to behave like Berserker, a fanatic cult of Teutonic warriors who dressed in wolf and bear skins. In the Baltic countries, in fact, their behavior was hardly distinguished from the rampages of the Wild Horde in Teutonic legend.

The wild man and the werewolf alike were metamorphosed from formidable forces in the pagan imagination, through the grotesque, almost psychopathic imagery of the Middle Ages, to become the derivative, often impotent and pathetic caricatures we find in movies and pulp literature today.

The legend of the werebeast is almost universal. In each country primitive beliefs in shapeshifting (the human ability to change to an animal form) combine with beliefs in sorcery to produce a fearsome local werebeast who goes about at night usually, but not always, slaying human beings. In Africa there were werehyenas, in Japan there were werefoxes, in South America there were werejaguars, in Norway there were werebears. In Europe there were werewolves.

The werebeast might be a sorcerer bent on killing an enemy, like the Navajo werewolf. He might be a victim under a sorcerer's curse, wandering melancholy about the countryside, as was said of werewolves in White Russia. Or he might be benevolent and protective, like Alphouns, the werewolf of a twelfth-century romance, *William of Parlerne*, who acted as a protector to the rightful heir to the Sicilian throne. There is nothing inherently evil in the idea of shapeshifting, which is why some benevolent werewolf stories survive. But as the wolf came to stand more and more for the bestial, for the perverse, for evil in every form, the simple phenomenon of shapeshifting was overshadowed by the presence of a terrible creature that preyed on everything human and, in the most voyeuristic stories, engaged in a level of violence and sexual depravity that had not the remotest connection with any animal but man himself. It is important to keep this in mind, because in looking to the "werewolves" of primitive ages there is a tendency to telescope backward ideas that only developed much later.

• • •

The werewolf of our legends took form, in part, in Greece. At the tip of the Balkan peninsula lies a landmass known as the Peloponnesus and at its center is a region known as Arcadia. According to Greek legend, Lycaon, the son of Pelasgus, civilized Arcadia and instituted the worship of Zeus there. Word later reached Zeus that Lycaon's many sons were lax in their religious duties and arrogant toward their father. Zeus decided to visit them, disguised as a day laborer, and see for himself.

When he came to Lycaon's house he was welcomed, but Lycaon's sons convinced their father to serve the stranger human flesh, to see if he might be Zeus in disguise. Nyktimos, one of the sons, was killed and his entrails were mixed with the meat of sheep and goats. A bowl of this was then set before the god. Zeus hurled the bowl to the floor, changed Lycaon and all his sons into wolves (except Nyktimos, whom he restored), and stormed out.

Still angry over Lycaon's blasphemy and incensed at the ways of men in general, Zeus unleashed a flood to drown them all. Deucalion's flood (named for the man who built an ark and escaped) destroyed Lycaon and his sons, but some survivors who later emigrated to Arcadia ritually killed people to satisfy the gods. These survivors were former residents of the country around Mount Parnassus. Ironically, they had been awakened on the night of the flood by the howling of wolves who led them to high ground. An Arcadian practice in later centuries, according to the geographer Pausanius, was to prepare a meal like the one served Zeus and set it before a group of shepherds. The one who found human entrail in his bowl ate it, howled like a wolf and, leaving his clothing hung on an oak, swam across a stream where he remained in a desolate region as a werewolf for nine years. If in that time he ate no human flesh he regained his human form.

This is the story Pliny tells in the *Historia naturalis*. He adds that an Arcadian youth named Damarchos who had become a wolf under these circumstances abstained from human flesh, regained his form, and later won a boxing match in the Olympic Games. Socrates alludes to the story in Plato's *Republic* when he says that a beneficent ruler (like Lycaon) is destined to become a tyrant if ever he tastes human flesh, that is, if he should ever arrange to have a political enemy murdered.

Lycaon's name is preserved in the scientific name for the Eastern timber wolf, *Canis lupus lycaon*, and in the name for a kind of delusion and melancholy in which a person believes himself to be a wolf but retains his human form—lycanthropy.

The origin of this story is vague. Most scholars shy away from regarding Zeus as a wolf-god to whom humans might have been sacrificed. They hold that he was a god of light and that the terms were, again, confused in Greek. The element of human sacrifice and the inclusion of wolves in the story may have come about like this. The Arcadians were an agricultural people. It may have been the custom for the reigning king to take his own life to propitiate the gods if the crops failed. In time, a modification of this practice was introduced whereby the king had someone else sacrificed in his place. To expiate his guilt at this, the king shared responsibility for the murder with those whom he invited to a ritual meal. One of this number was then chosen by lot to atone for the sin by being banished from human society—for nine years.

This is all plausible and probable. It may have been, too, that later the cult of Zeus was grafted onto an existing wolf cult in Greece that actually sacrificed human beings in an effort to placate wolves (the Arcadians kept flocks and the Peloponnesus was thick with wolves). Deucalion's flood, then, may represent the civilizing Hellenistic invasion that wiped out the practice of human sacrifice, leaving it to survive only in isolated places like Arcadia.

Whatever its origin and meaning, the story offers a perception of the wolf as bestial man who can, if he controls his animal appetite for nine years, attain the status of a human being. The connection between the outlaw or outcast and the wolf is also made clear.

We draw most of our werewolf tradition from northern and eastern Europe, but I chose this Greek legend to begin this section on werewolves because it is so succinct. It grew up among people who probably considered wolves enemies, and it voices one of the most persistent taboos in the folklore of Western man, that against eating human flesh. The wolf seen eating human carrion on a medieval battlefield was reviled because he was held to be sufficiently endowed to know that what he was doing was wrong but was base enough to do it anyway. The quintessential sinner.

A poignant aspect of the wolf's predicament emerges here. In a hunter society, like that of the Cheyenne, traits that were universally admired—courage, hunting skill, endurance—placed the wolf in a pantheon of respected animals; but when man turned to agriculture and husbandry, to cities, the very same wolf was hated as cowardly, stupid, and rapacious. The wolf itself remains unchanged but man now speaks of his hated "animal" nature. By standing around a burning stake, jeering at and cursing an accused werewolf, a person demonstrated an allegiance to his human nature and increased his own sense of well-being. The tragedy, and I think that is the proper word, is that the projection of such self-hatred was never satisfied. No amount of carnage, no pile of wolves in the village square, no number of human beings burned as werewolves, was enough to end it. It is, I suppose, not that different from the slaughter of Jews at the hands of the Nazis, except that when it happens to animals it is easier to forget. In the case of the werewolf, however, it must be recalled that we *are* talking about human beings.

Herodotus wrote that the Neurians who lived in present-day western Russia changed into wolves for a few days once a year. The Neurians were hunters who probably had a totemistic relationship with wolves and wore wolf skins in an annual ceremony; but this mention by Herodotus is commonly cited as evidence that early on there was a race of werewolves. Pliny and others mention a wolf cult at Mount Soracte near Rome. The members danced in wolf skins and walked through fire carrying the entrails of sacrificial animals. It is not hard to see how the propitiation of wolves who threatened flocks, combined with older totemistic relationships, easily created the impression of werewolves hundreds of years later.

The story of the werewolf in Petronius's *Satyricon* is often cited as evidence of a belief in werewolves in Rome at the time of Christ, but people tend to forget that the story was written to entertain. Any historical value is fortuitous. Petronius's tale is of a man who changes into a wolf and attacks a herd of cattle before being driven off with a pitchfork wound in the neck. The narrator in the story later finds his good friend suffering from a pitchfork wound in the same place. It is convincing evidence that he is, in Petronius's word, a *versipellis*, a skin changer. (This element—a wolf is wounded and a human being is later found with a similar wound—was the basis of proof in many werewolf trials.)

The werewolf stories from northern Europe typically were more robust, adventurous, and inventive than these classical Greek and Roman stories. Olaus Magnus writes in his *History of the Goths* that at Christmas werewolves gathered together for drinking bouts and forcefully entered houses for the purpose of raiding the wine cellar. The element of debauchery he introduced into the lore of the werewolf was probably adapted from the Teutonic legend of the Wild Horde that rode out at night astride wolves. Or from tales of the Berserker. That it took place at Christmas could mean Magnus's story was based on wild tales of the pagan midwinter festivals celebrating the return of the sun, or that it was Christianized so that the wolves were drunk on Christ's birthday, thus adding to the sacrilege.

Magnus also wrote that the werewolves of Livonia gathered at Christmas and, like the Arcadian werewolves, swam across a body of water to effect their transformation. They remained werewolves for twelve days, until the Epiphany, drank heavily, and at some point, says Magnus, gathered at the walls of an old castle where they engaged in leaping contests. The ones who couldn't jump the wall were beaten by the Devil.

Debauchery and sacrilege, which became common in werewolf stories later, are not the themes of early Teutonic werewolf tales. Violence is, however. In the Icelandic saga of the Volsungs, King Volsung's daughter Signy marries a king named Siggeir. Siggeir, whose mother is a werewolf, turns around and kills Volsung and puts his ten sons into stocks to feed his mother. The tenth son, Sigmund, escapes and Signy later bears him a son. One day Sigmund and his son come on a house in the woods where two men are sleeping. Hung on the wall over the head of each is a wolf skin. Sigmund believes the men are werewolves and that by donning the skins he and his son will be transformed for nine days. They put the skins on, agree not to kill more than seven men each, and go their separate ways. But the son kills eleven men and his angry father, still in wolf form, attacks and wounds him. His anger abated, filled with remorse, the father nurses his son's wounds. On the ninth day they regain human form, throw the wolf skins on a fire, and agree never to do such a thing again.

The Livonian wolves at the leaping wall.

Marie de France, writing in the latter part of the twelfth century, created the prototype of the sympathetic werewolf in a romantic narrative poem, or lay, called *Lai du Bisclavret*, "Bisclavret" being the name by which the werewolf was known in Brittany. In the story a French baron, besieged by his anxious wife, finally tells her that when he disappears for three days every week it is to roam the woods as a werewolf. Terrified, the wife induces her lover to follow the baron into the woods and steal his clothes. Without the clothes her husband cannot return to human form. This the lover does, and he and the wife are married while the baron's friends mourn his disappearance.

A year later the king is out hunting when his dogs overtake Bisclavret. The big wolf takes the king's stirruped boot in his paws and implores with his eyes for the dogs to be called off. The king orders the dogs away and returns home with the wolf, who becomes his tame and loving companion. Later, traveling in the vicinity of the baron's old castle with the wolf and his retinue, he is visited by the baron's wife. The wolf goes mad when he sees the woman, biting off her nose. The story of her betrayal comes out. She and her lover are banished and, with the

An Irish priest was on his way from Ulster to Meath when he was approached by a wolf who spoke to him. The wolf assured him that there was nothing to fear, it was just that his wife was dying and he wished the Last Rites for her. They were both victims of a curse pronounced on the people of Ossory by Saint Natalis, according to which every seven years two people had to don wolf skins and live as wolves. The priest was terrified but he followed the wolf into the woods. At some distance he found a female wolf lying ill beneath a tree. The priest stood frozen, *unable to act. The wolf reached down and rolled back the female's wolf skin and the priest saw underneath the bony torso of an old woman. No longer afraid, he heard her confession and gave her the Last Rites.*

The wolf accompanied the priest back to the highway, thanked him profusely and told him that if he lived out his seven years he would search the priest out and thank him properly.

The priest went on his way, satisfied he had done right.

—GIRALDUS CAMBRENSIS, 1188

return of his clothes, the baron regains his form and returns to his castle.

The werewolf of Marie de France's story is an involuntary one, a human being under a curse. By the time of the werewolf trials in the Middle Ages, an amalgamation of folklore and superstition had created such distinctions among types of werewolves and a body of lore on how transformations were affected and reversed. By then, too, a curtain of evil separated werewolves from their relatively benign origins. The imitative magic of the Pawnee wolf scouts had been reduced to voodoo.

Some werewolves became so voluntarily. A voluntary werewolf was a sorcerer who, typically, got the power of transformation from the Devil in a Faustian exchange. His transformation could be effected by donning a wolf skin or magic belt, by sipping water from the print of a wolf, by ingesting roots, by applying ointments, by drinking from certain streams, by charms, or by some action, such as swimming across a certain body of water or rolling around on the ground (epileptics were often taken for werewolves). An involuntary werewolf came to his form as the result of a family curse or a spell cast by a sorcerer—out of hate, for pay, or at the Devil's behest. A person also became a werewolf when he was born to a certain tribe, like the Seiar of Hadramaut, a Semitic people, or the residents of Ossory in Ireland. There is a Polish belief that a belt of human skin laid across the threshold of a house where a wedding is taking place will change all who step over it into wolves. And it was a general belief in Europe that those unfortunate enough to be born on Christmas Eve would be werewolves. Slavs believed those born feet first became werewolves, Scandinavians that the seventh girl born in a row to a family did. According to a legend from the Caucasus, a woman who committed adultery became a werewolf for seven years.

Elliot O'Donnell, a modern English author, writes in his book *Werwolves* that werewolves could be told "by the long, straight, slanting eyebrows, which meet in an angle over the nose, sometimes by the hands the third finger of which is a trifle longer; or by the fingernails, which are red, almond shaped and curved; sometimes by the ears, which are set low and rather far back on their head; and sometimes by a noticeably long, swinging stride, which is strongly suggestive of some animal." In human form the werewolf might show a vestigial tail between his shoulder blades and the Russians believed he had bristles under his tongue. In wolf form the werewolf was supposed to be tailless.

A werewolf regained human form by putting his clothes back on, taking the wolf skin off, or slipping the buckle of his wolf belt to the ninth hole. A werewolf could be cured if his wolf skin were burned, if he were slashed across the forehead three times and bled in a prescribed manner, or if he were addressed by his Christian name while being denounced as a tool of Satan. A werewolf named Peter Andersen in Denmark was apparently cured when his wife threw her apron in his face as he attacked her, as he had instructed her to do. Another was cured when his son threw a hat at him. They could also be caught and bound and exorcised with potions. According to O'Donnell, a common one was one-half ounce of sulfur, one-half ounce of asafetida or devil's dung, and one-quarter ounce of castor in clear spring water. Another was one-quarter ounce of hypericum compounded with three ounces of vinegar. These mixtures were used in sabbatlike settings by priests or friends of the victim, who was burned and beaten by young girls with ash switches in the process. Mountain ash, along with rye and mistletoe, were considered protection against werewolves.

The werewolf phenomenon might have languished in the folklore of the countryside but for two things: the wolf, *Canis lupus*, posed both a real and an imagined threat of major proportions in the medieval mind; and the legend of the werewolf suited the needs of the Inquisition, which did more to sustain the belief by fanatical persecution than any other agent or institution.

The Christian Church was historically embattled from the beginning. Without an enemy to fight, it had no identity. Until the time of the Christian emperors, the enemy was the state. Then it was the paganism of northern Europe. Then came the Crusades and the war against the infidel. After the reign of Charlemagne, the enemy was increasingly heresy, particularly reformism. By the time the Inquisition begins in the thirteenth century the perception of the Church about the enemy is clear: he is the heretic. Behind the heretic, like a puppet master, is the Devil. The wolf in the sheepfold. Once only a vague idea for theologians, the Devil has by now become a full-blown personality. As the Middle Ages begin he is a superhuman presence, as real as hogs tearing a child apart in a pigsty. The heretic is the means to destroy Christ's Church on earth. Only by destroying the heretic could the enemy be vanquished. Witches, sorcerers, and social reformers became the most visible enemies of the Church, and the most dangerous, because they could galvanize the ecclesiastical and political revolt incipient in the malaise of the Middle Ages. Witches, sorcerers, and the so-called possessed were brought before a mock court, which denounced them as heretics and killed them.

Allegations of witchcraft and sorcery—running around the countryside in a wolf skin killing children, or sending a pack of wolves to decimate the flocks of a good Christian—were charges rather easily sustained. Fundamental nonsense was taken for irrefutable evidence. The idle word of a neighbor, the gibberish of a village idiot, a shaving cut that showed up the morning after someone claimed to have driven off a wolf with a sharp stick—for these reasons and less thousands died at the stake. The hysteria and intimidation generated by swift, absolute, and irrevocable condemnation on the basis of mere shreds of evidence is what kept the Inquisition alive—and fed it victims. People wanted society to work smoothly, to be rid of whatever ailed it. They were easily drawn to simplification, to believing that werewolves, tearing around the countryside on the Devil's business, caused deformed children, disruptive harassment by the ruling classes, general ill fortune due to God's wrath, grisly murders, and so on. It was no coincidence that simultaneously there was a drive to wipe the wolf out in Europe, mounted as "the crying need of a civilized people."

The wolf and the look-alike werewolf became everyone's symbol of evil. (Oddly, the werewolf was hardly a concern of the Church before this time. The archbishop of Mainz had chided the Saxons in a sermon in 870 for a superstitious belief in shapeshifting. By 1270, however, the werewolf was the incarnation of the Devil and *not* to believe in the existence of werewolves was heretical.) The shepherds and the priests, with their respective flocks, hated wolves; the noble was bent on ridding his country of them to effect an air of civilization; Edgar of England imposed an annual tribute of three thousand wolves on the king of Wales; the landlord with his investments in livestock denounced them; the wives of the emerging middle class called the prostitutes wolves because they thought of them as wenches consuming the souls of their sons.

Terrorized by the number of sorcerers and witches the Inquisition found in their very midst, people responded in an orgy of accusation and counteraccusation. Historians of the period write that the hysteria was simply epidemic.

The excessive persecution of werewolves—where a witch might be hung, a werewolf was more often burned alive—had a formal basis. The supposition was, first, that sorcerers went about disguised as wolves because the wolf was the animal most hateful to good men; Church doctrine proclaimed that no sorcerer could harm men unless he were in contractual league with the Devil; the wolf, as the Devil's dog, became the form to do his work in. This symbolic logic was formalized in one of the most odious documents in all human history, the *Malleus Maleficarum*, published in 1487. Its title, *Hammer of Witches*, derives from a title sometimes bestowed on Inquisitors, Hammer of Heretics. One of the purposes of the book was to refute in tedious scholastic fashion every objection to the existence of werewolves.

The *Malleus* addressed itself mainly to proofs that those who became werewolves were in concert with the Devil and that the Church was acting properly in condemning them. From its pages superstition and folklore received an intellectual underpinning that made belief in werewolves not just a matter of Church doctrine but the intellectual fashion of the day. (Abjuring wolves, of course, had never really been out of fashion.) In a couple of places, the *Malleus* speaks directly about werewolves. Quoting both Leviticus ("If you don't keep my commandments I will send the beast of the field against you, who will consume your flocks") and Deuteronomy ("I will send the teeth of the beast down on them"), the *Malleus* states that wolves are either the agents of God, sent to punish the wicked, or agents of the Devil, sent with God's permission to harass good men. (That there was no middle ground where the wolf was his *own* animal clearly reveals the perception of the time.) Witches can change men into wolves, though the transformation is actually an illusion in the eye of the beholder because only God Himself can transform. A real wolf *(Canis lupus)* possessed by the Devil commits the mayhem. This was scholastic hairsplitting; werewolves were as real as their dead victims—as real as the Devil as far as the Church was concerned. That the Devil could create illusions only with the permission of God was simply poignant theology; it maintained God's supremacy over the Devil and gave purpose to human suffering. But, more importantly, to battle the werewolf brought one closer to God, and to burn the werewolf was to destroy a temple of evil in God's name.

One wonders if anyone shuddered at the fatuous logic—perhaps the *Malleus* would not have appeared if there were not terrible doubts to assuage. It is a commonplace of history that men condone violence for righteous causes and then feel guilty about it. It is also true that those who condemn violence most severely are sometimes its greatest voyeurs. Immediately after the execution of Peter Stump in Germany on March 31, 1590, for murder, incest, rape, and sodomy in the form of a werewolf, a pamphlet appeared describing his crimes in detail and dwelling on their perversity. Today we cannot judge what role such voyeurism played in the vigorous pursuit of werewolves in the Middle Ages.

Werewolfry also gave the upper classes an excuse for a sort of general housecleaning of undesirables. The trial in the 1570s of a hermit named Giles Garnier, who lived in a cave outside Lyon, is a good example. A wolf had apparently killed some children in the area. Garnier was found one day scavenging a dead body in the woods to feed his family. In

court, ignorant of his position at first, he was intimidated until he confessed to making a pact with the Devil, and to six or seven grisly child murders. He was burned alive without further ado at Dole, near Lyon, on
January 18, 1573. Montague Summers, an eccentric pedant and modern
apologist for the excesses of these witch-hunts, writes, "Hateful to God
and loathed of man, what other end, what other reward could he look for
than the stake, where they burned him quick, and scattered his ashes to
the wind, to be swept away to nothingness and oblivion." For all we
know, this was the fortune of a man whose only crime was being a beg-
gar.

A tailor who sexually abused children, tortured them to death, and
then powdered and dressed their bodies was burned as a werewolf in
Paris in 1598. Michel Verdun and Pierre Burgot were accused of sexual
relations with wolves in 1521 and executed. Another famous French case
involved a fourteen-year-old boy named Jean Grenier. He confessed to
being a werewolf, indicting also his father and a friend of his father. His
formal confession is gory, full of religious and sexual perversion. Condemned to death on September 6, 1603, he was transferred instead by
recommendation of clemency to a Franciscan friary in Bordeaux where
he spent the next eight years running around on all fours, completely
demented, physically deformed, and pathologically attached to wolf
lore.

Of what, exactly, he was a victim is a question that hurts the human
soul.

Among all the heretics and political enemies of state who were
marched through the courts and condemned as werewolves were an un-
ending number of the wildly insane, the epileptic, the simple-minded,
the pathologically disturbed, and the neurotically guilt-ridden. They
were condemned as society's enemies, but their connection with wolves
was tenuous in the extreme and that with werewolves highly imagined.

The point of examining all this is that these very same trials, this
period of hysteria, fixed in the human imagination the ghoulish and sexually perverse picture of the wolf/man that turns up hundreds of years
later in such pulp novels as *The Werewolf of Paris* and worse. Montague
Summers, immersed in the imagery of that time, writes: "The werewolf

loved to tear human flesh. He lapped the blood of his mangled victims, and with gorged reeking belly he bore the warm offal of their palpitating entrails to the sabbat to present in homage and foul sacrifice to the Monstrous Goat who sat upon the throne of worship and adoration. His appetites were depraved beyond humanity. In bestial rut he covered the fierce she-wolves. . . ." It is this twisted view from the Middle Ages that still feeds the human imagination, that preserves an image of the wolf that is not only without foundation in the natural world but almost completely a projection of human anxiety.

The werewolf has no counterpart in the sense that there is no strongly pervasive image of the wolf as a force for good. But the body of folk belief and folklore bearing on wolf children—human beings raised by nurturing female wolves after they have been abandoned by their parents—is, in a sense, the complementary image.

The history of wild, or feral, or wolf, children is long in legend and fact. The most famous, Romulus and Remus, are an enigma. Plutarch in *The Lives of the Noble Grecians and Romans* tells us that the most widely believed story of that time (the first century) was that they were the twin sons of a woman named Ilia, or Rhea, or Silvia. She was a Vestal Virgin, and when the children were born—Mars is supposed to have been their father—they were banished to the wilderness. A swineherd named Faustulus who was charged with taking them away took them home instead. His wife was rumored to be a loose woman (the Latin for both "prostitute" and "she-wolf" being *lupa* is given as the possible source of confusion). Other versions have the twins spending some time with wolves before Faustulus rescues them. The founder of the Turkish nation was also supposed to have been raised by wolves.

Rousseau wrote of the wolf child of Hesse, who turned up in 1344. Nine animal children—sheep children, bear children, cow children, and pig children—were classified *Homo ferus* by Linnaeus in 1758. He and others described nearly forty such children before the end of the nineteenth century. In the twentieth century there came a stream of reports of wolf children from India, and of baboon children, gazelle children, and monkey children from Africa.

These children were collectively referred to as wolf children because

WOLF GIRL

Although stories of wolf children in America are rare, there is a story told in Texas about a wolf girl who grew up on Devil's River, north of present-day Del Rio. The girl was, according to the story, born in May 1835 at the confluence of Dry Creek and Devil's River. The mother, Mollie Pertul Dent, died in childbirth and the father, John Dent, was killed in a thunderstorm at a ranch miles distant, where he had ridden for help. The child was never found, and the presumption was that she had been eaten by wolves near the Dents' isolated cabin.

In 1845, a boy living at San Felipe Springs (Del Rio) reported seeing "a creature, with long hair covering its features, that looked like a naked girl" attacking a herd of goats with several wolves. Similar reports were made by others during the ensuing year and Apache stories told of a child's footprints having been found a

number of times among those of wolves in that country, and so a hunt was organized.

On the third day of the hunt the girl was cornered in a canyon. A wolf with her was driven off and finally shot when it attacked the party. The girl was bound and taken to the nearest ranch, where she was loosed and closed up in a room.

That evening a large number of wolves, apparently attracted by the girl's loud, mournful, and incessant howling, came around the ranch, the domestic stock panicked, and in the mêlée the girl escaped.

She was not seen again for seven years. In 1852 a surveying crew exploring a new route to El Paso saw her on a sand bar on the Rio Grande, far above its confluence with Devil's River. She was with two pups. After that, she was never seen again.

That is the story they tell.

---

they were thought to have been raised by wild animals and because they behaved, in the eyes of human observers, like wild wolves. They hated to wear clothing, they had a penchant for raw meat, sought darkness during the day and roamed, instead, at night. They howled, ripped the flesh of those who tried to care for them, peeled back their lips to indicate displeasure, panted when they were hot, and ran around on all fours. It required only the barest stretch of the imagination, if such a child was found in the woods where there were wolves, to believe that the child had been raised by them.

Let me return to Jean Grenier, the disturbed child whose sentence was commuted. There is another, apparently factual, side to werewolfry that can be examined and that is the belief in lycanthropy as a pathological condition of melancholia and delirium, which has nothing to do with spells, the Devil, or eating human flesh. The idea has had some support among psychologists, but no case of lycanthropy can be clearly isolated from hysteria and superstition. Jean Grenier may have been such a victim. A man named Pierre de Lancre, who visited Grenier a year before he died, reported that he was lean and gaunt, that his hands were deformed, his nails like claws, and that he ran with great agility on all fours and ate rotten meat.

Had he turned up two hundred years later, Jean Grenier might have had a different fate. Had he in fact fallen into the hands of a gifted French teacher named Jean Itard—as did Victor, the wild boy of Aveyron—Grenier might have left us an explanation of others like him.

In the 1950s at the Sonia Shankman Orthogenic School of the University of Chicago, psychologists were treating nineteen children like Grenier. Some of them built dens in the corners of their rooms into which they crawled to eat the raw food they preferred. One of them, a girl, attacked one of the staff repeatedly, and so savagely that the woman required medical attention twelve times in as many months. The children licked salt for hours at a time and loped about the corridors at night, apparently with some pleasure. These, however, were not children rescued from the woods. They all came from middle-class homes in America. They were severely autistic.

The notion of the wolf child, a child actually raised by wolves, is a widespread belief. Because the wolf children described by various writers were all probably autistic or schizophrenic, suffering either congenital or psychological problems or both, the issue of whether authentic wolf-raised children ever existed seems a hopeless, not to say pointless, inquiry.

That people believed such things happened is undeniable, however, and it is not hard to see how such an idea took hold. Wolves likely did steal small babies occasionally, especially in India where they were left untended in the fields. But whatever ill they might have believed of wolves, most people also believed they were devoted and affectionate parents. It was quite plausible that wolves would care for children. Most cultures were aware that some animals, goats for example, nursed human infants, just as humans nursed young animals—puppies often—when the mother died.

Victor, the wild boy of Aveyron.

Victor of Aveyron, the most famous of all feral children, was humanely treated for years by the physician and speech therapist Jean Itard. Itard must have been a man of enormous energy and patience, and tremendous kindness. His success with Victor, who demonstrated most of the symptoms of so-called wolf children, was limited. The boy never learned to speak and he was confused by his sexual desires. He died at the age of forty. Itard's care of the boy, and his request of the French government that such children should not be abandoned in future as hopeless cases, is one of the most touching episodes in the literature of human care.

But the case of the rehabilitation of two Indian feral children, Amala and Kamala, presents us with something different. It is the only modern record which offers evidence of a direct link between wolves and wild children.

The Reverend J. A. L. Singh first saw Amala and Kamala about dusk on a Saturday, October 9, 1920, outside the village of Godamuri,

Saint Ailbe, a sixth-century Irish bishop, was born the son of a slave girl. Shortly after his birth he was taken out and deposited in the wilderness by order of his mother's owner. A wolf took compassion on him and cared for him until a huntsman found him. Years later, when he was Bishop of Emily, a gray wolf pursued by hunters ran into his house and laid her head on his lap.

"I will protect thee, old mother," said the bishop, drawing his cloak around the old wolf. "When I was little and young and feeble, thou didst nourish and cherish and protect me, and now that thou art old and gray and weak, shall I not render the same love and care to thee? None shall injure thee. Come every day with thy little ones to my table, and thou and thine shall share my crusts."

seventy-five miles southwest of Calcutta. He flushed three grown wolves from the base of an ant mound and inside, monkeyballed together in fear, he found two wolf cubs and two young girls. A few weeks later their den was excavated. Two of the three adult wolves present escaped. The third was shot. The two wolf cubs with the girls were sold in the market in Godamuri. Amala and Kamala (as they were later named) were placed in a cage in which they were unable to stand up and left in the care of a man who subsequently abandoned them. Singh returned five days later to find the girls lying in their own excrement, starving and thirsty. They were barely strong enough to suck water from the end of his handkerchief. After a seven-day journey wedged in the bottom of a bullock cart, they arrived at Singh's orphanage on November 4.

Amala died a year later, at about two and a half. Kamala, who was about eight when she was found, lived to be about seventeen. She died on November 14, 1929, at the orphanage, of uremic poisoning.

Amala and Kamala behaved in the manner of the severely autistic children described above, biting and howling, eating raw meat, preferring darkness, insensitive to heat and cold, keen of ear and nose, poor of eye. Like Victor of Aveyron they had difficulty with language. The thing that distinguishes them from other so-called feral children is that Amala never walked upright and it was years before Kamala did. This could have been, as one psychologist suggests, a regression to infant crawling behavior caused by the traumatic effect of the first two weeks after the children were taken from the wolf den.

The diary kept by the Singhs and a book written in praise of their work by a physician reveal that the Singhs were primarily concerned with civilizing Kamala by seeing to it that she wore clothing, ate with utensils, and attended regular religious services. They seemed less concerned with discovering her as a person.

The Singhs divided Kamala's actions into two categories: "wolf" and "human." They judged her progress by how many wolf ways disappeared and how many human habits were inculcated. It was the Singhs' orientation that Kamala had come to them as a bad creature and that she had to be turned into a good creature. Making a creature of God out of a creature of the Devil, in fact, is a note struck often in the diary. For all their kindness, there are elements of real barbarism in the Singhs' treatment. They shaved Kamala's head because they didn't like her to look "dirty." They bound her up so tightly in a loincloth in an effort to make her cover her genitals that she could not get it off to relieve herself.

There is a revealing conceit in the Singhs' diary. Mrs. Singh gave Kamala a backrub every morning and when Kamala responded by nuzzling her, she would note in the diary that Kamala was beginning to show "human affection." The first conceit, that such a demonstration of affection is uniquely human, is of course silly. The subtler conceit is that it was Mrs. Singh's decision to give Kamala the rubdown. Wolves in captivity routinely solicit scratching and other tactile attention from human beings.

Amala and Kamala could have been severely disturbed children, abandoned by their parents, who stumbled on the wolf den as a place of refuge. Such children, in fact, do show an uncommon fondness for animals, particularly dogs. (Singh says he saw the girls at the wolf den some days before he took them out, but that doesn't necessarily mean they were living there.)

There is no way to verify this story, although many scientists of the time believed Singh.

Why we should believe in wolf children seems somehow easier to understand than the ways we distinguish between what is human and what is animal behavior. In making such distinctions we run the risk of fooling

Mythic roots — the benevolent wolf mother, with Romulus and Remus

ourselves completely. We assume that the animal is entirely comprehensible and, as Henry Beston has said, has taken form on a plane beneath the one we occupy. It seems to me that this is a sure way to miss the animal and to see, instead, only another reflection of our own ideas.

The sense that there has to be a strong tradition of the benevolent wolf in literature, in art, or in folklore is a modern wish that must go wanting, for such a figure simply does not exist. There are benevolent wolves, and wolves that befriend those who treat them ill in literature, but not wolves who nurture, from whom people draw sustenance as perhaps Romulus and Remus did prior to their founding Rome.

But I think, somehow, that looking for the wolf-mother is the stage we are at now in history. If we go back to the time of Lycaon and follow the development of the wolf image through the Dark and Middle Ages to the present, the overriding impression is that of a sinister creature. But in the twentieth century, whether out of guilt or because we have reached such a level of civilization as to allow us the thought, we are looking for a new wolf. We seem eager to be corrected, to know how wrong our ideas about wolves have been, how complex the creature really is, how ultimately unfathomable. What we are looking for, I think, is a way to return mystery to animals, and distance and selfhood, and thereby dignity. To quote Beston again, we want to feel that animals "are not brethren, they are not underlings, they are other nations, caught with ourselves in the web of life . . ."

Almost like errant children, we seem to want forgiveness from wolves. And I think that takes great courage.

It may be reasonable to expect most people to dismiss the notion of a nurturing wolf as a naive person's referent, but that doesn't seem wise to me. When, from the prisons of our cities, we look out to wilderness, when we reach intellectually for such abstractions as the privilege of leading a life free from nonsensical conventions, or one without guilt or subterfuge—in short, a life of integrity—I think we can turn to wolves. We *do* sense in them courage, stamina, and a straightforwardness of living; we do sense that they are somehow correct in the universe and we are somehow still at odds with it.

As our sense of sharing the planet with other creatures grows—and perhaps that is ultimately the goal of natural history—the deep contemplation of wolves may be seen as part of an attempt to nurture the humbler belief that there is more to the world than mankind. In that sense, the wolf-mother is just now upon us, in a role a quantum leap removed from Romulus and Remus.

Thirteen

IMAGES FROM A CHILDHOOD

O NE fall afternoon a few years ago I stopped in at the Pierpont
Morgan Library in New York to see a special exhibition of children's literature. There were some early collections of *Aesop* and the animal fables of Jean de la Fontaine. And copies of the medieval epic
Reynard the Fox, in which Isengrim the Wolf plays such a major role. But
there was one thing I especially wanted to see: a presentation manuscript of Charles Perrault's *Histoires ou contes du temps passé*, a collection of
fairy tales published in France in 1697, containing the first written version of "Little Red Riding Hood." It was sitting on a stanchion, protected in a Plexiglas cube, not just something of value but palpable evidence of one of the better known villains of children's literature.

It is curious to find the wolf as a character in children's literature, for
all wolves in literature are the creations of adult minds, that is,

of adult fears, adult fantasies, adult allegories, and adult perversions. So the tendency to look on animal stories as simplistic is misleading. The wolf of Aesopian fable has changed little in twenty-five hundred years, but he is not just an unchanging symbol of bad behavior. He stands in the child's mind for something very real. It is Aesop's wolf, not Science's wolf—a base, not very intelligent creature, of ravenous appetite, gullible, impudent, and morally corrupt—that generations of schoolchildren are most familiar with. And it was through the fables of Aesop, Avianus, Babrius, and Phaedrus that many children of other centuries first encountered a moral universe beguiling in its simplicity and seemingly rich in worldly wisdom. Some children weaned on fable never inquired deeper into the animals than the stories led them, and so went through life believing the wolf evil, the fox sly, the bee industrious, and the ass foolish.

As adults, too, we often lump the wolves of all children's literature together. But the wolf of fable is really rather different from the wolf of the fairy tale. In fables—short, didactic, usually plotless aphorisms— the wolf's poor nature is ascribed to his having been born a wolf and it is possible to feel some sympathy for his predicament. Wolves are not hated in fables, the emotions elicited from the reader are not strong, the wolf is not hell-driven and malicious. He is not a complex beast at all. The wolf of fairy tale and folktale is a much fuller character, capable of diabolical evil and also, occasionally, of warmth and unflinching devotion. If the wolf of fable represents the perceptions of the conscious mind, the wolf of fairy tale represents the unconscious and becomes, as so frequently of late in analyses of "Little Red Riding Hood," a vehicle for sustaining the fantasies of the sexual unconscious.

The fable draws its morals and aphorisms from the easily observed world of nature, which is one reason its morals seem so apt. Fairy tales, on the other hand, proceed from abstractions and engage us at a deeper level. The fable is abrupt and cynical; the fairy tale is kinder, I think. It ministers to our anxious impulses and soothes us, despite occasional psychological darkness.

The wolf of fable and literature, then, should not be taken solely for the entertainment he affords to children. From Aesop to the novels of Jack London, he has laid claim to a far greater part of our imagination.

Now the hungry lion roars,
And the wolf behowls the moon.
A MIDSUMMER-NIGHT'S DREAM v.1.379

You may as well use question with the wolf.
THE MERCHANT OF VENICE iv.1.73

They have scared away two of my best sheep,
which I fear the wolf will sooner find
than the master.
A WINTER'S TALE iii.3.67

Since all is well, keep it so: wake not
a sleeping wolf.
2 HENRY IV i.2.174

If thou wert the wolf, thy greediness
would afflict thee, and oft thou
shouldst hazard thy life for thy dinner.
TIMON OF ATHENS iv.3.337

He's mad that trusts in the tameness
of a wolf, a horse's health,
a boy's love, or a whore's oath.
KING LEAR iii.6.20

Scale of dragon, tooth of wolf,
Witches' mummy.
MACBETH iv.1.22

'Tis like the howling of Irish wolves
against the moon.
AS YOU LIKE IT v.2.119

They will eat like wolves and fight like devils.
HENRY V iii.7.162

And now loud-howling wolves
arouse the jades
That drag the tragic melancholy night.
2 HENRY VI iv.1.3

As salt as wolves in pride.
OTHELLO iii.3.404

Thy desires
Are wolvish, bloody, starved, and ravenous.
THE MERCHANT OF VENICE iv.1.138

—JOHN BARTLETT, A.M.
from A Complete Concordance of Shakespeare

• • •

The fabulous literature of the Northern Hemisphere in which the wolf appears is, obviously, enormous. It is tempting at first to peruse such collections for insights into what people knew of wolves at different times and places, but as G. K. Chesterton wrote, in an introduction to Aesop, "The lion must always be stronger than the wolf, just as four is always the double of two . . . the fable must not allow for what Balzac called 'the revolt of the sheep.' " The wolf character, then, is more or less consistent. What *is* revealed by collections of fables is the political and social satire of an age, and which figures in history were taken for wolves in their time. Thus a Russian fable by Ivan Krilov, "The Wolf in the Kennel," which appeared in 1812, has a gray-coated wolf after a man's sheep, clearly the gray-coated Napoleon who had just invaded Russia.

The wolves met with in fable, however, were not actually stock characters. In the hands of various fabulists they were slightly different, according to the author, his intent, the audience he was writing to, and so on. So the wolf we find in Krilov shows more force and intelligence and is more rapacious. In a dark and excessively didactic collection by the Jewish writer Berekhiah ben Natronai ha-Nakdan, which appeared in the thirteenth century, the wolf is more sinister, more fundamentally wicked. In La Fontaine the wolf has more character and self-awareness than he does in earlier collections. Edward Moore, an eighteenth-century English dramatist, created in his fable "The Wolf, the Sheep, and the Lamb" a consciously evil, murderous beast who bargains with a sheep for her lamb, whom he takes as his bride. The lamb lives in terror as her husband slaughters sheep for his meals. Hunters almost shoot him one day and he accuses his lamb bride of treachery in setting them on his trail, which she has not done. Finally, in a rage he says: "Thou traitress vile, for this thy blood/Shall glut my rage, and dye the wood."

The fables we call "Aesop" today represent an oral tradition that, like the chapters of the *Physiologus*, was set down by more than one author. The earliest collection of Aesop we know of is one in iambic verse by the Latin poet Phaedrus. The earliest Aesop in Greek is one from the second century by Babrius, but it shows the effects of his having lived for a while in the Near East. The influence of fable collections from India, called the Fables of Pilpay or Bidpai and taken from the *Panchatantra* and the *Hitopadesa*, and stories of the Buddha in animal form from the *Jatakas*, show up more clearly in Aesopian collections after 1251, when Arabic versions of the Persian were finally translated into Spanish and Hebrew and, later, into Latin and other vernacular languages. (The jackal of these stories was grafted onto the wolf tradition in Aesop.) The fourth-century Roman poet Avianus based his very popular verse collection on Babrius, however, so the Eastern influence in collections of Aesop was fixed rather early, and there is some reason to treat the wolf of fable as therefore universal.

Whether Aesop ever lived at all is a matter of conjecture. He is thought by some to have been a freed slave who lived in Greece about 600 B.C., a man who used his fables to criticize indirectly the injustices of his day. Today few people in the Northern Hemisphere have not heard of him.

WOLF FABLES OF AESOP

THE DOG AND THE WOLF

Discouraged after an unsuccessful day of hunting, a hungry Wolf came on a well-fed Mastiff. He could see that the Dog was having a better time of it than he was and he inquired what the Dog had to do to stay so well fed. "Very little," said the Dog. "Just drive away beggars, guard the house, show fondness to the master, be submissive to the rest of the family and you are well fed and warmly lodged."

The Wolf thought this over carefully. He risked his own life almost daily, had to stay out in the worst of weather, and was never assured of his meals. He thought he would try another way of living.

As they were going along together the Wolf saw a place around the Dog's neck where the hair had worn thin. He asked what this was and the Dog said it was nothing, "just the place where my collar and chain rub." The Wolf stopped short. "Chain?" he asked. "You

mean you are not free to go where you choose?" "No," said the Dog, "but what does that mean?" "Much," answered the Wolf as he trotted off. "Much."

THE WOLF AND THE LAMB

One very hot day a Lamb and a Wolf happened to come on a stream at the same moment to quench their thirst. The Wolf was some distance upstream but called out asking to know why the Lamb was muddying the water, making it impossible for him to drink. The Lamb, quite frightened, answered as politely as he could that he could not have muddied the water as he was standing downstream. The Wolf allowed that that might be true. But he claimed he had heard the Lamb was maligning him behind his back. The Lamb answered, "Upon my word, that is a false charge." This irritated the Wolf extremely and drawing

Babrius, Avianus, and Phaedrus were the fabulists of record into the Middle Ages, when more free-ranging adaptations and original collections began to appear. Marie de France was writing fables in 1175. William Caxton was publishing Aesop in English for the first time about 1480. Even Leonardo da Vinci was trying his hand at fables. Renaissance scholars began to take a serious interest in fables as literature and, by the beginning of the seventeenth century, hundreds of writers were supporting themselves in part by writing them. Among the more widely circulated works were those of John Gay in England, Gotthold Lessing in Germany, and—by far the best known and most widely imitated—Jean de la Fontaine in France. La Fontaine, interestingly, was writing at a time when French intellectuals were debating the idea set forth by Des-

near the Lamb he said, "If it wasn't you then it was your father. It is all the same anyway." And so saying, he killed the Lamb.

THE WOLF AND THE MOUSE

A Wolf stole a sheep and retired to the woods to eat his fill. When he awoke from a nap he saw a Mouse nibbling at the remains. When the surprised Mouse ran off with a scrap, the Wolf jumped up and began screaming, "I've been robbed! I've been robbed! Stop this thief!"

THE SHEPHERD BOY AND THE WOLF

A Shepherd Boy was watching his flock near the village and was bored. He thought it would be great fun to pretend that a Wolf was attacking the sheep, so he cried out Wolf! Wolf! and the villagers came running. He laughed and laughed when they discovered there was no Wolf. He played the trick again. And then again. Each time the villagers came, only to be fooled. Then one day a Wolf did come and the Boy cried out Wolf! Wolf! But no one answered his call. They thought he was playing the same games again.

THE WOLF AND THE HUNTER

A hunter killed a goat with his bow and arrow and, throwing the animal over his shoulder, he headed home. On the way he saw a fine boar. He dropped the goat and let fly an arrow at the boar. The shot missed the heart and the boar fatally gored the hunter before he too expired.

A Wolf caught the smell of blood and found his way to the scene. He was beside himself with delight at the sight of all this meat, but he decided to be prudent, to start with the worst of it and finish with the softest, most delectable pieces. The first thing he determined to eat was the bow string. Taking it in his mouth, he began to gnaw. When it snapped the bow shaft sprung and stabbed the Wolf in the belly and he died.

---

cartes that animals were beastly machines without souls while men were a separate, mysterious creation. La Fontaine disagreed strongly, which makes what he has to say about the wolf in his fables of more than passing interest. I will return to him in a moment.

In 1818, Thomas Bewick published a collection of Aesop in England that featured his own marvelous woodcuts—his wolves have stunning, huge eyes and enormous feet—and Bewick's caricature of the wolf can serve as an example of the Aesopian character.

In spite of living in more enlightened times, Bewick wrote out of a tradition that was very strongly of the school of nature, not nurture, as befits the wolf of fable. His wolf was innately evil, irreconcilably and fundamentally corrupt, and not very intelligent. Interestingly, what passes for

THE WOLF AND THE CRANE

One day a Wolf got a bone stuck in his throat. He was unable to dislodge it and so he went around asking for someone to pull it out. Finally a Crane offered to help. He stuck his long bill down the Wolf's throat and extracted the bone. When the Crane asked for a reward, the Wolf said, "You are lucky I didn't bite your head off. That's all the reward you get."

THE WOLF HELPS THE DOG

A Dog, grown old in the service of his master and thought to no longer be of any use, was going to be turned out to finish his days alone. One day the Dog met a Wolf to whom he told his plight. The Wolf took pity and between them they devised a plan. The Dog would return to his master's residence and shortly thereafter the Wolf would attack the sheep fold. The Dog would drive him out, they would feign a ferocious battle, and the Wolf would be driven off. Thus would the Dog be redeemed in the eyes of his master.

Things went just as they had planned. The Dog was welcomed back, praised for his fierce loyalty and bravery, and promised food and a warm hearth until the day he died.

A week later the Wolf returned, asking the Dog for a return of the favor. The Dog was only too delighted to sneak him in to a banquet that evening where, by lying quietly beneath the tables, he could gorge himself royally on scraps from the table. This went very well, nothing suspected, until the Wolf had had too much to drink. He began to sing in a loud voice. The master of the house discovered him, and, surmising the ruse, booted both Dog and Wolf out the door.

THE WOLF AND THE SHEPHERDS

One evening a wolf passed near a sheep fold and smelled mutton cooking. He drew close and peered through the bushes. A lamb was roasting over the fire and the shepherds were discussing the good quality of the meat. If it was me that had done this, thought the Wolf, they would be after me with sticks and stones and curses.

cleverness in Bewick's fox is dishonesty in his wolf; and what for the fox is craft is for the wolf cheating. In the morals he appended to the tales, Bewick railed against ingratitude, against the lack of vigilance that lets despots come to power, against gullibility, and against impudence. The wolf serves him primarily as a symbol of impudence and corrupt power—despotism without a conscience. So, in "The Wolf and the Lamb," he puts the blame for such brutishness to blood, writing in his moral that "men of wolfish disposition and envious and rapacious tempers cannot bear to see honest industry raise its head." Which is one reason (in the story) why wolves kill lambs. It is their nature. At another point Bewick says the same of people, writing that certain groups, like wolves, have "blood tinctured with hereditary, habitual villainy and their nature leavened with evil." (On the other hand, in "The Dog and the Wolf," Bewick's personal aversion to tyranny and enslavement did force him to give us a noble wolf. He writes there of the "true greatness of soul" that the wolf displays.)

Ivan Krilov, a contemporary of Bewick, was the greatest of the Russian fabulists. There is a statue of him in the Summer Garden in Leningrad which is as famous as that of Hans Christian Andersen in New York's Central Park. Krilov's wolves, mostly because Krilov was a masterful storyteller, are among the richest in fable, much more vigorous and frightening than the wolves of European fable; it is tempting to conclude that he either drew them from or contributed to the terrible Russian angst over visions of wolf packs in howling pursuit of sleighs on lonely winter nights. But Krilov had a sense of humor. One of my favorite fables is "The Wolf in the Dust." A wolf anxious to steal a sheep from a flock approaches the animals from downwind under a cover of dust kicked up by the sheep. "Hey," says the sheepdog with the flock, when he sees the wolf, "there's no use your wandering around in the dust like that, it's no good for your eyes."

"I've got bad eyes anyway," yells back the wolf over the noise of the sheep drive. "But they say dust kicked up by sheep is an excellent cure for it. That's why I'm down here."

Jean de la Fontaine grew up in Château-Thierry and was familiar with animals and the world of nature before he began writing. His fables were well-crafted poems, highly satirical and much copied. The literary critics of his time disparaged the fable as a literary form, saying its subject matter was far too prosaic to warrant poetic treatment. La Fontaine disagreed; eventually he was admitted to the French Academy. The bickering in Parisian salons over the merit of La Fontaine's fables—their form, their morals, their satirical targets—precipitated discussion of one of the most hotly debated issues of the day: the nature of animals and their place in the universe.

By this time the pseudoscientific view of the bestiaries was waning and the science of natural history, benefitting from Francis Bacon's cry for a scientific method, was on the rise. Hobbes, who wrote in England but spent much of his time in France, was saying that man was little more than a cog to be politically manipulated, a little machine. René Descartes was delineating animals as "beast machines," creatures without souls and distinct from man. Rationalists of the time were creating a predictable and lifeless universe.

The idea of Cartesian dualism was one of the most pervasive themes of the seventeenth century, and its reverberations in zoology today are practically as strong as they were in Paris in the 1640s. It held that if an animal has no soul—if an animal is only a machine—then our approach to forms of life other than ourselves can be irresponsible and mechanistic. It was precisely this view that came to dominate the biological sciences and to give men who were otherwise much admired, like Audubon, the ethical space to shoot fifty or a hundred birds just to make a single, accurate drawing. The mechanistic approach to wildlife, further, led biologists to a tragic and myopic conclusion: that animals can be "contained," that they can be disassembled, described, reassembled, and put back on the shelf. This is an idea that is only now beginning to disappear in zoology.

La Fontaine disagreed violently with Descartes. He believed that animals not only had souls but were capable of rational thought. Montaigne, in a famous essay called "In Defense of Raymond Sebond," had written with penetrating skepticism about the dogmatic assumptions of this time. One of the evils he attacked most vigorously was the complacency with which scientists like Descartes approached animals. Montaigne argued against the compulsive desire to do away with something by describing it, and he perceived correctly that if you took the mystery out of animals they became nothing more than curiosities. He thought such behavior not only stupid but pathetically arrogant.

But these were isolated voices.

The fable enjoyed a renaissance in the century after La Fontaine's death before—a limited form to begin with—it exhausted itself as a form of social satire. It was replaced by longer beast epics like *Gulliver's Travels* and the stories of Reynard and Isengrim, which had enjoyed wide circulation since the fourteenth century.

Ysengrimus, a Latin poem of some sixty-six hundred lines, was written in about 1150 by Nivordus of Ghent in Belgium. It was the first literary recording of what by then was a growing oral tradition, stories based on the long-standing feud between Isengrim the wolf, who stood for the lower nobles, and Reynard the fox, a peasant hero. The French *Roman de Renart* was the product of several thirteenth-century authors and was immediately popular. Reynard's witty insults and subterfuge and his cavalier nose-thumbing delighted people who were oppressed. His scathing castigation of wealthy clergy and dull-witted nobility, of unpopular monarchs and political and ecclesiastical abuses, brought howls of approval. The story cycle usually began with Reynard's summons to the court of the king, a lion, to answer charges made against him by Isengrim and others. Reynard defends himself with devious wit and well-placed flatteries. When he has charmed and ingratiated himself with everyone but Isengrim, he volunteers for some adventure to prove his innocence. Off he goes and we subsequently see more of his guile and much of his cruelty. Isengrim is frequently killed in these stories.

Isengrim is forever Reynard's fool, but the tales have an odd flavor to them today. Isengrim, for all that he is duped, basically tells the truth and tries to lead a moral life. He is also loyal. Reynard is guileful and arrogant, utterly without human warmth, amoral and violent. He gets away with it all in the beginning but in later versions he is punished for his treachery. In *The Most Pleasant and Delightful History of Reynard the Fox: The Second Part* (1681), wit and comedy give way to brutality and evil, and in the end Reynard is killed along with Isengrim. And in *The Shifts of Reynardine, the Son of Reynard the Fox* (1684), Reynardine is hung for his evil-doing.

The brief glimpses we catch in the Reynard stories of a wolf with whom we can sympathize recall the heroic werewolf in William of Parlerne and the sympathetic wolves that surface occasionally in folktales, usually as guides, often of children. They show warmth, compassion, and self-sacrifice, contradicting the ghoulish image of the ravening beast.

There were single stories of the wolf and the fox that in time became detached from the Reynard cycle, as well as original creations, so that today there are a large number of fox and wolf stories. In most of them Fox outwits Wolf by getting him to do something foolish, like sticking

The wolf and the crane, illustrations of the Aesopian fable.

his tail in a hole in the river ice to catch fish, only to have it freeze there and break off.

The wolf of ethnic folktale is more varied than the wolf of fable and the Reynard stories. In the collections of Jacob and Wilhelm Grimm he seems one-dimensional and predictable, but in other collections he is articulate, sagacious, vicious, silly, and endearing by turns. Often, as in a collection of Georgian (Russian) folktales called *Yes and No Stories*, the wolf is treated miserably by ingrates but nevertheless continues to help them. In a famous Russian story, "The Firebird," the wolf helps the king's youngest son find a firebird that has stolen his father's golden apples. He secures a princess and a fabulous horse for the boy and protects him from his brothers, who want to kill him. Through it all the boy causes one problem after another, but the wolf stays by him.

The other side of the coin is the wolf who is himself helped but then turns on his helper, as in the fable "The Wolf and the Crane." In a Chinese story called "The Wolf of Chungshan Mountain," a scholar meets a wolf being pursued by hunters. He kindly offers him a hiding place in his bookbag. When the hunters are gone, he lets the wolf out. The wolf promptly declares his intention to eat the man. The scholar objects and they agree to have the matter debated by the first stranger they meet. The first stranger manages to get the wolf to crawl back in the bookbag by insisting on a complete reenactment of the scene. The stranger then clubs the wolf to death, praises the scholar for his compassion, and remonstrates with him for his foolishness. In other versions the wolf and his benefactor meet three strangers, each of whom says, yes, it is true, favors are soon forgotten in this world—and the wolf eats his erstwhile friend.

Wolf and dog stories form a genre all their own. Classic among them is the ancient Welsh tale of Gelert, a huge hound. Prince Llewelyn leaves Gelert to guard his infant son while he goes off hunting. A wolf creeps into the castle and a desperate struggle ensues, during which the infant's cradle is overturned. Gelert finally kills the wolf and falls down exhausted. When Llewelyn returns and sees the upended crib and Gelert smeared with blood, he is gripped with rage and drives the dog through with his spear. Only when he turns the crib over does he find his son asleep and see the dead wolf.

Observations on the hypocrisy of men and stories of wolves bent on realistic accommodation with man present us with a sympathetic character. In "The Old Wolf in Seven Fables," an aging wolf visits the shepherds around him, knowing his days are numbered. He asks the first one for enough sheep to satisfy his hunger in exchange for not terrorizing the flocks and killing more than he needs. No, says the shepherd. He asks the second one for six sheep a year. No. He asks the next for one sheep a year, and is accused of plotting and sent off. To a fourth he offers to act as watchdog against other wolves, to a fifth he promises to eat only sheep that die of natural causes, and to a sixth that he will bequeath him his wolf skin. Finally, spurned by them all, he turns around and wreaks havoc on the flocks of every one.

Many folktales stress the wolf's gullibility. In "The Wolf's Breakfast," a wolf has a dream of a fantastic breakfast and awakens famished. Intent on making it come true, the hungry wolf faces goats, swine, a cock, a goose, a mare and her foal, and a ram. He demands with foolish straightforwardness the life of each in turn, and each engages him in some diverting task long enough to escape. Cursing his endless stupidity he cries aloud for someone to chop off his tail as punishment. A huntsman, conveniently near, obliges. Thus we are cautioned not to put too much faith in dreams.

In a class almost by itself is Serge Prokofiev's *Peter and the Wolf,* a symphonic fairy tale in which the young Peter and a small bird capture a wolf who has eaten their friend the duck. When hunters on the wolf's trail arrive, Peter asks them to spare the wolf's life and take him to a zoo.

In an eerie, dreamlike native American story from the Pacific Northwest coast a boy named Sheem becomes a wolf. Abandoned by his brother and sister after the death of their parents, Sheem takes to following wolves in order to eat what they leave. The wolves feel kindly toward him and allow him to stay close. One afternoon his brother is fishing on a lake when he hears a child weeping. Paddling toward shore he recognizes Sheem, who now looks a little like the wolves. The young boy cries out to him, "My brother! My fate is near! My woes are ended! I shall be changed!" and so saying he becomes even more wolflike. The brother beaches the canoe and chases after Sheem, trying to gather him in his arms, crying in anguish: "Nee sheema! Nee sheema! My little

Before a wolf was brought into their classroom, a group of grade-school children were asked to draw pictures of wolves. The wolves in the pictures all had enormous fangs. The wolf was brought in, and the person with him began speaking about wolves. The children were awed by the animal. When the wolf left, the teacher asked the children to do another drawing. The new drawings had no large fangs. They all had enormous feet.

brother! My little brother!" But the boy eludes his grasp, alternately howling and calling out the names of his brother and sister as he runs. Soon he is a wolf completely and he bounds away.

The people of Lithuania tell of a wolf who promised to give up killing animals and to lead a holy life. Things went well until one day the wolf was going down the road and a gander came flapping up to him. He wrung its neck. "Geese shouldn't hiss at saints," he said.

The stories of "Little Red Riding Hood," "The Three Little Pigs," and "The Seven Little Goats" are perhaps the best-known fairy tales in which the wolf plays the role of an ogre. Of these the reader probably only needs to be reminded of the plot for the third: a wolf, uttering secret words he has accidentally overheard and imitating the voice of a mother goat, tries to get into a locked house where there are seven goats. They doubt whether it is their mother and ask the wolf to prove it by showing his white hooves in the window. The wolf raises his flour-dusted paws, the goats are convinced, and they let him in. He eats them all, save the smallest who hides in the grandfather clock. When the mother returns, the little goat tells her what has happened and with the help of a huntsman they track the wolf down. They find him asleep by a stream. The huntsman cuts him open, removes the young goats, stuffs the wolf with rocks, and sews him up. Awakened, the startled wolf jumps in the stream and drowns.

The sexual undercurrent in "Little Red Riding Hood" has been a topic of frequent allusion among psychologists for years, though Charles Perrault's original version presents an unresolved problem and is more a cautionary tale with a moral than a fairy tale. In Perrault's version the

wolf eats Red Riding Hood and that's that. In later versions Red Riding
Hood is rescued in various ways. According to a short history of the
story written by Iona and Peter Opie, in *Madame de Chatelain's Merry
Tales for Little Folk* (1868) a wasp stings the wolf, whose bark alerts a
tomtit, who warns a huntsman, who shoots an arrow that kills the wolf.
In an 1840s version, Red Riding Hood screams and her father rushes in
to save her. In a nineteenth-century version popular in Brittany the wolf
puts grandmother's blood in a bottle, which he gives to Red Riding
Hood to drink before killing her. In the Brothers Grimm the wolf eats
Red Riding Hood and falls asleep. His snores bring huntsmen, who
open his belly to get Red Riding Hood and her grandmother out and
then fill it with rocks, recalling again the wolf's antipathy for stones.
This is the version, I believe, that appears in a book with a delightful
title, published in 1760 in England: *The Top Book of All, For Little Misters
and Misses*.

James Thurber, in a 1930s version, has Red Riding Hood shooting the
wolf with a pistol she had hidden in her basket. Writes Thurber, "Moral:
It's not so easy to fool little girls nowadays as it used to be."

Bruno Bettelheim, in *The Uses of Enchantment*, analyzes "Red Riding
Hood" or, as the story is known in Grimm, "Little Red Cap," in sexual
terms. A prepubescent girl announcing her sexual availability with her
red cap is approached by a seducer, who entices her to forsake what Bettelheim calls the reality principle (staying on the path to grandmother's)
for the pleasure principle (going off to pick flowers). Red Cap picks flowers until she can't hold any more and then suddenly remembers her er-
rand. Thus we see her ambivalence about whether to live by the reality
principle or the pleasure principle. A similar scene occurs at grandmother's when she gets undressed and gets into bed with the wolf. She
doesn't know whether to stay and resolve the oedipal conflict or bolt
from the bed. The male nature, writes Bettelheim, is what Red Riding
Hood is trying to cope with, and for her it is split into two opposite
forms: the dangerous seducer and the rescuing father figure.

"It is as if Little Red Cap is trying to understand the contradictory

Red Riding Hood.

nature of the male by experiencing all aspects of his personality: the selfish, asocial, violent, potentially destructive tendencies of the id (the wolf); and the unselfish, social, thoughtful and protective propensities of the ego (the hunter).

"Little Red Cap is universally loved because although she is virtuous, she is tempted; and because her fate tells us that trusting everybody's good intentions which seems so nice, is really leaving oneself open to pitfalls. If there were not something in us that likes the big bad wolf, he would have no power over us. Therefore, it is important to understand his nature, but even more important to learn what makes him attractive to us. Appealing as naïveté is, it is dangerous to remain naïve all one's life."

Bettelheim goes on to say that what appeals in the wolf is his capacity to provide simultaneously tremendous excitement and great anxiety, the essence of the sexual act in the mind of a child for Bettelheim.

Erich Fromm has suggested that the wolf's eating Red Riding Hood represents both a hostile feminine view of the destructive nature of the sexual act, and a male desire to usurp the female role by having living beings inside it.

I think "Little Red Riding Hood" might be examined as an extended metaphor on another level. Like "The Three Little Pigs" and "The Seven Little Goats," this is a violent story. And the violence done to the wolf is socially acceptable. If one imagined cattlemen and woolgrowers as Red Riding Hood's avenging father, it would be easy to see sheep and cows as their little girls and the wolf as the lurking rapist. What makes this suggestion less than facetious is that the sort of outrage and the promise of violence stockmen manifested when they found a wolf-killed sheep is uncommonly like that manifested by men on hearing that a neighbor's child has been raped by an itinerant laborer.

Making Freudian connections between sex and violence in wolf terms can quickly land one in an analytical morass. The wolf is called female destructive and male destructive. He is called a threat to the male ego as well as a projection of the male ego. He is suavely seductive; he is brutally violent. The reader can do as well as I here. Our historically ambivalent vision of the wolf is, again, very evident. An odd thought that remains with all these stories is that as adults it is often only these violent tales of hedonistic, ravenous wolves that we most easily recall. Why that should be I do not know. Perhaps these were the stories our parents and teachers emphasized. In any case it seems disconcertingly clear that this is the wolf we are preoccupied with.

In an essay entitled "The Occurrence in Dreams of Material from Fairy Tales," Sigmund Freud recounts the childhood dream of a patient he calls the Wolf-man. The child was born, curiously, on Christmas Eve, 1886, in western Russia to an upper-middle-class family. He grew up maladjusted, and in psychoanalysis Freud traced his infantile neurosis through a boyhood dream that, Freud felt, derived in part from the child's having been frightened by the wolves in Red Riding Hood and other children's stories.

In the dream the boy is lying in bed at night. He is looking out over the foot of his bed through casement windows at a row of walnut trees. It is winter and the old trees are without leaves, stark against the snow. Suddenly the windows fly open and there sitting in a tree are six or seven wolves. They are white, with bushy tails, their ears cocked forward as though they were listening for something.

The boy awakes screaming.

Freud's analysis has not much to do with wolves, but the boy's dream is surely as eerie, as surreal, a vision of wolves as exists in any fairy tale.

The place of wolves in literature would not be complete without at least an allusion to the body of fiction that bears on wolfish themes, though the basis for much of it will by now be clear. There are the *Jungle Stories* of Rudyard Kipling, perhaps best known, featuring Mowgli, the boy adopted by wolves. Frank Norris, a turn-of-the-century exponent of naturalism, developed "lycanthropy mathesis" as a state of moral degeneration and severe depression in *Vandover and the Brute*. Werewolfry was a minor but staple theme of popular literature in America until the thirties, and I have already mentioned Guy Endore's *The Werewolf of Paris*. G. W. M. Reynolds wrote a Victorian thriller called *Wagner the Wehrwolf* that was wildly popular in magazine installments in 1846/47. Guy de Maupassant in a strange and crude short story called "The Wolf" features two pathologically insane brothers in hot pursuit of a wolf. One brother has been struck by a limb during the chase and his head crushed. His dead body is strapped crosswise in his own saddle. When the wolf finally turns to fight, the live brother props the dead one up in some rocks to watch. Then, hysterical with power, he throws away his weapon and strangles the wolf. H. H. Munro (Saki) wrote a werewolf story of charm and humor in "Gabriel-Ernest," featuring a sixteen-year-old nature boy; and his "The She-Wolf" is an amusing drawing-room farce in which a stuffy matron is apparently changed into a wolf. There is a maniac in John Webster's *The Duchess of Malfi* who believes himself a mad wolf and a lycanthropic character of Gothic horror appears in Charles Robert Maturin's *The Albigenses*. The English novelist Algernon Blackwood wrote a number of bloody werewolf stories.

Daniel Defoe's *Robinson Crusoe* and Willa Cather's *My Antonia* contain archetypal wolf scenes: in the former it is a fantastic battle in the Pyrenees, in the latter a reminiscence about a bride and groom thrown to the wolves one wintry night by the driver of a pursued sleigh. This is the most oft-repeated wolf scene in literature, its apotheosis being the scene in Robert Browning's "Ivan Ivanovitch" in *Dramatic Idylls*, where the mother throws her children to the wolves.

The American poet Hamlin Garland captured some of the bitterness of life in the Upper Midwest in the nineteenth century and some of the hatred directed at wolves by those people when he wrote:

> His eyes are eager, his teeth are keen
> As he slips at night through the brush like a snake
> Crouching and cringing, straight into the wind
> To leap with a grin on the fawn in the break.

And in a poem called "The Wolves," another American poet, Galway Kinnell, speaks of buffalo hunters and wolves in such a way as to leave the hunters saddled with the bestial imagery usually put to the wolf. D. H. Lawrence was very much taken with the animal life of the American Southwest. In "Autumn at Taos" he compares the ash gray sage of the desert mesas to a wolf's back, describing it as a kind of land fur. In "The Red Wolf," a pueblo seer calls Lawrence a thin red wolf of a paleface, recalling Northern Plains Indian allusions to the East, the direction from which Lawrence has come, as the place of the wolf and the color red. Robinson Jeffers penned my favorite two lines about the wolf:

What but the wolf's tooth whittled so fine
The fleet limbs of the antelope.

I have indicated already that the oral literature of native Americans was rich with wolf stories. The Indian wolf, of course, was not the European wolf, though the familiar theme of shapeshifting—which nineteenth-century Europeans frequently took for werewolfry when they heard these Indian stories—is common. George Bird Grinnell recorded many wolf stories among the Blackfeet, Pawnee, and Cheyenne. One of the most haunting is "Black Wolf and His Fathers," in his *By Cheyenne Campfires*. A man left to die in a pit is rescued by two wolves—one white, one rabid. During a long journey to the Place of the Wolves, the white wolf must keep constant guard so that the rabid wolf won't attack the man. With the white wolf's help, the man is later adopted by the wolves. When he returns to his tribe, he kills the two women who left him to die in the pit and offers their bodies to the wolves. Grinnell also has a similar story in *Blackfoot Lodge Tales* entitled "The Wolf-man."

But if there is one writer whose name must be linked with the wolf it is of course Jack London. He was obsessed by them. *Call of the Wild* and *White Fang* are widely known. In the former a dog regains its "wolfish heritage" in Alaska, and in the latter a wolf is tamed. The character of Wolf Larsen in *The Sea-Wolf* is probably a projection of London's own personality. His first story collection was entitled *The Son of the Wolf*.

London named his dream house, never completed, Wolf House, and delighted in being called Wolf, the name his perhaps homosexual friend George Sterling gave him. (Literary allusions to homosexual lovers as "wolves after lambs" are not rare. Plato, in *Phaedrus*, writes, "The eager lover aspires to the boy just as the wolf desires the tender lamb.") London was accused of being homosexual because of his aggressive displays of drinking and forcing himself on women, behavior that he thought proved his masculinity. In a poignant scene a month before he died, London asked his wife to have a watch he had given her inscribed "Mate from Wolf," and lamented that she did not call him more often by that name.

London's novels show a preoccupation with "the brute nature" in man, which he symbolized in the wolf. In *The Sea-Wolf*, Larsen's internal war is between his brutish and civilized natures, though the idea of the brute as London presents it is admirable. But it is, ultimately, a neurotic fixation with machismo that has as little to do with wolves as the drinking, whoring, and fighting side of man's brute nature. London, one of the most frustrated and perhaps tragic figures in American literature, nevertheless struck responsive chords with his themes. Few twentieth-century American authors have been as widely translated and appreciated outside America.

Even so swift and cursory a glance at wolves in literature as this reveals that—except for a few stories here and there where a writer wasn't bound by the conventions of fable or the happy endings of fairy tales—the role of the wolf is fairly predictable. London's wolves and wolfish men seem more serious-minded and are more engaging because he was writing about a facet of human nature—the bestial side, the wolf side of man—and was not content to let the wolf stand simply as a stock symbol.

The possibility has yet to be realized of a synthesis between the benevolent wolf of many native American stories and the malcontented wolf of most European fairy tales. At present we seem incapable of such a creation, unable to write about a whole wolf because, for most of us, animals are still either two-dimensional symbols or simply inconsequential, suitable only for children's stories where good and evil are clearly separated.

Were we to perceive such a synthesis, it would signal a radical change in man. For it would mean that he had finally quit his preoccupation with himself and begun to contemplate a universe in which he was not central. The terror inherent in such a prospect is, of course, greater than that in any wolf he has ever written about. But equally vast is the possibility for heroism, humility, tragedy, and the other virtues of literature.

Fourteen

A HOWLING AT TWILIGHT

A T the southern end of the Acropolis in Athens stand the ruins of the Lyceum. Philologists argue about the origin of the name but it seems probable that the building was once used as a place of worship for Apollo, the Wolf Slayer. Apollo was a patron of shepherds, and Pausanias, a second-century Greek author, writes that it was Apollo who directed shepherds to put out meat laced with bark poison to kill wolves.

In later years the Lyceum became a gymnasium, then a hall where Aristotle, among others, taught. At the time he was lecturing, Aristotle was writing a text on animals, and in the section on wolves he included the story of Apollo's birth on the Island of Delos. Apollo's mother, Leto, disguised as a wolf and accompanied by a pack of wolves, had made the trip from the land of the Hyperboreans to Delos to escape detection by the jealous Hera, wife of Zeus, who was Apollo's father.

How Apollo became the major figure in Greek mythology associated with wolves is still something of a mystery. As a patron of shepherds he was supposed to kill them, but he also took on the form of a wolf to fight, as in the *Aeneid*, where he destroys the sorcerers of Rhodes. His temple at Argos commemorates a battle between a wolf and a bull, as does a bronze relief at his temple at Sicyon. And there is also a bronze wolf at his most famous shrine, the Oracle at Delphi. One explanation for the Delphic wolf is that a wolf once killed a temple robber at some distance from the shrine and then led worshipers to the kill. They recovered what had been stolen and cast a statue of the wolf in bronze to honor him. Coins issued at Argos, a patron city of Apollo, were adorned with wolves from at least the fifth century B.C.

Apollo, then, was associated with wolves, but this is not a strong theme in Greek mythology. He was more widely known as a sun god. I have already referred to the confusion over the Greek words for "light" and "wolf." Perhaps they were genuinely confused, or perhaps they are related in a way philologists cannot understand. Adding to the confusion is the epithet "wolf-born," used to describe the circumstances of Apollo's birth, but also used to refer to a place, Lycia, where the cult figure, Apollo, originated. In the *Iliad*, for example, Apollo is most beloved of the Lycian warriors. So, in literature, the terms "Lycean Apollo," "wolf-born Apollo," and "wolfish Apollo" are sometimes interchanged. In *Agamemnon* Cassandra invokes Apollo as a wolf slayer. Jocasta in *Oedipus Rex* and Electra in *Electra* seek reassurance in Lycean Apollo. The chorus in *The Seven Against Thebes* asks him to fight their enemies: "Be wolf to them wolf-slayer! With gnashing of the teeth requite them."

Before the Hellenistic invasion, both hunting and agricultural people with ties to the wolf (totemistic in the case of the hunters, perhaps pro-pitiatory in the case of the shepherds) lived in Greece. As the worship of Apollo was slowly grafted onto the beliefs of both by the Hellenistic in-vaders, Apollo came to be associated with the protection of sheep among agriculturists and with warrior virtues among hunters. Hence Apollo's somewhat contradictory wolf-hater–wolf-admirer image.

The classicist Richard Eckels suggests that after wolves had been re-duced in numbers in Greece people became sentimental about them and, along with the crow, they became sacred to Apollo, who was now supposed to protect them. I don't think this is any more likely than that Osiris was a wolf god, as some have suggested. A culture that raises sheep and cattle (and is troubled by wolves well into modern times), that produces Aesop's fables and most of the antipathetic wolf lore of the Western world, does not suddenly become sentimental about wolves. As for Osiris and the other Egyptian gods sometimes identified with the wolf, this is likely a case of confusion with the jackal.

The wolf that shows up in Apollonian legend is one that is familiar to us. The wolf of the Norsemen is something quite different. In that mythology we encounter some elements already familiar: the wolf in association with light, with war, with witches, and with Loki, the trickster. But the wolves of Teutonic mythology are overpowering in these roles.

Imagine you are standing on the shores of the Baltic Sea on a cold, wintry day. The thick gray clouds stretch to the horizon. The sea is torn into scraps of whitecaps by a relentless wind that causes you sometimes to reach out to keep your balance. A roar begins to build in your ears, as though you were in a dark tunnel at the approach of a train. With a screeching explosion it is beside you, a gigantic woman astride an enormous gray wolf, its eyes glowing like two moons, a snake around its head for a bridle. When one of the Nordic giantesses, Hyrrokin, arrived at the funeral of Balder, four Berserker struggled to hold her wolf in check while she broke the enormous funeral ship Hringhorn loose from the sand.

That was the wolf of the Norse. They called him the gray horse of the giantesses, the dusky stallion of the night rider.

Nordic wolves were the companions of the Norns, the Teutonic fates. The Finns called them Rutu's hounds, dogs of the death spirit. The ruler of all the gods, Odin, kept two wolves always at his side, Geri and Freki. They accompanied him in battle together with his two ravens, and tore the corpses of the dead. Thus Wolfram, from *Wolf-hraben*, "wolf-raven," was a great warrior's name, and to see a wolf and a raven on the way to battle augured victory. Rudolf, from *Ruhm-wolf*, was another warrior name, meaning "victorious wolf." And Wolfgang meant "wolf going before," a hero whose coming was announced by the appearance of wolves.

I have alluded to the fanatic Berserker in connection with the European werewolf tradition, but there is nothing in southern Europe to match the stature of Fenris, Skoll, and Hati, the Nordic death wolves.

Fenris was the son of Loki and Angur-boda, a giantess. Two other children were born of this illicit marriage: Hel, whom Odin cast down into the earth to rule the dismal realm of the walking dead; and Iormungandr, an enormous serpent Odin banished to the sea. Odin took Fenris to Asgard, home of the gods, where he hoped to have the wolf's friendship and allegiance. But Fenris grew to such a size there that the gods were soon afraid to approach him. It was decided to chain the wolf to the earth to guard against trouble, and for this purpose a great chain, Laeding, was forged. By cajoling and flattering the pleasant-tempered wolf they managed to get the chain on him—only, they said, so he could show his great strength by breaking it. Fenris stretched, as if he had been

Fenris howling at Götterdämmerung.

taking a nap, and the chain fell to the ground in pieces. The gods returned with Droma, the strongest chain they could make, and managed
to get Fenris to submit to being bound again. It took him a moment, but
Fenris snapped the links of Droma, too.

Now frightened and wondering how long Fenris would remain good-
natured, the gods sent to the land of the dwarfs for a chain of prodigious
strength. The dwarfs fashioned a slender rope, smooth as silk, from the
spittle of birds and the murmurings of fish, from the anguish of bears
and the footsteps of cats, from a woman's beard and the roots of a mountain. The rope was called Gleipnir. It was so strong, they said, nothing
could break it. If it was tested, it would only become stronger.

Fenris eyed Gleipnir with suspicion. He agreed to be tied up only if
someone would first put his hand into his mouth as a pledge. Tyr, a war
god, stepped forth and placed his hand between Fenris's jaws. The wolf
was bound. He leaned into the bonds but they did not break. He put all
his strength to them but they did not even begin to stretch. In a rage he
crushed Tyr's hand, tearing it off at the wrist, which thereafter became
known as the wolf joint.

With Fenris subdued, the gods put the end of Gleipnir through an
enormous rock and tied it to a boulder which they threw into the sea.
Fenris began to howl. The howling started deep inside him and the
sound shook the earth. One of the gods took his sword and drove it into
the roof of Fenris's mouth, wedging the butt against his lower jaw, so
that he could not howl. The blood that gushed forth became the river
Von.

It was Fenris's fate to remain thus chained like his father Loki and the
giant Hel-hound Garm until the end of the world when Gleipnir would
burst and he would be loosed to lead an army against Odin and the rest
of the Aesir.

The sign that the end had come would be the eclipse of the sun and
moon. Each day Sun and Moon were pursued by the enormous wolves
Skoll, Hati, and Managarm. Kept by Angur-boda, fed on the bone marrow of murderers and adulterers, of which there was no end, they grew
stronger and stronger. Each day they got closer to Sol (Sun) and Mani
(Moon) until one day their jaws closed around them and the life was
crushed out of them. Their blood dripped from the wolves' jaws and

poured down on the earth. The stars began to fall out of the sky. This was *Götterdämmerung*, the Twilight of the Gods. Fenris was released. Loki and Garm broke their chains, and at the same moment the dragon Nidhug gnawed through the root of the world tree and the earth was split with the tremor. Then Heimdall, one of the Aesir, sounded the alarm on his horn Giallar, and the sound was heard the world over. At Asgard the Aesir armed themselves, and, mounting their horses, crossed the great rainbow bridge to Vigrid, where the last battle would be fought.

Loki's serpent son Iormungandr churned the sea to boiling before he crawled out onto the battlefield. One of the great waves stirred by his tail broke the Death Ship, Nagilfar, loose from the shore. It was made from the nail parings of the dead and Loki was at its helm. In another ship were the Frost Giants. Hel came up through a breach in the earth with Garm and the dragon Nidhug, who flew over the battlefield raining corpses from beneath his wings. The skies burst apart and there was Surtur with his sword of flame, igniting the earth. Fenris arrived, breathing fire, his eyes blazing, to stand with Garm, with Hel and Loki and the Death Horde, against Odin, Thor, Tyr, and the rest of the Aesir.

At a signal the battle began. The gods fought with exemplary valor but were doomed from the beginning. Fenris met Odin with jaws so wide they took in everything between earth and sky and Odin was swallowed alive. Loki killed Heimdall but fell mortally wounded. Tyr drove his sword through Garm's heart, but not before the Hel-hound tore him open. Thor struck Iormungandr a death blow and staggered back unharmed, only to be drowned in the flood of venom that poured from the serpent's jaws. Odin's son Vidar, seeing his father slain, rushed at Fenris and planting a foot in his mouth grabbed the wolf's shaggy head and ripped the jaws apart.

Surtur's fire leaped higher and higher, consuming the forests and fields. Fire roared through the nine kingdoms of Hel and boiled the waters of the ocean, until the earth lay still and smoking.

In time, under the light of a new sun, grasses began to grow. Flowers bloomed. The waters ran again. Two human beings, a woman named Lif and a man named Lifthrasir, whose descendants would spread over the earth, came out of a dark wood which the fires had not destroyed.

• • •

At the beginning of the second Christian millennium, the Icelandic sailor Leif Ericsson was exploring the eastern coast of North America, from Newfoundland possibly to as far south as what we today call Virginia. Perhaps he sailed into the Upper Bay and observed the granite and forests of Manhattan Island. We have no way of knowing. Perhaps he and his men camped on the beaches of southern New Jersey and filled their water casks with the dark cedar water that would stay fresh in the barrels for more than a year. We do not know. But Ericsson would have seen wolves. He would have seen their tracks on the beaches everywhere he went. He would have seen them watching from the woods as his ship rolled in the breakers. He would have heard their howls as his men stepped ashore.

Out of Ericsson's sight, beneath the southern horizon, south of Libra and Scorpio, was a constellation of 159 stars. It was known in Europe as The Beast or The Wild Animal. The Assyrians called it the constellation of The Beast of Death, and its brightest star The Star of the Dead Fathers. It was incorporated by some into the constellation to the east, the Centaur, and regarded as a sacrificial offering, so that it came to be known as The Victim.

It was also known by the name it still carries—Lupus.

Had Ericsson and his men gone farther south than historians believe they did, been one evening anchored in the Florida Keys, they would have seen a midnight sun burning in the southern sky where Lupus was, the stellar fire of a supernova that took place some time in the year 1006.

The chances are good that Ericsson did not see the supernova. The chances are that he regarded the Indians and the trees and the warmth of the seasons and went on his way, knowing not at all what would take place in this new world, what would die here and then be born again.

You can, if you have access to a very good telescope, still observe the remnant of the supernova in Lupus. It is now the most delicate gossamer of filamentary nebulosity. Wisps of red and blue silhouetted against blue-black interstellar space.

It is as though someone had cried out.

Epilogue

ON THE RAISING OF WOLVES
AND A NEW ETHOLOGY

Dᴜʀɪɴɢ the time I was researching this book, my wife and I raised two hybrid red wolves at our home in the woods in Oregon. These two wolves, Prairie and River, triggered many of the perceptions in this book and it was my association with them that first alerted me to the possibility of human error in the judgment of animals.

I am wary of situations in which wild animals are penned for the sake of human analysis. And yet I cannot deny that this experience, our experience, was extraordinary. It opened my eyes to my own human biases, to the gaps in my formal education with regard to animals, and to my own capacity for pity, anger, and a sense of helplessness where wild animals are concerned.

I would like in this epilogue to share some of these episodes. I don't think they belong in the foregoing chapters because, strictly speaking, they amount to little more than the author's experiences with his pets. But, with some clarification of my point of view, they have a place here.

I am not an authority on wolves. I do not think my experiences are universal, and I do not wish to encourage other people to raise wolves. Wolves don't belong living with people. It's as simple as that. Having done it once, naïvely, I would never do it again. Most people I know who have raised wolves feel the same way. All too often the wolf's life ends tragically and its potential for growth while it lives is smothered. I am grateful for the knowledge I have gained but if I'd known what it would cost I don't think I would have asked.

Prairie and River came to us from a wildlife park through the intervention of a friend and were three weeks old when they arrived. We bottle-fed them and, as is usually the case with young wolves, or dogs, they were intensely interested in everything around them. Canines use their mouths, I think, in much the same way we use our hands, especially when they are young. They are not trying to eat everything they encounter, they are simply trying to get a feeling for whatever it is. And the wolves felt everything. By the time they were six weeks old we had anything we valued stored three feet off the floor.

In these first few weeks, Prairie and River howled mournfully, perhaps sensing their parents' distance or their isolation from others like themselves. They ate ravenously and seemed always to be at one of two extremes: sleeping, sprawled like beanbags in the middle of the floor, or tearing through the house in pursuit of each other or imaginary beings. When they were seven weeks old they had a single, short, bloody fight during which the female, Prairie, got the best of the male, River. We never saw another fight as serious, though which animal usually deferred to the other afterward changed several times.

They never tried to harm us when they were puppies (or later), though they jerked at our hair hard enough almost to wrench it from our skulls, and they would scratch us inadvertently with their claws and sharp milk teeth. And though we were not afraid of them when they got larger, they occasionally tried the imaginations of our friends with their antics. One day a woman left her infant son on a blanket on our living-room floor and turned her back to talk with us. Behind her were the wolves, whose hiding place was under the wood stove. The pups came out into the open (overcoming their fear of a strange adult), anxious to get a closer look at the baby, a living creature (I was thinking they were thinking) close to their own size and, more importantly, one who also lived in that twelve-inch-high zone next to the floor where they lived.

With great hesitancy, ready to flee at the first sign of discovery, jabbing the air nervously, high and low, for some clue to the creature, they finally got up to the edge of the baby's blanket. Anxious to draw the baby into their world but still afraid of the adult whose back was turned only inches away, they took an obvious but frightening step—they took hold of the baby's blanket and began pulling him away. At that moment the mother turned around and the surprised wolves—scrambling frantically for traction on the hardwood floor—bolted for their hideout under the wood stove.

Another time, when they were about a year old, Prairie and River "attacked" Sandy, my wife. We had had friends to dinner and we wanted them to see the wolves before they left. It was very late, so we took a flashlight and led them out through the woods. The wolves had been asleep but they jumped up as we drew near. We were at the fence for only a few minutes, sweeping the flashlight around their pen, before we said good night to our friends and they departed.

I felt guilty about waking the wolves up, about invading their privacy. I wouldn't wake a child up for friends to see in the middle of the night. Sandy and I exchanged some thoughts about this and she went back to the pen without the flashlight. I went into the house. As she entered the pen the wolves immediately began to push her around, slamming against her with their bodies and soft-biting her arms and legs. They were fast enough and strong enough, of course, to have hurt her seriously, but they didn't. Our intuitive feeling was that they were angry. Other people who have worked with wolves in enclosures have had similar experiences. It is almost as if the animals were warning you of the limits of friendship. What makes the message so strong, of course, is that it's coming from an animal that can kill you.

Although I am familiar with wild country, I learned, I think, several remarkable things simply by walking in the woods with River and

Prairie and paying attention to what they did. We took them out on leashes. They often sought out ridges, high on the slopes of the mountain valley where we lived. I assumed at first that it was for the view but later it seemed it was for another reason as well. Here the air currents that moved strongly upslope in the afternoon reached them intact, not broken up, with the olfactory information they carried scattered, as happened when the winds blew through the trees.

The wolves moved deftly and silently in the woods and in trying to imitate them I came to walk more quietly and to freeze at the sign of slight movement. At first this imitation gave me no advantage, but after several weeks I realized I was becoming far more attuned to the environment we moved through. I heard more, for one thing, and, my senses now constantly alert, I occasionally saw a deer mouse or a grouse before they did. I also learned the several thousand acres we walked in well enough to find my way around in the dark. I never moved as quietly, or with the grace that they did, not with my upright stance and long limbs that caused my body to become entangled, and the ninety-degree angle at my ankle that caused my feet to catch. But I took from them the confidence to believe I could attune myself better to the woods by behaving as they did—minutely inspecting certain things, seeking vantage points, always sniffing at the air. I did, and felt vigorous, charged with alertness.

They moved always, it seemed one day, in search of clues.

After these experiences, when I came in contact with Eskimo perceptions of the wolf I was much quicker to understand that the Eskimo "sees" differently from the way I see, and that I would likely never see as well in the wild as the Eskimo did, any more than I would ever see as well in the woods one day as Prairie and River.

There were moments of pain and embarrassment with the wolves, times when we sensed how awful the pen must have been for them, as large as it was. The smoke from a slash fire at a logging site would drift through. They would sense fire but have nowhere to run. Deer would appear, and the wolves would race excitedly up and down, looking for a way out. A loose board would make a banging noise in a storm and terrify them. There were other incidents, though, ones that could almost make up for these. To see them leaping for falling leaves in October. To sleep with them in the pen at night and feel them drifting by, just brushing your fingertips with their fur.

I would often sit out in the woods next to the pen on sunny afternoons, reading and making notes. I enjoyed being around them.

One summer day, when the wolves were a little more than two years old, someone let them out. We never found out who. I think it must have been someone who believed all wild animals should be free but who did not know that wild animals raised in captivity are no longer wild. River was shot and killed by a man who told us later he wasn't sure what kind of animals they were but they looked wild and were trying to play with his neighbor's dogs, so he thought they might be rabid. With River lying there dead, Prairie bolted for the deep woods. The next day, when we got home (we were away at a funeral), she responded to Sandy's howling and came to her, lay down at her feet, trembling and disoriented.

Prairie's depression and disorientation lasted for weeks, long enough for us to consider putting her to sleep. Finally, with the aid of a young dog who befriended and supported her, she came around.

We buried River. While I was digging the grave I thought of all the wolves I had met and how many of those were dead. Killed by other wolves in pens that did not let an ostracized animal escape. Killed in scientific experiments. Poisoned by people who hated wolves. Shot by neighbors who feared them. Wolf pups that had been killed by animal caretakers because there were simply too many to be fed and housed, and no one had taken the responsibility to isolate the sexes when the females were in estrus. Killed by people who professed a love for wolves but who, because the wolf puppies wouldn't housebreak like dogs, or because they didn't look royal blooded enough after losing an ear or the tip of a tail in a fight, didn't want them around.

I didn't know what to say to the man who killed River. I didn't know what to say to River. I just stood there in an afternoon rain trying to remember what I'd learned in his presence.

I think, as the twentieth century comes to a close, that we are coming to an understanding of animals different from the one that has guided us for the past three hundred years. We have begun to see again, as our primitive ancestors did, that animals are neither imperfect imitations of men nor machines that can be described entirely in terms of endocrine secretions and neural impulses. Like us, they are genetically variable, and both the species and the individual are capable of unprecedented behavior. They are like us in the sense that we can figuratively talk of them as beings some of whose forms, movements, activities, and social organizations are analogous, but they are no more literally like us than are trees. To paraphrase Henry Beston, they move in another universe, as complete as we are, both of us caught at a moment in mid-evolution.

I do not think it possible to define completely the sort of animals men require in order to live. They are always changing and are different for different peoples. Nor do I think it possible that science can by itself produce the animal entire. The range of the human mind, the scale and depth of the metaphors the mind is capable of manufacturing as it grapples with the universe, stand in stunning contrast to the belief that there is only one reality, which is man's, or worse, that only one culture among the many on earth possesses the truth.

To allow mystery, which is to say to yourself, "There could be more, there could be things we don't understand," is not to damn knowledge. It is to take a wider view. It is to permit yourself an extraordinary freedom: someone else does not have to be wrong in order that you may be right.

In the Western world, in the biological sciences, we have an extraordinary tool for discovery of knowledge about animals, together with a system for its classification; and through the existence of journals and libraries we have a system for its dissemination. But if we are going to learn more about animals—real knowledge, not more facts—we are going to have to get out into the woods. We are going to have to pay more attention to free-ranging as opposed to penned animals, which will require an unfamiliar patience. And we are going to have to find ways in which single, startling incidents in animal behavior, now discarded in the winnowing process of science's data assembly, can be preserved, can somehow be incorporated. And we are going to have to find a way, not necessarily to esteem, but at least not to despise intuition in the scientific process, for it is, as Kepler and Darwin and Einstein have said, the key.

The English philosopher Alfred North Whitehead, writing about human inquiry into the nature of the universe, said that in simply discussing the issues, the merest hint of dogmatic certainty is an exhibition of folly. This tolerance for mystery invigorates the imagination; and it is the imagination that gives shape to the universe.

The appreciation of the separate realities enjoyed by other organisms is not only no threat to our own reality, but the root of a fundamental joy. I learned from River that I was a human being and that he was a wolf and that we were different. I valued him as a creature, but he did not have to be what I imagined he was. It is with this freedom from dogma, I think, that the meaning of the words "the celebration of life" becomes clear.

Afterword

A REAQUAINTANCE WITH WOLVES

The high desert of eastern Oregon ranged off under a bright crescent moon in long swells, like an inland ocean. I was driving home from Burns, a ranching town in Oregon's dry plateau country, headed for the Cascade Mountains and a temperate rainforest on the far side of those volcanic peaks, where my house sits by a river. Twenty minutes or more would pass between one oncoming vehicle and the next. At the farthest reach of my truck lights, coyotes skipped the road. Twice I saw small herds of antelope silhouetted against the clear sky.

Despite the warm, insular confinement of the truck, the sound of its engine, and whir of tires on the two-lane blacktop and macadam, I felt included in the silent nightscape of chilled winter land I was moving

287

through. It was fenced, to be sure, but the absence of any building and the moon's pale light suggested, still, uncorralled nature.

The rolling uplands of scattered juniper, sage, and rabbit brush to either side of the road were likely as wolfless on this night as they had been before white settlement, one of the few, odd corners of North America to have virtually no history of wolves, according to wolf historian Stanley Young. A hundred miles away to the northeast, in the wide basins and wooded foothills of the Blue Mountains, however, wolves had turned up at least three times since 1999. They had swum the Snake River from Idaho, to make their appearance in a land where the last wolf had been trapped out more than fifty years before. Of the three, one was struck and killed by a vehicle on Interstate 84, south of Baker City in May 2000. A second, a radio-collared female, was captured by state, federal, and Nez Perce tribal biologists on the Middle Fork of the John Day River in February 1999 and returned to her home range in central Idaho. The third, a male, was shot in October 2000 north of Ukiah, Oregon, and some suggested, left to be found.

Each of these three wolves—and chances are good there were others, never seen or reported—was a descendant of animals introduced into Idaho's Salmon River backcountry in 1995 and 1996 by the federal government. Their unanticipated appearance in eastern Oregon had instantly stirred mixed and powerful emotions across the state. Many people in the two largest urban areas, Portland and Eugene, initially saw these dispersing wolves as a favorable omen, a tenuous symbol of reconciliation between human and nonhuman worlds. Residents of predominantly rural eastern Oregon, however, were nearly unanimous in their demand that the state do something to keep such migrating wolves away. They viewed these creatures as a serious economic threat to livestock operations and to sport hunting, a major component of tourism in that part of Oregon. In the rising and acrimonious statewide debate, they charged that wolves would ruthlessly kill pets in the suburbs and argued that their presence would degrade the value of ranch land.

That winter night, driving across the desert, I was coming home from one of fourteen regional town hall meetings arranged by Oregon's Department of Fish and Wildlife, each meant to solicit public opinion about which approach the state might take to wolves wandering into Oregon from Idaho. The strident objections I'd heard to this animal's establishing a presence in the state, raised by virtually all of the nearly one hundred peo-ple in attendance in Burns that night, were so vehement, so biologically naive, so seemingly beyond negotiation, I remember thinking the meeting could as easily have taken place in 1902 as 2002.

The consensus sentiment was: Kill them, or they will harm us.

It is difficult to summarize what we have learned about wolves in the twenty-five years since this book was written, partly because wolves are studied in a more politicized environment today. For example, recent genetic research suggests that the eastern timber wolf (at present *Canis lupus lycaon*, but tentatively *Canis lycaon*) may be a separate species from the gray wolf *(Canis lupus)*, one more closely related to the red wolf *(Canis rufus)*. This speculation has affected public debate about the reintroduction of wolves to their former habitat in the northeastern United States as well as debate about the intent of certain provisions in the Endangered Species Act. Such a contesting of scientific opinion likely would not have taken place twenty-five or thirty years ago.

The most striking—and uncontested—reassessment of our under-standing of wolf ecology in recent years has been prompted by long-term studies of predator/prey relationships. The effect wolves have on the size of prey populations, we now know, is much more complicated than originally imagined. In short, wolves *limit* the size of prey populations but they do not *regulate* them. Grizzly bears, for example, where they are pres-ent, play a larger role in the population dynamics of moose and caribou than anyone previously suspected.

While wolf researchers continue to refine our conceptions of wolf biology, behavior, and ecology (looking, for instance, for the causes of infant mortality or speculating on the resolution of social tensions in a pack), we have arguably seen the most significant change in our under-standing of the wolf in another area—wolf-human relations. This change has come about largely as a result of wolves' increased contact with humans (1) in areas where large wolf populations are intact, protected, or well managed (Alaska, Canada, and Minnesota); (2) where smaller, natu-rally occurring wolf populations are recovering (Montana, Wisconsin, and Michigan); and (3) in areas where wolves have been reintroduced.

Red wolves, the first species of wolf to be successfully reintroduced, were released in North Carolina, mostly in and around Alligator River National Wildlife Refuge, beginning in 1987. Gray wolves, after early attempts in various locales failed, were successfully reintroduced in 1995 and 1996, when the U.S. Fish and Wildlife Service placed thirty-five wolves from British Columbia and Alberta in former wolf habitat in central Idaho and released another thirty-one in the Yellowstone country of Wyoming. These two populations have thrived, and wolves in Yellowstone National Park have provided researchers in the lower forty-eight states with extraordinary new opportunities for study. Gray wolves were also reintroduced in Arizona and New Mexico in 1998, and a federal plan for their release in northern New England and upstate New York was drawn up in 1992.

Increased human contact with wolves over the past three decades has led to a reconsideration of their reputedly always-benign response to the presence of human beings. The topic of much greater interest to most, however, and an area of intense scientific curiosity, has been wolf reintroduction. Whether the reintroduction of the wolf makes good all-around biological sense remains an open question; the successful reintroduction of these creatures in several regions, however, has signaled the appearance of something new—an active human desire now to share wild land with wolves, bears, and other large predators, perhaps not incidentally emerging in a country that historically has been this animal's most systematic foe.

It is easy, I think, to underestimate the emotional impact wolf reintroduction has had on many Americans. For some, considering the near maniacal way in which the animal was once hunted down, it's been like reconciliation with a bad dream. Scientists contend we will never be able to completely restore the ecosystems in which wolves once lived, but many now feel that we've been able at least to restore some sense of our own dignity by successfully implementing and managing wolf reintroduction programs.

The decades following the publication of Adolph Murie's *The Wolves of Mount McKinley* (1944) and Stanley Young and Edward Goldman's *The Wolves of North America* (1944) saw an enormous growth in our general understanding of the biology and ecology of wolves, and we developed a greatly expanded appreciation of the complexity of their behavior. This awakening pointed directly to a reassessment of our relationship with wolves and, I believe, led straight to considering the feasibility of reintroduction.

Today, along with the usual stream of data from field and laboratory studies, work that scientists have traditionally relied on, most professional researchers, with some notable exceptions, are willing to take seriously the amplifying views of indigenous people about wolves, building on the pioneering work of Robert O. Stephenson with Nunamiut Eskimos in Alaska's Brooks Range. They are also more willing to consult with scholars in folklore, mythology, history, and human psychology on the development of wolf management and wolf reintroduction programs. The fieldwork of scientists in Europe, the Middle East, and Asia has further deepened our knowledge of the wolf's ability to adapt successfully to human encroachment in previously wild environments.

Our awareness of wolves, as a result, has become quite complex. We better comprehend how our own behavior and preconceptions affect our understanding of what they do, and our overall relations with them are now more informed by ethical considerations.

You wouldn't have guessed, of course, at the Harney County Senior Center in Burns that December night, that such a profound shift in awareness had occurred. (The anger and frustration directed against wolves at some of the other town hall meetings in Oregon, I later learned, was even greater.) But in fairness to many of those testifying in Burns, the wolf itself, *Canis lupus*, was not the focus of their fulminations but rather what the wolf's protected status and its deliberate reintroduction symbolized for the majority of those who attended the meeting. Along with many other rural Americans, these Oregonians shared a sense that they were being financially compromised and socially marginalized by the recent development of ecologically based land-use policy decisions across the United States. They also felt, generally, that these policies were too environmentally restrictive and that they were developed mostly by "city people," persons innocent of the day-to-day realities of rural life.

A second, closely allied group of Americans—if they can, indeed, be separated out as a second group—spoke that night about their conviction that they were being chronically thwarted and endlessly manipulated by the federal government because of their way of life. Some in this group were instantly hostile toward the suggestion of any kind of toleration of potential threats to their grazing privileges on public land, should that land be seen to have some other public use, such as water conservation or wildlife protection.

The modern controversy over wolf protection, wolf management, and wolf reintroduction, in other words, has stirred a discomfitting examination of both our romance with wild wolves and our nostalgia about the ranching life.

Looking back over the twenty-five years since this book was first published and wondering where we've gotten in our dealings with these animals, I feel compelled to offer only a couple of thoughts. At the opening of the twenty-first century, the wolf is a much less demonized animal than it was when Stanley Young was writing. This is largely due to the wide dissemination of a body of scientific research on wolves and on a growing sophistication among lay people about ecology in general. The wolf, however, continues to generate more adamant positions and to trigger more powerful emotions than any other large predator in the northern hemisphere, especially if the question is about where wolves might fit in a landscape shared closely with humans. Some folklore about wolves, both that which attributes nobility to them and that which seizes upon them as an embodiment of evil, is so deeply entrenched that its adherents completely shut out the emerging insights of field biologists, historians, religion scholars, and other researchers in the social sciences and humanities. In their rigid stances they are impervious even to reason. Why this is so remains one of the most interesting questions in wolf research, partly because it's so representative of large-scale political forces at work today in American culture.

A second thought is that with the reintroduction of wolves, we've demonstrated that we're more capable now of living in a give-and-take relationship with the natural world than we once were. This bodes well for all animals, ourselves included. It means we're willing to consider biological information alongside economic data and human social needs in the development of public policy and management programs.

Finally, if one strain of wolf research in recent decades would seem to call for clarifying comment, it would be the study and promotion of dominance hierarchies in wolf packs. While a sometimes convenient tool of analysis, the notion of sex and age hierarchies has led too many people to make specious assumptions about wolf behavior. Interpreting wolf interactions too strictly along these lines, like placing too strong an emphasis on the significance of a predator's "territory," requires many large mammals to carry the freight of human constructs, including "ownership" and "authority," baggage no animal should be asked to bear.

Many of us now seem to subscribe to the idea that wild animals are not mechanisms. They cannot be summed up, any more than Homo sapiens can be summed up. Wild animals are intricately fitted in the world, an intricacy that, many speculate, goes further and deeper than the catch nets of Homo sapiens' neurological capacity to conceive.

Reality is a mystery, to put it another way, and bound to remain so. And it may be as good an idea to live within the mystery as it is to stand outside it, possessed of the notion that it can be explained.

We have been moving steadily in recent years toward another sort of reconciliation, that with our own ecology and biology. We wonder now whether our national and local politics should reflect, far better than they have, what we are learning about the kind of environment our bodies fundamentally require. The growth of much of this thinking, curiously, can be traced directly to the long-term, exacting, and thoughtful fieldwork being done by women and men studying animals in their natural habitats, a range of creatures, at some level, not so different from ourselves. Wild animals, living beyond fiscal economies, disinterested in the nation-state, requiring no technologies, no growth in their rates of consumption in order to abide and proliferate, yet able to experience emotional states somewhere in the realm of our own, remind us that we are rooted in an absolute need for good water, clean air, and unadulterated food. And, not incidently, in a requirement for diversity. Diversity, many now suspect, is not merely a characteristic of life, either biological life or cultural life. It is a condition necessary *for* life.

It would not be inappropriate or sentimental in the context of this book, considering the scope of what has happened in wolf studies in recent years, to thank this enduring creature, *Canis lupus*, for standing by while we continue to pursue a complex and difficult aspiration, the implementation of a universal justice that would include all we see living around us.

Barry Lopez
McKenzie River, Oregon
2003

BIBLIOGRAPHY

Only selected background and reference works are listed here. Several large bibliographies already exist for material in the first section. Sources for the second section are too diverse to list completely. Much of the most important research material for the third section is unpublished in theses and dissertations or stored in the files of historical societies. Research material for the fourth section is simply too voluminous to present economically. For a researcher with a specific inquiry directed through the publisher, I will do whatever I can to help locate a source.

Books and articles sufficiently identified in the text are, for the most part, not mentioned below.

1: Canis lupus *Linnaeus*

The most recent, reliable collection of scientific papers on the wolf is L. D. Mech and L. Boitani, eds., *Wolves: Behavior, Ecology, and Conservation* (Chicago: University of Chicago Press, 2003), but see also two earlier collections edited by Harrington and Paquet (1982) and Carbyn (1995) cited in the bibliographic notes under "Afterword." Mech (rhymes with "each") also wrote *The Wolf: The Ecology and Behavior of an Endangered Species* (N.Y.: Natural History Press, 1970) and *The Wolves of Isle Royale* (Wash., D.C.: U.S. Department of the Interior, Fauna of the National Parks of the United States, Fauna Series 7, 1966), both works rich with field observations. The only criticism that might be made of Mech's long-term, dedicated research is that his ideas now too throroughly dominate the field.

I have quoted several times from Adolph Murie, *The Wolves of Mount McKinley* (Wash., D.C.: U.S. Department of the Interior, Fauna of the National Parks, Fauna Series 5, 1944). The book is more than thirty years old but still good science and pleasant reading. Other works I used as background for these chapters include *Ecological Studies of the Timber Wolf in Northeastern Minnesota*, edited by L. D. Mech and L. D. Frenzel (St. Paul, Minn.: U.S. Department of Agriculture, North Central Forest Experiment Station, Forest Service Research Paper NC-52, 1971); R. F. Ewer, *The Carnivores* (Ithaca, N.Y.: Cornell University Press, 1973); J. P. Scott and J. L. Fuller, *Dog Behavior: The Genetic Basis* (Chicago: University of Chicago Press, 1965); a collection of papers edited by Michael Fox, *The Wild Canids: Their Systematics, Behavioral Ecology and Evolution* (N.Y.: Van Nostrand Reinhold, 1975); and several books on animals associated with the wolf, including John Kelsall, *The Migratory Barren-Ground Caribou of Canada* (Ottawa: Canadian Wildlife Series 3, Queen's Printer, 1968) and books on convergent evolution, including Hans Kruuk, *The Spotted Hyena* (Chicago: University of Chicago Press, 1972). While it was not originally available in book form, a collection of papers from a symposium on wolves in *American Zoologist* (7: 221–381, 1967) may be treated as such. A collection of papers published in 1979 to which I had early access is *The Behavior and Ecology of Wolves* (New York: Garland STPM Press), the proceedings of a symposium on wolves held at the University of North Carolina at Wilmington, May 23–25, 1975, edited by E. Klinghammer.

There are several popular treatments of wolves by writers with a background in wildlife biology, including Farley Mowat's fictionalized account, *Never Cry Wolf* (Boston: Little, Brown, 1963) and Lois Crisler's *Arctic Wild* (N.Y.: Curtis Books, 1958). *Never Cry Wolf* is dated but still a good introduction. Less adventuresome and personal is R. J. Rutter and D. H. Pimlott, *The World of the Wolf* (Phila.: Lippincott, 1968). The anecdotal and perhaps exaggerated accounts of Ernest Thompson Seton are still worth reading, both in *Lives of Game Animals* (Garden City: Doubleday, 1929) and *Life Histories of Northern Animals* (N.Y.: Scribners, 1909). The works of Stanley Young so earnestly mix fact and fiction that, taken strictly for science, they are problematic, and I have therefore cited them below with materials for Section III.

Young's bibliography in *The Wolves of North America* (Wash., D.C.: American Wildlife Institute, 1944; and Dover reprint, 1964) is enormous but undisciplined and, at points, inaccurate. More valuable are Mech's and Boitani's bibliography in *Wolves* and Fox's in *The Wild Canids*.

Several books that treat the wolf in Russia and Asia have been translated for the National Science Foundation by the Israel Program for Scientific Translations (IPST), Jerusalem. They include G. A. Novikov, *Carnivorous Mammals of the Fauna of the USSR* (Moscow, 1956, and Jerusalem, IPST, 1962); S. I. Ognev, *Mammals of Eastern Europe and Northern Asia* (Leningrad, 1931, and Jerusalem, IPST, 1962); and S. U. Stroganov's *Carnivorous Mammals of Siberia* (Moscow, 1962, and Jerusalem, IPST, 1969). They suffer slightly from the inclusion of popular opinion and in Ognev's case an avowed hatred of wolves.

There are a number of excellent papers on wolf ecology and behavior. Several that one might enjoy reading in full, which I have touched on only briefly, are: R. O. Stephenson and R. T. Ahgook, "The Eskimo Hunter's View of Wolf Ecology and Behavior" in *The Wild Canids* (pp. 286–91); R. Henshaw, L. Underwood, and T. Casey, "Peripheral Thermoregulation: Foot Temperature in Two Arctic Canines" (*Science* 175: 988–90, March 3, 1972); C. A. Nielsen, *Wolf Necropsy Report: preliminary pathological observations* (Juneau: Alaska Department of Fish and Game, Special Report, Federal Aid in Wildlife Restoration, July 1977); R. Schenkel, "Expression Studies of Wolves" (*Behaviour* 1: 81–129, 1947); R. P. Peters and L. D. Mech, "Scent-Marking in Wolves" (*American Scientist* 63 (6): 628–37,

1975); H. Kruuk, "Surplus Killing by Carnivores" (*Journal of Zoology, London* 166: 233–44, 1972); E. Zimen, "Social Dynamics of the Wolf Pack" in *The Wild Canids* (pp. 336–62); W. O. Pruitt, "A Flight Releaser in Wolf-Caribou Relations" (*Journal of Mammalogy* 46: 350–51, 1965); P. Marhenke, "An Observation of Four Wolves Killing Another Wolf" (*Journal of Mammalogy* 52:630–31, 1971); R. G. Bromley, "Fishing Behavior of a Wolf on the Taltson River, Northwest Territories" (*The Canadian Field-Naturalist* 87 (3): 301–3, 1973). Robert Stephenson's papers, which offer both the results of field work and comments on Nunamiut wolf observations, include a series of annual Wolf Reports (Federal Aid in Wildlife Restoration, 1972, 1973, 1974, 1975) and *Characteristics of Wolf Den Sites* (Federal Aid in Wildlife Restoration, 1974), all published by the Alaska Department of Fish and Game, Juneau.

For background on the red wolf (*Canis rufus*), see G. A. Riley and R. McBride, *A Survey of the Red Wolf* (Wash., D.C.: U.S. Department of the Interior, Fish and Wildlife Service, Special Scientific Report No. 162, 1972); J. L. Paradiso and R. M. Nowak, *A Report on the Taxonomic Status and Distribution of the Red Wolf* (Wash., D.C.: U.S. Department of the Interior, Fish and Wildlife Service, Special Scientific Report No. 145, 1971); and J. H. Shaw and P. Jordan, "The Wolf That Lost Its Genes" (*Natural History* 86 (10): 80–88, December 1977).

C. H. D. Clarke, "The Beast of Gévaudan" (*Natural History* 80 (4): 44–51, 66–73, April 1971) and Vilhjalmer Stefansson's *Adventures in Error* (N.Y.: Robert M. McBride, 1936, and Gale Research Company reprint, Detroit, 1970) provide a good survey of the question of wolf predation on humans, but see the papers by McNay under "Afterword."

Articles on the ecology and behavior of the wolf are produced regularly and will no doubt refine or even refute points in this section in the future. *Wildlife Index* and *Biological Abstracts* are continually updated sources of the most recent information and are available at most large libraries with scientific holdings.

II: And a Cloud Passes Overhead

Several pertinent observations on the Nunamiut are contained in the series of papers by Stephenson mentioned above. For information of a more general nature see R. Rausch, "Notes on the Nunamiut Eskimo and Mammals of the Anaktuvuk Pass Region, Brooks Range, Alaska" (*Arctic* 4 (3): 147–95, 1951) and Nicholas Gubser, *The Nunamiut Eskimo: Hunters of Caribou* (New Haven: Yale University Press, 1965). I used several books as general background in chapter 4, among them Richard Nelson, *Hunters of the Northern Ice* (Chicago: University of Chicago Press, 1969). Edmund Carpenter, *Eskimo Realities* (N.Y.: Holt, Rinehart and Winston, 1973) provides insight into the Eskimo's different way of seeing, as does James Gibson, *The Perception of the Visual World* (Boston: Houghton Mifflin, 1950). For some specific information, see J. Kleinfeld, "Visual Memory in Village Eskimo and Urban Caucasian Children" (*Arctic* 24 (2): 132–38, 1971).

For background on the Naskapi I relied on Georg Henriksen, *Hunters in the Barrens: The Naskapi on the Edge of the White Man's World* (St. John's, Newfoundland: Memorial University of Newfoundland, 1973) and Frank Speck, *Naskapi: The Savage Hunters of the Labrador Peninsula* (Norman, Okla.: University of Oklahoma Press, 1935). On sacred meat and the Animal Master see Speck's book and two articles by A. Hultkrantz: "Animals Among the Wind River Shoshoni" (*Ethnos* 26: 198–218, 1961) and "The Owner of the Animals in the Religion of the North American Indians: Some General Remarks" in A. Hultkrantz, ed., *The Supernatural Owners of Nature* (Stockholm: Almquist & Wiksell, 1961).

For some interesting elaboration on the idea of a conversation of death, see J. Eisenbud, "Evolution and Psi" (*Journal of the American Society for Psychical Research* 70: 35–53, 1976). On territorial hunting see D. S. Davidson, *Family Hunting Territories in Northwestern North America* (N.Y.: Museum of the American Indian, Heye Foundation, 1928); F. Speck, "The Family Hunting Band as the Basis of Algonkian Social Organization" (*American Anthropologist* 17 (2): 289–305, 1915); and B. Smith, "Predator-Prey Relationships in the Southeastern Ozarks—A.D. 1300" (*Human Ecology* 2 (1): 31–43, 1974). Comparable data on behavioral adaptations of deer under pressure from humans and wolves respectively can be found in H. Hickerson, "The Virginia Deer and Intertribal Buffer Zones in the Upper Mississippi Valley" in *Man, Culture and Animals: The Role of Animals on Human Ecological Adjustments*, A. Leeds and A. Vayda, eds. (Wash., D.C.: American Association for the Advancement of Science, 1965) and L. D. Mech, "Population Trend and Winter Deer Consumption in a Minnesota Wolf Pack" in *Pro-*

ceedings of the 1975 Predator Symposium, R. L. Phillips and C. Jonkel, eds. (Missoula, Mont.: Montana Forest and Conservation Experiment Station, 1977).

Black Elk Speaks by John Neidhardt (Lincoln, Neb.: University of Nebraska Press, 1961), *The Sacred Pipe* by Joseph Epes Brown (Norman, Okla.: University of Oklahoma Press, 1953), and *Seeing With a Native Eye*, Walter Capps, ed. (N.Y.: Harper & Row, 1976), convey a general impression of the world view of native Americans. Many diverse observations on Indian attitudes toward animals are recorded in the indexed 32 volumes of *Early Western Travels, 1748–1846*, edited by Reuben Thwaites (Cleveland: A. H. Clark, 1904–1907). Of particular interest are the journals of Maximilian, Prince of Wied (volumes 22, 23, and 24).

For the Cheyenne and Pawnee who figure so prominently in the text see, respectively, *The Cheyenne: Their History and Ways of Life* by George Bird Grinnell (Lincoln, Neb.: University of Nebraska Press, 1972, 2 volumes) and Gene Weltfish, *The Lost Universe* (N.Y.: Basic Books, 1965). See, too, Grinnell's story collections: *Pawnee Hero Stories and Folk-tales* (Lincoln, Neb.: University of Nebraska Press, 1961); *By Cheyenne Campfires* (Lincoln, Neb.: University of Nebraska Press, 1971); and *Blackfoot Lodge Tales* (Lincoln, Neb.: University of Nebraska Press, 1962). For ritual use of the wolf skin see Thomas Mails, *The Mystic Warriors of the Plains* (N.Y.: Doubleday, 1972). Bird Shirt's story is from *American: The Life Story of a Great Indian, Plenty-Coups, Chief of the Crows* by Frank Bird Linderman (N.Y.: John Day, 1930) and used with permission. Additional information is in William Wildschut, *Crow Indian Medicine Bundles* (N.Y.: Museum of the American Indian, Heye Foundation, 1960). Material on the Bella Coola is from *The Bella Coola Indians* by Thomas F. McIlwraith (Toronto: University of Toronto Press, 1948). The stories about Kills in the Night and Ghost Head at the end of chapter 5 are recounted more fully in, respectively, *Pretty Shield: Medicine Woman of the Crows*, by Frank Bird Linderman (Lincoln, Neb.: University of Nebraska Press, 1972) and *The Sioux: Life and Customs of a Warrior Society* by Royal B. Hassrick et al. (Norman, Okla.: University of Oklahoma Press, 1964).

Much additional information is in the many indexed volumes of the University of Oklahoma's Civilization of the American Indian series.

For general background on the dog in Indian cultures see G. Wilson,

"The Horse and the Dog in Hidatsa Culture" (*Anthropological Papers of the American Museum of Natural History* 15: 125–262, 1924); G. Allen, "Dogs of the American Aborigines" (*Bulletin of the Museum of Comparative Zoology at Harvard College* 63 (9): 431–517, March 1920); and W. D. Matthew, "The Phylogeny of Dogs" (*Journal of Mammalogy* 11 (2): 117–38, 1930). The Crow story of the wolf and the dog is from R. H. Lowie, "Myths and Traditions of the Crow" (*Anthropological Papers of the American Museum of Natural History* 25: 224–25, 1918).

The story of the Sleeping Wolf fight is recounted in George Hyde, *The Life of George Bent* (Norman, Okla.: University of Oklahoma Press, 1968). For information on Navajo werewolves see W. Morgan, "Human Wolves Among the Navajo" (Yale University Publications in Anthropology, no.11, 1936) and "Southwest Witchcraft" (*El Palacio*, The Quarterly Journal of the Museum of New Mexico 80 (2), 1974).

The story of Laugher is adapted from James Willard Schultz's manuscript in the special collections library at Montana State University. Different versions of the story of Woman Who Lives with Wolves appear in Hassrick's *The Sioux*, and elsewhere. The Pawnee origin story is from Weltfish.

For the Makah Wolf Ceremony, see Alice Ernst, *The Wolf Ritual of the Northwest Coast* (Eugene, Ore.: University of Oregon Press, 1952). The Captive Girl Ceremony is, again, from Weltfish. The Sunrise Wolf Bundle Ceremony can be found in full in Alfred Bowers, *Hidatsa Social and Ceremonial Organization* (Wash., D.C.: Bureau of American Ethnology, Bulletin no. 194, 1965).

Many of these works contain helpful bibliographies.

III: The Beast of Waste and Desolation

For the general development of ideas in chapter 7, I relied in part on John Rodman, "The Dolphin Papers" (*North American Review* 259 (1): 13–26, 1974). Roderick Nash's ideas are in his *Wilderness and the American Mind* (New Haven: Yale University Press, 1967). Both the Rodman article and Nash's book are heavily footnoted and mention is made of most major works, classical and modern, bearing on the themes of hatred of the beast and fear of wilderness.

Records of animal trials and a general discussion of related philosophical issues are in E. Evans, "Bugs and Beasts Before the Law" (*Atlantic Monthly* 54: 235–46, August 1884). Pertinent points in Descartes's arguments are in his fifth discourse in *Discourse on Method* (N.Y.: Penguin, 1968).

An account of Courtaud, highly embellished, is in E. T. Seton, *Great Historic Animals, Mainly About Wolves* (N.Y.: Scribners, 1937). A work on human wolf predation with some apparent basis in fact is John Pollard, *Wolves and Werewolves* (London: R. Hale, 1964).

The problems wolves face in trying to survive in captivity are reported regularly in *Zoological Record*. For a personal treatment see Lois Crisler, *Captive Wild* (N.Y.: Harper & Row, 1968).

Information on wolf hunting with dogs in Russia and America comes largely from popular magazines of the period, including various issues of *Scribner's Magazine, Outdoor Life*, and *English Illustrated Magazine*. In general, outdoor magazines of the period covered (roughly 1850 to the present) are an excellent guide to attitudinal changes concerning the wolf. Especially useful, and mentioned in the text, are copies of *The Alaska Sportsman* from the 1930s, and *Outdoor Life*, which began publication in 1897. Roosevelt's quote on hunting wolves with dogs, at the beginning of chapter 8, is from "A Wolf Hunt in Oklahoma" (*Scribner's Magazine* 38 (5): 513–32, 1905).

Material on hunting wolves with eagles is from Remmler's own account, "Reminiscences of My Life with Eagles" (*Journal of the American Falconer's Association* 9, 1970), but I am indebted to Stephen Bodio, Harry Reynolds, and Alberto Palleroni for clarifications. The Tamworth incident is from Charles Edward Beals, *Passaconaway in the White Mountains* (Boston: R. G. Badger, 1916). The Saturday-afternoon wolf killing is distilled from Charles Harger, "Hunting Wolves by Automobile" (*World Today* 16: 429–32, April 1909). The O'Connor book is *The Big Game Animals of North America* (N.Y.: Outdoor Life/E. P. Dutton, 1961). See also his "Wolf" (*Outdoor Life* 127 (4): 72–75, 144–45, 148–49, April 1961). The aerial hunting incident quoted is from Russell Annabel, *Hunting and Fishing in Alaska* (N.Y.: Knopf, 1948). The James H. Bond book, *From Out of the Yukon*, was published by Binfords and Mort, Portland, Ore., in 1948.

Research material listed in Stanley Young's enormous bibliography in *The*

Wolves of North America served as the basis for chapter 9. I also relied heavily on his *The Wolf in North American History* (Caldwell, Idaho: The Caxton Printers, 1946); on the many, diverse accounts and attitudes expressed in the indexed volumes of Thwaites's *Early American Travels, 1748–1846*; and on several articles: W. Petersen, "Wolves in Iowa" (*The Iowa Journal of History and Politics* 38 (1): 50–93, 1940) and an updated, edited version by Petersen (*The Palimpsest* 41 (12): 517–64, December 1960); A. Bowman, "Wolves: Being Reminiscent of My Life on an Eastern Montana Ranch" (typed manuscript 591. B68, 1938, in collections of the Montana Historical Society, Helena); E. Curnow, "The History of the Eradication of the Wolf in Montana" (unpublished master's thesis, University of Montana, Missoula, 1969); and G. D. Hendricks, "Western Wild Animals and Man" (unpublished doctoral dissertation, University of Texas, Austin, 1951).

The quote from Dodge is from *The Hunting Grounds of the Great West* by Richard Irving Dodge (London: Chatto and Windus, 1878). Webber's encounter with wolves is given full treatment in *Romance of Sporting; or Wild Scenes and Wild Hunters*, by C. W. Webber (Philadelphia: Lippincott, Grambo and Co., 1854). The quote from Taylor is in *Twenty Years on the Trap Line*, by Joseph Henry Taylor (Bismarck, N.D.: 1891). The Pattie, Maximilian, and several other quotes are from volumes in Thwaites.

The article on Caywood referred to is A. H. Carhart, "World Champion Wolfer" (*Outdoor Life*, 84 (3): 22–23, 74–75, 1939).

Roger Caras tells the story of the Custer Wolf in *The Custer Wolf: Biography of an American Renegade* (Boston: Little, Brown, 1966). The story of the Currumpaw Wolf is from E. T. Seton, *Wild Animals I Have Known* (N.Y.: Scribners, 1926). Information on wolf control in Canada was kindly provided by Ron Nowak from his unpublished manuscript "The Gray Wolf in North America."

Commentaries by trappers I felt most important for my purposes were: A. R. Harding, *Wolf and Coyote Trapping* (Columbus, Ohio: A. R. Harding Pub. Co., 1909); Ben Corbin, *Corbin's Advice; or the Wolf Hunter's Guide* (Bismarck, N.D.: The Tribune Co., 1900, copy at North Dakota Historical Society, Bismarck); Bud Dalrymple, *The Grey Wolf of South Dakota* (Altoona, Pa.: Altoona Tribune Co., 1919, copy at Montana Historical Society, Helena); and *L. Louck's Successful System of Trapping Wolfkind* (n.p., n.d., copy at Minnesota Historical Society, Minneapolis).

IV: And a Wolf Shall Devour the Sun

Source material for this section was by far the most diverse, ranging through mythology, literature, and history, and in the light of this my annotations here are even more restricted in comparison with those above.

Francis Klingender alludes to the story of the Wolf of Gubbio in a seminal work for these chapters, *Animals in Art and Thought to the End of the Middle Ages* (Cambridge, Mass.: Massachusetts Institute of Technology Press, 1971). The Florence McCulloch work referred to is her *Medieval Latin and French Bestiaries* (Chapel Hill, N.C.: University of North Carolina Press, 1960). The T. H. White book is *The Bestiary: A Book of Beasts* (N.Y.: G.P. Putnam's, 1954). See also Anne Clark, *Beasts and Bawdy* (N.Y.: Taplinger, 1975) and Joseph D. Clark, *Beastly Folklore* (Metuchen, N.J.: Scarecrow Press, 1968). Much of the anecdotal material for these chapters came from Sir James Frazer, *The Golden Bough: A Study in Magic and Religion* (London: Macmillan, 1911–15, 12 volumes, third ed.) and his *Folklore in the Old Testament: Studies in Comparative Religion, Legend and Law* (London: Macmillan, 1918, 3 volumes); L. H. Gray, *Mythology of All Races* (Boston: Marshall Jones and Co., 1916–32, 13 volumes); Beryl Rowland, *Animals with Human Faces* (Knoxville, Tenn.: University of Tennessee Press, 1973); Herbert Seager, *Natural History in Shakespeare's Time* (London: E. Stock, 1896); Richard Eckels, *Greek Wolflore* (Philadelphia: University of Pennsylvania, 1937); and Thomas Jackson Peart, *Animals and Animal Legends in English Medieval Art* (unpublished doctoral dissertation, University of Wisconsin, 1955).

The incident at the end of chapter 11 is recounted in full in C. E. Johnson, "A Note on the Habits of the Timber Wolf" (*Journal of Mammalogy* 2: 11–15, 1921).

For chapter 12, Montague Summers, *The Werewolf* (Secaucus, N.J.: Citadel Press, 1966), despite its bias, is requisite. Elliot O'Donnell, *Werwolves* (London: Methuen & Co., 1912) provides some balance. John A. MacCulloch's article, "Lycanthropy," in the *Encyclopedia of Religion and Ethics* (N.Y.: Scribners, 1908–1926, 8: 206–20) is a helpful synthesis. For a bibliography see George F. Black, *A List of Works Relating to Lycanthropy* (New York Public Library, 1920).

The Richard Bernheimer work referred to is *Wild Men in the Middle*

Ages (Cambridge, Mass.: Harvard University Press, 1952). For more on William of Parlerne, see Kate Tibbals, "Elements of Magic in the Romance of William of Parlerne" (*Modern Philology* I (3): 355–71, January 1904). I relied on Robert Graves, *The Greek Myths* (Baltimore: Penguin, 1955, 2 volumes) for the story of Lycaon. For two examples in modern popular literature stressing themes of sexual violence and spiritual malevolence as they apply to werewolves, see, respectively, *The Werewolf of Paris*, by Guy Endore (N.Y.: Farrar and Rinehart, 1933), and *The Prey*, by Robert Arthur Smith (N.Y.: Fawcett, 1977).

The severely autistic children and conditions at the Orthogenic School of the University of Chicago are discussed in Bruno Bettelheim, "Feral Children and Autistic Children" (*The American Journal of Sociology* 64 (5): 455–67, March 1959). Jean Itard's *The Wild Boy of Aveyron* (N.Y.: Appleton-Century-Crofts, 1962) details Itard's association with Victor, and the opening chapters of Harlan Lane's *The Wild Boy of Aveyron* (Cambridge, Mass.: Harvard University Press, 1976) develop a remarkable picture of Victor's life before he came to Itard. Also see Lucien Malson's *Wolf Children and the Problem of Human Nature* (N.Y.: Monthly Review Press, 1972). For the paragraphs on Amala and Kamala I relied on *Wolf Child and Human Child* by Arnold Gesell (N.Y.: Harper, 1941) and *Wolf Children and Feral Man* by J. A. L. Singh and R. M. Zingg (N.Y.: Harper, 1942).

The stories in chapter 13 are drawn from more than fifty collections. For Bewick, I used a reprint of the 1818 edition of *The Fables of Aesop with Designs on Wood by Thomas Bewick* (London: Paddington Press, 1975). For Reynard, I used an 1895 edition of *The Most Delectable History of Reynard the Fox*, Joseph Jacobs, ed. (N.Y.: Schocken Books, 1967). Iona and Peter Opie, *The Classic Fairy Tales* (N.Y.: Oxford University Press, 1974), Thomas Noel's *Theories of the Fable in the Eighteenth Century* (N.Y.: Columbia University Press, 1975), and *Early Children's Books and Their Illustration*, Gerald Gottlieb, ed. (N.Y.: Pierpont Morgan Library/David R. Godine, 1975) are useful guides.

Freud's case is detailed in *The Wolf-Man*, Muriel Gardiner, ed. (N.Y.: Basic Books, 1971).

Notes on Jack London's fascination with wolves are in Jon Yoder, "Jack London as Wolf Barleycorn" (*Western American Literature* 11 (2): 103–19, August 1976).

For Götterdämmerung, I relied on *Myths of Northern Lands* by H. A. Guerber (N.Y.: American Book Company, 1895). The supernova in Lupus was photographed in 1976 for the first time and is discussed in "The Optical Remnant of the Lupus Supernova of 1006" by Sidney van den Bergh (*The Astrophysical Journal, Letters*, 208 (I), II: L17, August 15, 1976).

Afterword

For background on the Oregon wolf hearings, see, for example, "When Wolves Move In" (*The* [Portland] *Oregonian*, 10 November 2002) and "Bills Aim to Prevent Wolves' Return" (*The* [Eugene] *Register-Guard*, 9 April 2003). The orientation packet prepared by the Oregon Department of Fish and Wildlife and distributed to attendees before each of its town hall meetings is "Town Hall" (Portland, Ore.: Oregon Department of Fish and Wildlife, November 2002). A summary of those meetings is set forth in "Exhibit H: Summary of Wolf Town Hall Meetings" (Portland, Ore.: Oregon Fish and Wildlife Commission, 7 February 2003) and "Exhibit C: Wolf Alternatives and Update" (Newport, Ore.: Oregon Fish and Wildlife Commission, 20–21 March 2003).

Information on the wolves that migrated into Oregon in 1999 and 2000 is in "Town Hall" and "Exhibit H: Summary of Wolf Town Hall Meetings," above.

The Idaho and Yellowstone reintroductions are summarized in E. E. Bangs and S. H. Fritts, "Reintroducing the gray wolf to central Idaho and Yellowstone National Park" (*Wildlife Society Bulletin* 24: 402–413, 1996) and E. E. Bangs, et al., "Status of Gray Wolf Restoration in Montana, Idaho, and Wyoming (*Wildlife Society Bulletin* 26: 785–98, 1998). See also "The Reintroduction of Gray Wolves to Yellowstone National Park and Central Idaho: Final Environmental Impact Statement" (Helena, Mont.: U.S. Fish and Wildlife Service, 1994) and C. M. Mack and J. Holyan, "Idaho Wolf Recovery Program: Restoration and Management of Gray Wolves in Central Idaho. Progress Report 2002" (Lapwai, Idaho: Nez Perce Tribe, Department of Wildlife Management, 2003).

For a review of the taxonomy of the eastern timber wolf see P. J. Wilson, et al., "DNA Profiles of the Eastern Canadian Wolf and the Red Wolf Provide Evidence for a Common Evolutionary History Independent of the

Gray Wolf" (*Canadian Journal of Zoology* 78: 2156–66, 2000). For a reassessment of the effect of wolf predation on the population of prey species see R. D. Boertje, et al., "Predation of Moose and Caribou by Radio-Collared Grizzly Bears in East and Central Alaska" (*Canadian Journal of Zoology* 66: 2492–99, 1988) and two monographs by W. C. Gasaway, et al.: *The Role of Predation in Limiting Moose at Low Densities in Alaska and Yukon and Implications for Conservation*, Wildlife Monographs, no. 120 (Bethesda, Md.: The Wildlife Society, 1992) and *Interrelationships of Wolves, Prey, and Man in Interior Alaska*, Wildlife Monographs, no. 84 (Bethesda, Md.: The Wildlife Society, 1983).

Baseline material for assessing the recovery of naturally occurring wolf populations in the contiguous United States is provided in B. Lopez, "Wolves in the Lower Forty-Eight" (*Journal of the North American Wolf Society* 2 (2): 10–17, 1976). For a summary of the red wolf reintroduction program, see M. K. Phillips, et al., "Restoration of the Red Wolf" in L. D. Mech and L. Boitani, eds., *Wolves: Behavior, Ecology, and Conservation* (Chicago: University of Chicago Press, 2003). The wolf recovery program in Arizona and New Mexico is analyzed in P. C. Paquet, et al., "Mexican Wolf Recovery: Three-Year Program Review and Assessment" (Albuquerque, N.M.: prepared by the IUCN-SSC Conservation Breeding Specialist Group for the U.S. Fish and Wildlife Service, 2001). See also M. K. Phillips, et al., "Living Alongside Canids: The Extermination and Recovery of Red and Gray Wolves in the Contiguous United States" in D. Macdonald and C. Sillero, eds., *Canid Biology and Conservation* (London: Oxford University Press, in press) and relevant papers in L. N. Carbyn, et al., eds., *Ecology and Conservation of Wolves in a Changing World* (Edmonton, Alberta: Canadian Circumpolar Institute, 1995).

The federal plan for reestablishing the wolf in the northeastern United States is *Recovery Plan for the Eastern Timber Wolf* (Minneapolis and St. Paul: U.S. Fish and Wildlife Service, 1992). Also see J. Elder, ed., *The Return of the Wolf: Reflections on the Future of Wolves in the Northeast* (Hanover, New Hampshire: University Press of New England/Middlebury College Press, 2000).

Growing public interest in encountering wild wolves, together with expanding wolf populations, has led to more frequent human-wolf contact, including some unprovoked attacks. See M. E. McNay, "Wolf-Human

Interactions in Alaska and Canada: A Review of the Case History" (*Wildlife Society Bulletin* 30: 831–43, 2002) and supporting material in M. E. McNay, "A Case History of Wolf-Human Encounters in Alaska and Canada," (*Wildlife Technical Bulletin* 13, Juneau, Ak.: Alaska Department of Fish and Game, 2002).

Robert O. Stephenson's papers include "Nunamiut Eskimos, Wildlife Biologists, and Wolves" in F. H. Harrington and Paul C. Paquet, eds., *Wolves of the World: Perspectives of Behavior, Ecology, and Conservation* (Park Ridge, N.J.: Noyes Publications, 1982) and with B. Aghook, "The Eskimo Hunter's View of Wolf Ecology and Behavior," cited above in section I.

For a recent overview of the history of human attitudes toward wolves, including the impact of such attitudes on current wolf management policies, see S. H. Fritts, et al., "Wolves and Humans" in *Wolves: Behavior, Ecology, and Conservation.* Also, see M. A. Nie, *Beyond Wolves: The Politics of Wolf Recovery and Management* (Minneapolis: University of Minnesota Press, 2003) and a series of papers about modern human perceptions of wild animals by S. Kellert, including, with M. Black, et al., "Human Culture and Large Carnivore Conservation in North America" (*Conservation Biology* 10: 977–90, 1996).

INDEX

Italicized numbers indicate illustrations.
Numbers followed by an *m* indicate marginalia.

aardwolf, 17
Abyssinian wolf, 18
Adams, James Capen, 175
Adams, John, 142
adaptability, 13, 15, 21, 291
admiration for wolf,
    28–29, 85–86, 104,
    114, 163, 166, 169,
    257
Adventures in Error (Ste-
    fansson), 70
Aelian, 221

Aeneid (Vergil), 272
Aesop's fables, 217, 248,
    250, 251, 253, 254,
    254*m*–56*m*, 255,
    260. *See also* individ-
    ual titles
agricultural vs. hunting
    views of wolf, 102,
    233
Ahgook, Robert, 60,
    80–81
Ahtena, 109

Ailbe, Saint (bishop of
    Emily), 246*m*
Alaska, 1–3, 13, 18, 19, 21,
    25, 26, 30, 37, 60,
    66, 72, 79, 99, 143,
    159–60, 162–63,
    195, 224
Alberta, Canada, 99, 194,
    290
Albertus Magnus, 219, 222
Albigenses, The (Maturin),
    268

albino wolf, 21
Allen, Durward, 39
Alligator River National
    Wildlife Refuge,
    289–90
alpha animals, 31–32, 33,
    44, 49, 52, 90
Alphouns, 230
amaguk, 79, 87–88
Amala and Kamala,
    245–47
American Fur Trading
    Company, 177
Andean wolf, 17–18
Andersen, Peter, 237
Angur-boda, 274, 275
Animal Master, 90–91, 93,
    132
animal trials, 145
annual cycle of wolf pack,
    36–37
antelope, 59, 99, 105, 195,
    269
Anthus family, 205–6
Apollo, 210, 271–72
Arapaho, 105
Arcadia, 205–6, 231
Arikara, 105
Aristotle, 215–16, 219,
    271
Arizona, 290
Asia, wolves in, 14, 291
Asian wolf, 13*m*, 15
Assiniboin, 99, 115
attacks on men. *See* man,
    as prey
autistic children, 244, 246
"Autumn at Taos"
    (Lawrence), 268
Avianus, 253, 254

Babrius, 253, 254
Bailey, Vernon, 189
balsam root, 117
barking, 39–40, *42*
Barthe, Angela de la, 228

Bartholomew of England,
    221, 222
battues, 149, 171
Bauterne, Antoine de,
    70
Bear in the Flat, 104
bears, 27, 67, 69, 81, 87,
    104, 289
beast epics, 258–59
"beast machine," 147, 255,
    258
beasts of Gévaudan. *See*
    Gévaudan, beasts of
beaver, 54, 177, 177*m*
behavior. *See* specific types
behavior, evolution of, 81
Bella Coola, 4, 104, 106,
    121
Beowulf, 141
Berekhiah ha-Nakdan,
    253
berkuts. *See* eagles hunting
    wolves
Bernheimer, Richard,
    229
Berserker, 230, 234
bestiaries, 205, 216, *217*,
    219–21, 257
Beston, Henry, 248, 249,
    284
beta animals, 34
Bettelheim, Bruno,
    264–66
Bewick, Thomas, 255–57
Bible, wolf in, 141, 184,
    210, 214, 218, 226,
    240
Bidpai, 253
Billings (Canadian
    hunter), 176
biological sciences, 3, 16,
    224, 288, 289,
    290–91, 293
    as metaphor, 77–78,
    79–80
    as tool, 284

Cartesian dualism in,
    258
cf. Nunamiut percep-
    tions, 78–85, 291
research affected by
    wolf killing in, 72
Bird Shirt, 106–8
Bisclavret (Marie de
    France), 235
Blackfeet, 117*m*, 123, 124,
    269
Black Plague, 208
"Black Wolf and His
    Fathers," 269
black wolves, 21, 22, 66,
    83
Blackwood, Algernon, 268
Blanca, 192–93
Blind Bull, 103
Blue Mountains, 288
Bond, James, 164–65
Boone and Crockett Club,
    163
bounties, 151, 158, 187,
    194–95
    fraud and, 188–89, 198
    hunting for, 25*m*, *165*,
    168, 179–87, 184,
    186–87
    laws, 171–72, 181–83
    on dogs, 173*m*
    paid, 182–83
Bowstring men, 118
breeding, 26, 31–33
Bridger, Jim, 177*m*
British Columbia, 25, 30,
    194, 195, 290
British Columbia wolf, 21
British Isles, 13, 147, 171,
    172, 208, 236,
    236*m*, 239, 246*m*
Browning, Robert, 268
buffalo, 54, *55m*, 58, 60,
    96, 99, 174, 177,
    179
Burgot, Pierre, 241

Byron, George Gordon, 225
bystander phenomenon, 62

caching, 63
Caddo, 105
Call of the Wild (London), 269
Cambrensis, Giraldus, 236m
Campbell, Joseph, 5
Canada, 13, 15, 21, 25, 30, 58, 70, 71m, 88, 93, 99, 194–95
Canidae, 17
Canis (wolf ancestor), 17
Cape hunting dog, 18, 39
Captive Girl Ceremony, 132
captive wolves, *151*, 152, 184
    behavior in, 29, 32–33, 41–43
    and dogs, 69
    extrasensory communication in, 50–51
    feeding habits of, 41, 95, 96
    as gene pool, 16
    red wolves as, 279–83
    scapegoat animal among, 52
    training eagles to hunt with, 156
    vocalization among, 39
caribou, 4, 67, 101, 194
    as Naskapi prey, 88–93
    as sacred meat, 90, 93
    as wolf prey, 3, 54, 58, 59, 60–61, 85
Caribou House, 93, 123
Carpenter, Edmund, 87
Carpenter, Louis, 119
Carson, Lawrence, 163
Cartesian dualism, 258

Cascade Mountains wolf, 13m, 21
Cather, Willa, 268
cattle, 138, *181*, 273. *See also* livestock industry
Caxton, William, 254
Caywood, Bill, 187–88
chase, 25, 60–61, 84
chase-without-death, 101
Chaucer, Geoffrey, 225
Cherokee, 105, 109
Chesterton, G. K., 252
Cheyenne, 103, 105, 113
Cheyenne Wolf Soldiers, 115–20
children's literature, 250–51
China, 13
Chinese wolf, 13m, 15
coat. *See* pelage
cognitive mapping, 48–49
coins with wolf image, 272
Collectanea rerum memorabilium (Solinus), 216
color, 4, 10, 21–24, 83
Colorado, 187, 188
communal care of pups, 35–36
communication, systems of, 4, 24, 38–52. *See also* specific types of
conservation of energy, *60*, 60–61, 89
"conversation of death," 62, 94–95
copulatory tie, 26, 196
Corbin, Ben, 184–86
Courtaud, 149–50
Cowan, Ian MacTaggart, 16
"cowardice" of wolves, 147–48, 175–76. 184m
coyotes, 14, 17, 67, 69, 196

Cree, 99, 124
Crisler, Lois, 152
Crow, 106, 110, 110m–111m, 113, 118
Curnow, Edward, 181
Curran, James, 70
Currumpaw Wolf, 192–93
Custer, George Armstrong, 154

Dakotas, 168
Dall sheep, 54, 195
Dante, 205
Danube River Valley, 14
death, appropriateness of, 95
deer, 55, 59, 99, 101, 159, 195
Defoe, Daniel, 268
Delphi, bronze wolf at, 272
den raiding, 185, 188, 191, 197
dens, 10, 27, 82, 85
deodants, law of, 46
Department of Fish and Wildlife, 288
Descartes, René, 147, 254–55, 258
description, physical, of wolves, 18–26
"Destruction of Sennacherib, The" (Byron), 225
Deucalion's flood, 231
Devil, the, 140, 145, 204, 209, 210, 213, 221, 225, 234, 236, 238, 239, 240, 241
Devil's dog, 239
diet, 54–55
digestion, 53–54
dingo, 17
dire wolf, 17

diseases, 29–30
named after wolf, 216*m*
dispersal, 13, 16, 36, 64–65
distances traveled, 4, 25, 25*m*
distribution, 12–14
Divina commedia (Dante), 205
Dodge, Colonel Richard, 176
"Dog and the Wolf, The" (Aesop), 254*m*, 257
dogs, 17, 69, 197, 209
bounty on, 173*m*
coursing with, 153–54, 156, 168, 172
feral, 14, 69, 150, 172–73, 197
as prey, 2, 69
in tales, 110*m*–11*m*, 261
cf. wolf, 19, 26, 52
dogs of the Death Spirit, 273
dog-wolf hybrids, 69, 71, 110*m*
domestic stock, 94–95, 181, 223*m*
attitudes toward, 138, 181, 184–85, 190, 266, 273
lack of prey signals in, 94–95
in Middle Ages, 208
by outlaw wolves, 191–92
predation on, 146, 150, 171–73, 182
See also cattle; livestock industry
dominance behavior, 47
dominant/submissive relationship, 44–45
Down's syndrome, 227
Duchess of Malfi (Webster), 268
ducks, 37, 54

eagles, 62
hunting wolves, 155–56
east, direction of wolf, 102, 268
Eckles, Richard, 272
ecological relationships, 10, 63, 67–73, 104. *See also* individual animals
Eddas (Icelandic sagas), 210
Edgar of England, 147, 208, 239
Edmund, Saint, 205, *206*
elusiveness, 65–66, 100
encyclopedias, 206, 221–23
Endangered Species Act, 152, 198, 289
Endore, Guy, 267
endurance, 25*m*
Ericsson, Leif, 277
Eskimos, 38, 113, 123
killing wolves, 109
perceptions, 82, 87
on predation, 181
as prey, 69
See also Nunamiut
etymological associations, wolf and light, 209–10, 272
Europe, 13, 30, 70, 72, 147, 149–50, 154, 155, 156, 171, 228, 237, 239, 291. *See also* individual countries; Middle Ages
European wolf, 15, 19
evolution, 16–17
extinction, 14, 16, 134
extinct populations, 13, 14
extrasensory communication, 50–51

fables, 226, 251–57, 258, 254*m*–56*m*. *See also* individual titles

fabulists, 251–57
facial gestures, 44–47
fairy tales, 251, 263–66
Falkland wolf, 18
Faustulus, 242
feeding habits, 29, 41, 53–55
female wolves, 22–23, 32–33, 33*m*, 39, 40, 49, 66–67, 82, 83, 100, 192–93
Fenris, 210, 274, 274–75, 276
feral children. *See* wolf children
fiction, wolves in, 267–70
Field and Stream magazine, 144, 186
fighting, 10, 27, 51–52, 66, 100
Finland, 72
"Firebird, The," 261
Fish and Wildlife Service, U.S., 290
fishing, 54
Flatheads, 100
folk beliefs, 29, 216, 223, 223*m*, 229
in bestiaries, 205, 219, 220–21
in encyclopedias, 206, 222
about werewolves, 236–37
See also plants associated with wolves; medicine, wolf parts as
folklore, 121, 145, 214, 220*m*, 291, 292
folk rhymes, 210
folk tales, 110*m*–11*m*, 261–63, 269. *See also* individual titles
food sharing, 3, 29
footpads, 20

fox, 63, 67, 69
fox, and wolf, in fable,
    256, 259–61
France, 150, 240, 245,
    258, 259, 264
    idioms, 219, 220*m*
    werewolves in, 235,
    241
Francis, Saint, 212, *214*
Freki, 273
Freud, Sigmund, 267
Freudian associations, 266
friendliness among wolves,
    28, 37
Fromm, Erich, 266
fur, 19, 108. *See also* pelage

"Gabriel-Ernest" (Saki),
    268
gait, 9, 24
Galen, 215
games. *See* play
games named for wolf, 113
Garland, Hamlin, 268
Garnier, Giles, 240–41
geese and wolf folktale,
    263
Gelert, folktale of, 261
generosity in wolves, 29
George, Saint, 223*m*
Geri, 273
Germany, 13, 150, 225, 240
gestation, 26, 215
Gévaudan, beasts of,
    70–71
Ghost Head, 112
Gibson, James, 87
Glacier National Park,
    13
glandular secretions,
    49–50
Gleipnir, 275
Goldman, Edward, 14,
    223, 290
gold rushes, 178, 180
Goldstream Valley, 2

gorging, 53
Götterdämmerung, 210,
    275–76
government hunters,
    187–88, 189–92,
    193–94
gray wolf, 289, 290
Great Britain. *See* British
    Isles
Great Plains wolf, 13*m*,
    134, 175–80
Greece, 205–6, 231,
    271–73
Greenland wolf, 13*m*
greeting, 12
Grenier, Jean, 241, 243–44
Grey, Zane, 193
Grimm, Jacob, 221, 261,
    264
Grinnell, George Bird,
    179
growling, 40
Gubbio, wolf of, 212,
    214
Gubser, Nicholas, 80

Haida legends, 92*m*
Hall, Edward T., 82
Hammond, Jay, 144
Haqibana, 105
Ha-sass, 130
Hati, 274, 275
hearing range, 43
Henriksen, Georg, 88
Henrie, Captain Dan,
    176–77
heretics, 238
Herodotus, 233
*Hesitant Wolf and Scrupu-
    lous Fox* (Kennerly),
    226
Hidatsa, 104, 106, 112
    wolf bundle transfer
    rite, 133
*Histoires ou contes du temps
    passé* (Perrault), 250

History of the Goths (O.
    Magnus), 234
Hitler, Adolf, 225
Hobbes, Thomas, 258
homeopathic imitation,
    104, 106–8
Hopi Snake Dance, 128
Hornaday, William T.,
    184*m*
horses, 94, 124, 179, 220
hour of the wolf, 209
howling, 11–12, 27, 38–39,
    40, 41, 42, 280
    descriptions of, 11–12,
    39, 39*m*
    frequency of, 10, 81
    in myths, 115–17, 231,
    275
    and native Americans,
    38, 85, 103, 112,
    129, 209
    responses to, 156, 175
Huidekoper, Wallis, 190
hunting
    aerial, 3, 140, 144,
    159–60, 162, *165,*
    166, 197–98
    big game, 139, 164–65,
    194, 195, 288
    buffalo, 55*m*, 96, 177,
    268
    coursing, 153–54, 168,
    172
    government hunters,
    187–88, 189–92,
    193–94
    predator control, 139,
    141, 148*m*—49*m*,
    169, 171–74,
    181–83, 288
    recreational killings,
    151, 152
    righteousness of killing
    wolves, 140, 141,
    142, 144, 146,
    161–63

hunting *(cont.)*
    sport hunting, 153–66
    torture, 139–40, 152,
        196
    traps, 108–9, 172, *189,*
        190–91, 192
    wolfers, *155,* 168,
        178–80, 184–85,
        186
    See also killing of
        wolves; trappers;
        wolfing
hunting as a sacred activ-
    ity, 91–92, 93–96
hunting by wolves, 3, 36,
    38, 55–63, 93–96,
    222
hunting methods
    Naskapi, 88–89
    native American/wolf
        correspondences, 99
    Nunamiut, 82–83
hybrid swarm, 14

Icelandic sagas, 234
Idaho, 288, 290
idioms, 208, 209, 219,
    220*m*, 221, 226
imitation of wolves, 85,
    101, 104, 105,
    106–8, 110, 111–12,
    118, 129, 130–31
"In Defense of Raymond
    Sebond" (Mon-
    taigne), 258
India, 19, 245
Indians. *See* native Ameri-
    cans
initiation ceremonies,
    129–32
injuries, 10, 30
Inquisition, 206, 208, 219,
    238–39
interactions with other
    animals. *See* individ-
    ual animals

interbreeding, among sub-
    species, 14–16
intuition, 284
Ireland, 236, 236*m,*
    246*m*
Isengrim the wolf, 250,
    259. See also *Ysen-
    grimus*
Isidore of Seville, 218
Isle Royale, Lake Supe-
    rior, 13, 25, 64, 72
Italy, 13
Itard, Jean, 244, 245
"Ivan Ivanovitch" (Brown-
    ing), 268

jackals, 17, 253, 273
Jamestown, Va., 171
Japan, 14
jaws, crushing power of,
    26
Jeffers, Robinson, 268–69
John Jay River, 288
Johnson, Eugene, 224
Jungle Stories (Kipling),
    267

Kamala, 245–47
Kendrick, Senator John
    B., 148*m*–49*m*
Kennerly, Karen, 226
*Key to Animals on which
    Wolf and Coyote
    Bounties are Paid*
    (Bailey), 189
killing of wolves
    on federal land, 187,
        190–94
    on Great Plains,
        177–81
    methods of, 108–9,
        139, 155, 157,
        190–93, 196
    in Middle Ages, 239
    by native Americans,
        108–9

reasons for, 138–52
rites of atonement for,
    109
after war, 150
See also battues; den
    raiding; hunting;
    poisoning; predator
    control; strychnine;
    trappers; wolfing
Kills in the Night, 110
Kinnell, Galway, 268
Kiowa, 118
Kipling, Rudyard, 267
Kleinfeld, Judith, 82
Klukwalle (Makah cere-
    mony), 129
Krilov, Ivan, 252, 253, 257
Kruuk, Hans, 56
Kwakiutl, 109, *130*

La Fontaine, Jean de, 250,
    253, 254–55, 257,
    258
Lai du Bisclavret (Marie de
    France), 235–36
Larsen, Wolf, 269
Laugher, 124–28
Lawrence, D. H., 268
legends, 4, 92*m*, 103,
    133*m*, 210
Leto, 271
Lewis, Meriwether, 174
lex talionis, 145
"light" and "wolf",
    209–10, 219, 272
literature, wolves in, 205,
    267–70
litter size, 27–28
Little Red Riding Hood,
    206, 250, 251,
    263–66, 265, 267
Little Wolf, 120
*Lives of the Noble Grecians
    and Romans, The*
    (Plutarch), 242
livestock industry, 180,

181, 185–86, 195,
288, 291
in Montana, 181–83
Llewelyn, Prince, 261
Loki, 210, 273, 274, 275,
276
London, Jack, 269–70
lone wolves, 13, 16, 38, 60,
64, 65, 105
longevity, 29
Lorenz, Konrad, 29
lupa, as term, 219, 226,
242
Lupton, Richard, 221, 222
Lupus (constellation), 277
Lupus erythematosus, 216*m*
lycanthropy, 232, 243–44.
See also shapeshifting;
werewolves
Lycaon, 231–32
Lyceum, 271
lynx, 67

McCulloch, Florence, 218
mai-cob, 123
Maine, 14
Mainz, archbishop of (A.D.
870), 239
Makah Wolf Ritual,
129–32
male wolves, 3, 28, 29, 32,
44, 49, 52, 66, 103,
193
*Malleus Maleficarum
(Hammer of
Witches)*, 206, 219,
239–40
man as prey, 4, 69–70,
123, 240
attacked by wolves,
69–71, 149, 176–77,
177*m*, 221, 268, 281
dead on battlefields,
144, 150, 208, 232,
273
verification of, 70

Managarm, 275
Mandan, 114
maned wolf, 17
mange, scarcoptic, 183
Manifest Destiny, 142, 184
Manitoba, 71*m*
Marie de France, 235–36,
254
markings, 24, 45–47, 47
Mars, 210, 242
masks, wolf, 129–31, *131*
Mather, Cotton, 142
mating, 26, 32–33, 36
Maturin, Charles Robert,
268
Maupassant, Guy de, 267
Maximilian of Wied, 175
"meat drunk," 53
Mech, L. David, 57, 62,
65, 67–68, 72
medicine, wolf parts as,
105–6, 108, 110–12,
213, 222
medicine animal, wolf as,
105
Mekiana, Justus, 81
Mexican wolf, 13*m*, 195
Mexico, 13, 195–96
Michigan, 13, 72
Middle Ages, 205, 206–11,
254
enemies of Church in,
238–41
medicine in, 213, 215
werewolves in, 226,
227–30, 238–41
wild man in, 228–30
Minnesota, 13, 21, 100,
101, 139, 150, 151,
156–57
Mokoshan, 90
Montaigne, Michel de,
258
Montana, 13, 168, 197
cattle industry in,
181–83

Montana Stock Growers'
Association, 190
moon, 38
"Moonlight, Wolf," *174*
Moore, Edward, 253
moose, 55–56, 57
mortality, 29–30. *See also*
pups
Mount McKinley
National Park, 26,
66, 72
Mowat, Farley, 38
Mowgli, 267
Munro, H. H. (Saki), 268
Murie, Adolph, 25, 26, 37,
38, 39, 63, 72, 224,
290
music and wolves, 221
My Antonia (Cather),
268
mythology, Teutonic, 210,
221, 234

names derived from wolf
animal, 17–18, 209*m*
disease, 216*m*
game, 113
native American, 106,
118, 119, 120,
120*m*, 121
Norse, 273–74
plant, 113, 208
Nash, Roderick, 141, 143
Naskapi, 88–93, 95, 113,
123
Naskapi/wolf correspon-
dences, 89–90
Natalis, Saint, 236*m*
native Americans
correspondences with,
99–101, 103–4,
104–5, 169–71, 191
cosmology of, 102
and death, 95, 119
elusiveness among, 100
fear of wolves by, 123

native Americans (*cont.*)
  identification with wolf
    by, 101, 105, 112,
    118, 129–30,
    132–34
  integration into envi-
    ronment of, 104–5
  killed by wolves, 4
  killing of wolves by,
    108–9
  names for wolf among,
    106, 118, 119, 120,
    120*m*, 121
  rituals of, 109, 120–21,
    128–32, 169. *See also*
    individual names
  stock lost to strychnine
    by, 179
  tales of, 92*m*,
    110*m*–111*m*,
    121–22, 133*m*, 210,
    262, 269
  view of animals by, 86,
    102, 104
  warriors among,
    114–20
  wolf parts used by, 104,
    105–6, 108, 109–12,
    114–15, 120–21,
    172
  women and wolves
    among, 120–21
  See also individual
    tribes
natural histories, 213–15,
  257
  development of,
    215–21
Navajo werewolves,
  123–24
Neurians, 233
Newfoundland wolf, 14
Newhouse, Sewell, 190
Newhouse traps, 189–90,
  190
New England, 290

New Mexico, 192, 290
New York, 290
Nez Perce, 105, 288
Nitaina, 124–28
Nivordus of Ghent, 259
Norns, 273
Norris, Frank, 267
Norse mythology,
  273–76
North Carolina, 289
northwest coast tribes,
  101, 105, 113,
  128–32, 262
Northwest Territories, 194
Notable Things (Lupton),
  222
Nuliayuk, 123
Nunamiut, 3, 22–23, 59,
  78–86, 110*m*
  acuteness of, 81–83
  hunters among, 82
  observations of wolf by,
    81, 291
Nyktimos, 231

"Occurrence in Dreams
  of Material from
  Fairy Tales, The"
  (Freud), 267
O'Connor, Jack, 160–61
Odin's wolves, 273
O'Donnell, Elliot, 237
Olaus Magnus, 234
"Old Wolf in Seven
  Fables, The," 262
old wolves, 3, 66–67, 86,
  87–88, 89–90,
  262
olfaction, 48–50
Omaha, 65, 101
omega animal, 52
Ontario, Canada, 194,
  195
Opie, Iona and Peter,
  264
oracle, wolf as, 103

Oregon, 287, 288–89, 291
Oregon Trail, The (Parkma
  n), 176
Orton, Alda, 39
Osiris, 273
Oto, 107
Ouachita National Forest,
  141–42
Outdoor Life magazine,
  160, 187
outlaw wolves, 149–50,
  188, 191–93, 193*m*
Owl Friend, 115–17

packs
  characteristics of, 34
  identity of, 36–37
  size of, 26, 70, 176
  structure of, 34–35
  variability by season of,
    36
  See also social structure
paramilitary terminology,
  32
parasitism, 29
Parkman, Francis, 176
"Parson's Tale, The"
  (Chaucer), 225
Pattie, James O., 176
Pausanius, 231
Pawnee, 65, 101, 102,
  110–13, 132–33
  creation legend of,
    133*m*
  Wolf Man, 132
  Wolf Star, 210
payment, wolf parts as,
  147, 172, 208, 239
Peck, Robert, 179
pelage, 11, 19, 21–24. *See
  also* black wolves;
  white wolves
pelts
  as medicine, 222
  native American uses
    of, 104, 105, 106–8,

109–12, 120–21,
123
as payment, 172
value of, 21, 80, 177,
179
werewolves and, 123,
233, 234
See also wolfing
*Perception of the Visual
World, The* (Gib-
son), 87
Perrault, Charles, 250,
263–64
Peter and the Wolf
(Prokofiev), 262
Peters, Roger, 48–50
Petronius, 233
Phaedrus (fabulist), 254
Phædrus (Plato), 269
Physiologus, 213–14, 215,
216–19
Pimlott, Douglas, 16, 62
plants associated with
wolves, 109, 112,
113, 117, 121, 208,
216, 220, 222
and werewolves, 237
Plato, 231, 269
play, 4, 11, 37, 67–68, 84
Plenty Coups, 106
Pliny, 205, 216, 218, 219,
231, 233
Plutarch, 216, 221, 242
poetry, wolves in, 252*m*,
259, 268–69
poisoning of wolves, 139,
194–95, 271. *See also*
government
hunters; strychnine
populations, of wolves,
13–14, 184–85,
193–94, 195–96,
289. *See also* extinct
populations
postural communication,
43–48, *44*, *45*

body gestures, 47
facial expressions, 44,
47
markings, 24, 45–47,
47
piloerection, 43
reassurance displays, 48
pouncing, 10, 36
Prairie (name of wolf),
279–83
predation on domestic
stock. *See* domestic
stock
predator control, 139, *141*,
148*m*–49*m*, 169,
171–74, 181–83,
288. *See also* individ-
ual methods
predator/prey signals
announcement of avail-
ability, 58
between buffalo and
wolf, 57–59
"conversation of death"
in, 62, 94–95
Kruuk on, 56–57
prey, 10, 54–55, 59, 61,
289
bystander phenomenon
in, 62
as factor in territory,
55, 64, 100–1
location of by wolves,
66–67
See also individual
types; killing of
wolves; surplus
killing
prey selection, 4, 54–55,
58–59, 61–62
"conversation of death"
in, 94–95
Nunamiut on, 84–85
private property, 147,
196
Prokofiev, Serge, 262

Pueblo Indians, 99, 128
Pulliainen, Erkki, 72
pups, *28*, *34–35*
behavior in, 28–29, 35,
280–81
communal care of,
35–36
diseases of, 27
growth of, 36
killing of, 185, 188,
191, 197, 224
learning in, 31, 33*m*,
35, 36, 50
mortality of, 27, 29, 51
raised in captivity, 16,
279–83
social structures of, 27,
28–29, 35, 48
vocalizations of, 40–43
purification ceremony for
women, 120–21
Pythochares, legend of,
221

Quebec, 93, 195
Quimby, General, of
Sandwich, 157–58

rabid wolves, 69, 71, 71*m*,
194–95, 208, 269
Blackfoot cure for bite
of, 123
distinguished by track,
83
ravens, 3, 10, 67–68, *68*,
82, 85, 105, 273
red, color of wolf, 102,
106, 118, 120, 124,
268
"Red Wolf, The," 268
red wolves, 14, *15*, 19, 25,
30, 54, 152, 279–83,
289–90
regurgitation, 35, 41, 48, *91*
Remington, Frederic, *174*
Remmler, F. W., 156

rendezvous sites, 33*m*, 36
reintroduction of wolves, 289–90, 292
resting behavior, 11
retribution, law of, 145
reward for man as wolf prey, 70
Reynard the fox, 250, 259
Reynolds, G. W. M., 267
ritual preparation for hunt, 90
River (wolf name), 279–83
Robinson Crusoe (Defoe), 268
Roman Church, 205, 208, 213, 214, 238–39
Romulus and Remus, 226, 242, 248, *248*
Roosevelt, Theodore, 142, 153–54
Rousseau, Jean-Jacques, 242
Russell, Jeffrey, 227, 229
Russia, 13, 21, 53, 153–54, 155, 156, 237, 261

sacred meat, 92–93, 95–96
saints and wolves, 205, 206, 209, 212, *214*, 246*m*
Saki. *See* Munro, H. H.
Salmon River, 288
Scandinavia, wolves in, 13
scapegoat, wolf as, 52, 140, 184, 226, 227, 233
scent glands, 24, 49
scent marking, 49–50
scent posts, 10, 49
scent rolling, 50, 51, *51*
Schenkel, Rudolph, 44, 47, 81
Scripture, 141, 184, 210, 214, 218, 226, 240
Sea-Wolf, The (London), 269–70

"Sea Wolf, The" (Haida folktale), 92*m*
Seiar of Hadramaut, 236
sensory activity, 10, 11, 50, 85, 281–82
separate reality of other organisms, 285
Seton, Ernest Thompson, 69, 192–93
"Seven Little Goats, The," 263
sexual hierarchies, 31–32, 34–35
sexual imagery associated with wolves, 219, 226, 239, 242, 251, 263, 264–67, 269
sexual maturity, 29
shadings. *See* markings
Shakespeare, William, 210, 252*m*
shapeshifting, 205–6, 230, 234, 239, 262–63, 269, 272
"Sheem," 262–63
sheep, 59, 138, 172–73, 220–21, 273
industry, 172–73, 182
and wolf, 225
"Shepherd Boy and the Wolf, The," 255*m*
"She-Wolf, The" (Saki), 268
Shoshoni, 99
Sigmund, 234
Singh, Rev. J. A. L., 245–47
Sioux, 110*m*, 112, 113, 116*m*, 121
size, 10, 18–19, 36, 263*m*
Skoll, 274, 275
Sleeping Wolf, 118–19
Small Ankles, 133–34
smelling. *See* olfaction
Snake River, 288

social structure, 31–37
among captive wolves, 32–33, 292–93
as dynamic, 33
females in, 32
Naskapi/wolf, 89–90
in pack, 34–36
sexual hierarchies, 31, 292
Solinus, 216, 219
Son of the Wolf, The (London), 269
songs, 104, 116*m*, 117*m*, 129
Sonia Shankman Orthogenic School, 244
Soracte, Mount, 233
sourwood, 109
South Dakota, 192
Spain, 30
Speck, Frank, 92
speed, 11, 25*m*
Spirit of the Caribou, 90
sport hunting, 153–66. *See also* wolfing
stare, 4, 62, 175, 219
starvation, 152
Stefansson, Vilhjalmer, 70
Stephenson, Robert, 79, 81–82, 83, 290
stockmen
associations, 190, 191
as avengers, 266
losses by, 182, 191, 192
stones and wolves, 219, 221, 264
"Strafing Arctic Killers," 144
strychnine, 139, 178, 179–80, 190
Stump, Peter, 240
submissive behavior, 44–45, 47, 48
subspecies, 14*m*, 14–16
summer activity, 10, 13, 37

Summers, Montague, 241–42
Sun Dance ritual, 128
Superior National Forest, 50
Supernova (Lupus), 277
supracaudal gland, 24, 49
surplus killing, 4, 54, 55*m*, 56–57, 95
Swan's Head, 106–8
sweet grass, 112
swimming, 25
symbol, wolf as, 142, 143, 205, 210, 226, 239

Tamworth, New Hampshire, wolf siege at, 157–58
Tasba, 105
Tasmanian wolf, 18
Taylor, J. H., 179
teeth, 25–26, 67, 222, 263*m*
temperature regulation, 19–21
temples of Apollo, 272
Tepehuanan Indians, 196
territory, 63–67, 292
   marking of, 48–49
   sharing of, 65
   trespass in, 51, 65, 66
   variability of, 64–65
territory, native American/wolf correspondences, 85, 99–101
Texas, 14, 152, 243*m*
theriophobia, 140
"Three Little Pigs, The," 263
Three Toes of Harding County, 192
Thurber, James, 264
timber wolf, 289
Tlingit, 101
Tomarctus, 17
Topsell, Edward, 222

track, 10, 20, 20*m*, 83
transplanting wolves, 72
trappers, 39*m*, 162–63, 164, 187, 188, 192
   on Great Plains, 177–78
   reminiscences of, 196–99
Trapper's Guide (Newhouse), 190
traps. *See* hunting
travel, 10–12, 21, 25, 66
Troilus and Cressida, 210
tse-ka, 129
Tuberville's Booke of Hunting, 223
Turkey, 242
Twelve Days, 229–30, 234
Twenty Years on the Trapline (Taylor), 179
twilight, 209, 210
Twilight of the Gods, 275–76
Tyr, 275

Ungava Bay, 93
ungulate diseases, 58
Uses of Enchantment, The (Bettelheim), 264

Vandover and the Brute (Norris), 267
Vargamors, 229
Verdun, Michel, 241
Victor of Aveyron, 244, 245, *245*
Vidar, 276
vocalizations, 38–43, *42*, *43*. *See also* individual types
Volsungs, 234
Von, River, 275

Wagner the Wehrwolf (Reynolds), 267
Wallace, Dave, 168–69, 196

Washington, George, 172–73
Weasel Bear, 116*m*
Webster, John, 268
weight, 18–19, 36
werebeasts, 230
werewolves, 205–6, *235*, 236*m*, 226–42
   beliefs about, 124, 150, 208, 236–37
   benevolent, 230
   characteristics of, 233–34, 237
   involuntary, 236–37
   in literature, 230, 235–36, 267–68
   Lycaon as, 231–32
   in *Malleus Maleficarum*, 239
   among the Navajo, 123–24
   persecution of, 208, 227–28, 239–41
   as projection of humans, 226, *228*, 230, 232–33
   voluntary, 236
   cf. wild man, 228–30
   women as, 229
   See also lycanthropy; shapeshifting
Werwolves (O'Donnell), 237
White, T. H., 221
White Fang (London), 269
Whitehead, Alfred North, 284–85
White Sage, 121
white wolves, 21–22, 175, 176, 191, 220*m*, 267, 269
wilderness, 140–44
wild man, 206, 228–30
wild woman, 229
William of Parlerne, 230
Williams, O. W., 159

Williams, Roger, 142
willows, 102, 132
winter activity, 11, 36
Witchcraft in the Middle Ages (Russell), 229
"Wolf, The," 267–68
"Wolf and the Crane, The" 256*m*, 260
"Wolf and the Hunter, The," 255*m*
"Wolf and the Indian Dog, The," 110*m*–11*m*
"Wolf and the Lamb, The," 254*m*–55*m*, 256
"Wolf and the Mouse, The," 255*m*
"Wolf and the Shepherds, The," 256*m*
wolf bands, 105, 115–20
Wolf Belly, 119
wolf berries, 113
wolf bundle, 107, *107*, 132
wolf children, 242–48, *245*
    of Hesse, 242
wolf cults, 232, 233
wolfers. *See* hunting
wolf farming, 185
"Wolf Girl" (of Texas), 243*m*
"Wolf Helps the Dog, The," 256*m*
Wolf House, 269
wolf hunting. *See* killing of wolves
Wolf Hunters, The (Grinnell), 179
wolf imagery, 113, 144, 155, 206, 209, 225–27

in fable, 251
in Middle Ages, 210–11
in poetry, 268–69
sleighs pursued by wolves, 155, 257, 268
in World War II, 226
wolf management, 288–84, 290, 291–92
    federal policies for, 291
    see also reintroduction of wolves
wolfing, 178–80
    for sport, 153–66
"Wolf in the Dust, The," 257
"Wolf in the Kennel, The," 252
wolflike canids, 14
Wolf Man (Cheyenne), 119
Wolf-man (Freud patient), 267
"Wolf-man, The," 269
wolf moss, 113
wolf mother, benevolent, 226, 246*m*, 248–49
"Wolf of Chungshan Mountain, The," 261
Wolf Road, 132
wolf's bane, 208
"Wolf's Breakfast, The," 262
"wolf's head, the," 208
Wolf Star, 133*m*
Wolf Star (Pawnee), 102
wolf star (Sirius), 132

"Wolf, the Sheep and the Lamb, The," 253
"Wolf Tracker," 193
"Wolves, The," 268
wolves as individuals, 3, 18, 34, 82–84
wolves as prey, 27, 29
"Wolves Eating Caribou," *84*
wolves killing wolves, 4, 29, 51–52, 66, 100
Wolves of Mount McKinley, The (Murie), 224, 290
Wolves of North America, The (Young, Goldman), 223, 290
Woman Who Lived with Wolves, 121–22
Wood Buffalo National Park, 58
Wyoming, 71*m*, 290

yearling wolves, 28, 36, 85, 101
Yellow Wolf, 118
Yellowstone National Park, 290
Yes and No Stories, 261
Young, Arthur, 172–73
Young, Stanley, 180, 192, 223, 288, 290, 292
Young Wolf Medicine Society, 120
Ysengrimus, 259
Yukon, 195
Yury, Saint. *See* George, Saint

Zeus, 231, 232
Zimen, Eric, 169

ILLUSTRATION CREDITS

Page 8: Adult female, by John Bauguess.

Page 76: Pre-Columbian wolf mask, Key Marco, Florida. From collections of the University Museum of the University of Pennsylvania.

Page 136: Skull of three-year-old male, from Brooks Range, Alaska, by John Bauguess.

Page 202: Representation of the beast of Gévaudan, illustrator unknown, 1756. From *The Werewolf*, by Montague Summers. © 1966 by University Books, Inc. Published by arrangement with Lyle Stuart.

The photographs on pages 8, 22, 23, 24, 34–35, 40, 41, 44, 45, 46, 91, 103, 125, 136, 151, and 190 are by John Bauguess.

Page 15: Barry Lopez.

Page 20: James Cloutier.

Page 28: Barry Lopez.

Pages 42 and 43: Fred H. Harrington. Art by Donald Johnson.

Pages 51, 60, and 68: Barry Lopez.

Page 84: Peter Niego.

Page 96: Courtesy of National Collection of Fine Arts, Smithsonian Institution.

Page 107: Museum of the American Indian, Heye Foundation.

Page 117: From Walter McClintock, *The Old North Trail: Life Legends and Religion of the Blackfeet Indians,* by permission of the University of Nebraska Press.

Page 130: Museum of the American Indian, Heye Foundation.

Page 141: U.S. Fish and Wildlife Service, photograph courtesy of the Wildlife Management Institute.

Page 155: Courtesy of North Dakota Game and Fish Department and Mrs. Ted Pope, Amidon, North Dakota.

Page 161: Walter M. Baumhofer.

Page 165: Minnesota Department of Natural Resources.

Page 174: Courtesy of Addison Gallery of American Art, Phillips Academy, Andover, Massachusetts.

Pages 181 and 183: National Archives.

Page 207: The Pierpont Morgan Library.

Page 214: Agence TOP, Paris.

Page 217: The Pierpont Morgan Library.

Page 228: By Dorothy Fitch, from *Book of Fabulous Beasts,* by A. M. Smyth (London: Oxford University Press, 1939).

Page 235: By Maurice Sand, from *The Werewolf,* by Montague Summers. © 1966 by University Books, Inc. Published by arrangement with Lyle Stuart.

Page 245: Courtesy of Harvard University Press.

Page 248: City Museum, Leeds, England.

Page 260: Clockwise from upper left: by Thomas Bewick, from *Fables of Aesop with Designs on Wood by Thomas Bewick,* © 1975 Paddington Press Ltd.; by Alexander Calder, the Metropolitan Museum of Art, gift of Monroe Wheeler, 1949; by Charles H. Bennett, from *Fables of Aesop,* compiled by Willis L. Parker, J. J. Little and Ives Co.; by Arthur Rackham, from *Aesop's Fables,* compiled by V. S. Vernon Jones, William Heinemann Ltd.

Page 265: By Gustave Doré. From *French Fairy Tales.*

Page 274: By Hans Gerhard Sørensen, from *Of Gods and Giants,* by Harald Hveberg, Forlaget Tanum, Norli a.s.

Barry Lopez was born in Port Chester, New York, in 1945. He grew up in agricultural Southern California and New York City, went to college in the Midwest, and settled on the McKenzie River in rural western Oregon in 1970. His work has taken him to nearly fifty countries and to remote parts of Antarctica, Australia, North America, and Africa.

His articles, essays, and short stories have been widely anthologized and translated, and he has collaborated with painters, composers, architects, photographers, and other artists on a variety of projects. His books include *Arctic Dreams*, winner of the National Book Award; the novella-length fable *Crow and Weasel*; and collections of short stories *(Field Notes, Light Action in the Caribbean)* and essays *(Crossing Open Ground, About This Life)*.

He is the recipient of the John Hay and John Burroughs medals and other honors.